Mac OS X Lion Made Simple

Axely Congress

Apress®

Mac OS X Lion Made Simple

ISBN-13 (pbk): 978-1-4302-3768-6

ISBN-13 (electronic): 978-1-4302-3769-3

President and Publisher: Paul Manning
Lead Editor: Michelle Lowman
Development Editor: James Markham

Coordinating Editor: Kelly Moritz
Compositor: MacPS, LLC
Indexer: BIM Indexing & Proofreading Servies
Artist: SPi Global
Cover Designer: Anna Ishchenko

Distributed to the book trade worldwide by Springer Science+Business Media, LLC., 233 Spring Street, 6th Floor, New York, NY 10013. Phone 1-800-SPRINGER, fax (201) 348-4505, e-mail orders-ny@springer-sbm.com, or visit www.springeronline.com.

For information on translations, please e-mail rights@apress.com, or visit www.apress.com.

Apress and friends of ED books may be purchased in bulk for academic, corporate, or promotional use. eBook versions and licenses are also available for most titles. For more information, reference our Special Bulk Sales–eBook Licensing web page at www.apress.com/info/bulksales.

I would like to dedicate this book to my family, which gave me the courage and confidence to write this book and supported me throughout the entire process. I would also like to send a special thanks to my Mom, Dad, and my Love, Yolanda, for their relentless efforts to assist me in every way imaginable, as well as for helping me keep my life together.

Contents at a Glance

Contents v
About the Author ix
About the Technical Reviewer x
Acknowledgments xi
Part I: Mac OSX Lion Quick Start Guide 1
Getting Around Quickly 3
Part II: Introduction 13
Welcome to Mac OS X Lion! 15
Part III:You and Your Lion 19
Chapter 1: Getting Started With Lion 21
Chapter 2: Getting Around in Lion 29
Chapter 3: Understanding Lion Application Menus and Shortcuts 55
Chapter 4: Making iWork '09 Work 79
Chapter 5: Using the Mac App Store 97
Chapter 6: Finding Life in iLife 109
Chapter 7: Essential Utilities 135
Chapter 8: It's a Jungle Out There: Safari and the Internet 157
Chapter 9: Mail and Other Ways to Say Hello 175
Chapter 10: Keeping Things Safe: Time Machine and Security 191
Chapter 11: Automating Tasks and Customizing Lion 209
Index 225

Contents

Contents at a Glance iv
About the Author ix
About the Technical Reviewer x
Acknowledgments xi

Part I: Mac OSX Lion Quick Start Guide 1
Getting Around Quickly 3
The Ports on a MacBook Pro 4
The MacBook Pro's Keyboard 6
Navigating Lion 8
The Finder 10
Using the Trackpad 11
Part II: Introduction 13
Welcome to Mac OS X Lion! 15
Lion, the Name 17
Navigating this Book 17
Part I: Quick Start Guide 17
Part II: Introduction 17
Part III: Mac OS X Lion Made Simple 17
Quickly Locating Tips and Notes 18
Feedback! 18
Part III: You and Your Lion... 19
Chapter 1: Getting Started With Lion 21
Navigating the Desktop 21
Getting to Know Your Icons and Applications 25
Summary 28
Chapter 2: Getting Around in Lion 29
Using the Finder 30
The Window View Options 33
The Icon View 33
The List View 33
The Column View 34
The Cover Flow View 35

Finder Preferences....35
The General Tab....36
The Labels Tab....38
The Sidebar Tab....39
The Advanced Tab....40
The Finder App's Right-Click Options....41
Stacks....43
Stack Viewing....46
Airdrop....47
Bluetooth—the Airdrop Alternative....49
Using Launchpad....52
Spotlight Searching....53
Summary....54
■ Chapter 3: Understanding Lion Application Menus and Shortcuts....55
General Application Menus....55
The Finder....55
Reviewing the File Menu....58
Drilling Down on the Edit Menu....58
Exploring the View Menu....59
Zipping Around the Finder's Go Menu....60
Safari....64
iTunes....72
Exploring iTunes' File Menu....73
Using the Controls Menu....73
Accessing the iTunes Store via the Store Menu....74
Manipulating Resources with the Advanced Menu....74
Summary....77
■ Chapter 4: Making iWork '09 Work....79
The iWork '09 Suite....79
Pages....80
Using Pages....80
Navigating Pages....81
Looking More Closely at Pages' Inspector....86
Numbers....91
Keynote....94
Summary....96
■ Chapter 5: Using the Mac App Store....97
The Mac App Store....98
Keeping Your Apps Up to Date....100
Securing Your Identity....101
App Components and Purchasing....103
Purchasing an App....103
Application Information....104
The Application's Origins....104
Application Image Previews....105
Finding Similar Applications....106
Summary....107

Chapter 6: Finding Life in iLife 109

iMovie 110
- The iMovie Menu 111

The iMovie Interface 112
- Selecting the Right Template 113
- Breaking Down iMovie's Interface 114
- Prepping Your Video Content for Editing 117

iPhoto 120
- Getting Started 120
- iPhoto's Faces and Places 122
- Additional Features in iPhoto 124
- Editing in iPhoto 124

GarageBand 126
- The GarageBand Interface 126
- Welcome Window Pane 126
- GarageBand's Primary Interface 130
- Track and Share 133
- Summary 133

Chapter 7: Essential Utilities 135

Enhancing Your Experience with Utilities 136

Monitoring Your System 136
- Scrutinizing System Resources 138

Maintaining Hard Drive Health 138
- Beyond Disk Utility 140

Data Security 142
- Augmenting Lion's Built-in Data Security 143
- Customizing Your Input Devices Further 148

Staying Organized 150
- Leveraging iCal's Features with Other Utilities 151

Summary 155

Chapter 8: It's a Jungle Out There: Safari and the Internet 157

The Safari Interface 158
- Understanding the Address Entry Bar 158
- Searching with Google 159
- Search Alternatives and Bookmarking 161
- Using Top Sites 162
- Tabbed Browsing 164

Safari Preferences 165
- General 166
- Appearance 167
- Bookmarks 167
- Tabs 168
- RSS 168
- Autofill 169
- Advanced 169

Safari Privacy and Security 170
- Security Recommendations 171

Surfing Privately 171
Safari's Extras.....172
Summary 174
Chapter 9: Mail and Other Ways to Say Hello 175
Using Mail 176
Mail's Interface 176
Reviewing Mail's Main Menu Functions 177
Other Noteworthy Mail Items 178
E-mail Contextual Menus 181
Smart Mailbox 181
Composing a Message 182
Attachments 182
Fonts 183
Photo Browser 183
Stationery 184
Other Communication App Alternatives 185
iChat 185
FaceTime 186
Skype 187
Summary 188
Chapter 10: Keeping Things Safe: Time Machine and Security 191
Time Machine Overview 191
Setting up Time Machine 192
Using Time Machine 194
Using Time Capsule for Network Storage 194
Retrieving Data 195
Versions 198
Using Versions 199
Backup Alternatives 202
Super Flexible Backup 202
Carbon Copy Cleaner 204
Using Carbon Copy Cloner 204
Securing Your Lion 207
Cloud Storage and Physical Security 207
Summary 208
Chapter 11: Automating Tasks and Customizing Lion 209
Understanding Automation 210
The Basics of Automator 210
Example 1: Automating Text Audio 213
Example 2: Automating Internet Downloads 218
Customizing Lion 220
Folder Organization 221
Indexing with Spotlight 222
Customizing the Screen Saver 223
Summary 224
Index 225

About the Author

Axely Congress is the founder and CEO of MacMoral, a computer network engineering consulting company that deploys high end Mac-based infrastructures to SLBs, government, and educational institutions. He has been a successful entrepreneur since 2005, and a decorated educator of computer networking, and engineerring since 1994. He is also the co-founder, of Omnymbus, a distributed remote desktop cloud computing company. Axely spent time in the Air Force as a computer work group manager and Chief of communications and networking at Mildenhall AFB England. Axely can be reached at axely@macmoral.comcom.

About the Technical Reviewer

Originally from Owasso, Oklahoma, **Jesse Cole Guthery** moved to Phoenix Arizona to attend College College where he received a Bachelor of Arts in Film/HDTV Production in 2007. While working as an Apple Technician at Collins College he received his M.F.A. from Full Sail University in Media Design. Jesse currently works for the Salt River Project in Phoenix, Arizona as an HD Post-Production Coordinator. Jesse also is an Apple Certified Macintosh Technician, and Apple Certified Final Cut 7 Professional.

Acknowledgments

I would like to thank a few of my Ph.D instructors who have helped me grow as a learner throughout the last two years: Dr. Dunn, Dr. Irlbeck, Dr. Lane, and Dr. Mike. Without their guidance and encouragement, this book simply would not have been possible. To my brothers, Mikee and David, I want to say thanks for always having my back in life. Also, thank you to Ronda Lobato and Dolores Burns for being the most supportive and awesome friends a guy could have.

I would also like to thank Michelle and Kim for their patience and understanding as I went through the learning curve associated with understanding the book-writing process. Again, thank you.

Finally, I would like to thank Richard and Jan Forrest, who have been my dearest friends throughout the last five years. They have given me every chance in the world to be a success and urged me to push the boundaries of my talent and creativity to reshape technology and my life.

Part I

Mac OSX Lion Quick Start Guide

Welcome to the Mac OS X Lion Quick Start Guide. This guide will help you become more comfortable using the Lion OS, introducing you to some of its most-used functionality and helping you quickly grasp a few basic concepts that are at the core of how Lion works. This guide will also walk you through using some of the built-in utilities and tools that can make your computing life much easier. You should refer to this Quick Start Guide whenever you need to reference the fundamental aspects of using the Lion OS. The information contained in this guide will give you the tools you need to set your Lion free, enabling you to explore endless possibilities that are limited only by your imagination.

Getting Around Quickly

This Quick Start Guide is intended to help you understand some of the basic elements and actions necessary to start using your Mac proficiently. What you read in this book can help you drastically reduce the learning curve associated with using the Lion operating system (OS) for the first time. This guide will also serve you well as supplemental material, and it can make learning how to use Lion a fun and interesting experience. Refer to this starter guide whenever you need to refresh yourself on the basics of the Lion OS.

Over the past five years, the interfaces of the various iterations of Mac OS X have remained very similar. There are subtle differences between the different versions; however, there are not enough differences to make any seasoned Mac user flinch. Apple's goal with Lion has been to modify, not reinvent its Mac OS X user interface (UI). If you have used OS X Leopard or Snow Leopard, then you will notice minor adjustments here and there to make things a little more accessible for the end user; however, the overall changes are minor. In this section, we'll take a look at Lion's UI, so that you can get a good feel for where things are and what they do. Succeeding chapters in this book will cover the UI in depth. This guide will cover everything you need to get going in the right direction.

Another important aspect of using Lion is learning how to interact with the physical mechanics of your MacBook or iMac. For example, this book will teach you how to add devices and look up Lion's built-in keyboard shortcuts. Your Mac's keyboard and peripheral ports play a significant role in allowing you to interact properly with the underlying OS. Learning where certain keys and ports are will help you get the most out of the Lion OS. Let's begin by taking a quick glance at common Mac ports; we'll use a current MacBook Pro as a reference model.

The Ports on a MacBook Pro

One of the most important things to know is how to plug in your MacBook Pro's power cord (see Figure Q-1).

> **NOTE:** Plugging the cord into the wrong port by accident could create havoc on your Mac, so make certain that you plug your power cable into the right port.

Figure Q-1. *A MacBook Pro's power plug-in port*

You will also want to be aware of the RJ-45 port, which is for cable networking. This port is useful when you do not have access to wireless networks, but you do have access to a network switch or router that can provide Internet and/or network access (see Figure Q-2).

Figure Q–2. *A MacBook Pro's networking port*

If you plan on using any external drives for something like **Time Machine** (see Chapter 9: "Mail and Other Ways to Say Hello" for more information on this app), then you will need to use your Mac's built-in FireWire or USB ports (see Figure Q-3).

Figure Q–3. *A MacBook Pro's external FireWire and USB ports*

Finally, a MacBook Pro includes an Express Card slot, which also serves as a high speed peripheral interface slot. This is your Mac's fastest port, and it can be used to extend the functionality of your Mac with devices such as external RAID disks (redundant array of inexpensive disks). RAID disks allow you to configure multiple disks in different configurations for high performance applications that require speed and redundancy (see Figure Q–4).

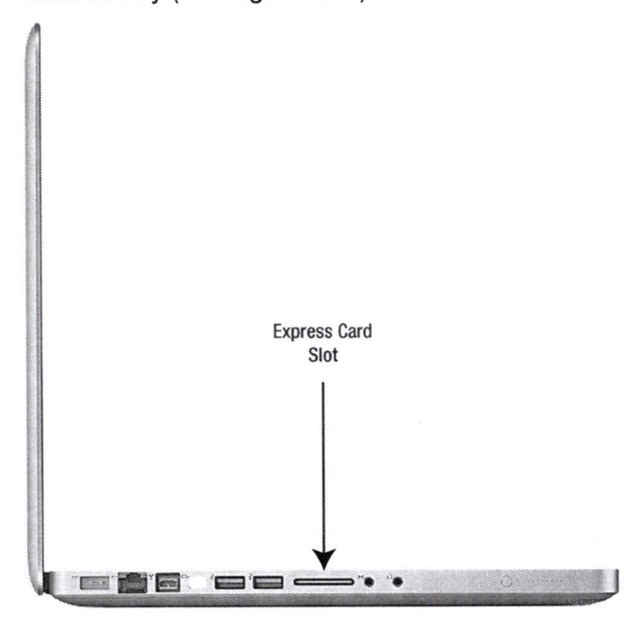

Figure Q–4. *A MacBook Pro's Express Card port*

The MacBook Pro's Keyboard

Regardless of which Mac you have, it is essential that you be able to navigate and understand your keyboard's layout. Mac keyboard layouts are similar to those seen on standard Windows keyboards; however, there are some significant differences, as well. Let's briefly explore a Mac keyboard's special key functions. Understanding these will make it much easier to follow along with the built-in shortcuts and other features discussed in this book.

Figure Q–5 shows a top-down view of the standard Mac keyboard layout, as seen on a MacBook Pro. Note the highlighted group of keys at the bottom of the keyboard. These are special keys that simplify accessing much of your Mac's functionality.

Figure Q–5. *Your Mac keyboard's special keys*

Zooming in on the area highlighted in Figure Q–5 reveals the **Command**, **Option**, **Fn** (**Function**), and **Control** keys, along with the **Space Bar** (see Figure Q–6).

Figure Q–6. *Zooming in your Mac keyboard's special keys*

You will use these keys to control much of the essential and hidden functionality of the Lion OS. Typically, you will use them in combination with other keys. In this book, you will see them referred to when using software-specific functions and built-in Lion system utilities. It is a good idea to become familiar with these keys because you will use them time and time again for shortcuts and other system tasks. Do not worry about memorizing any of the shortcuts or system specific functions referred to by this book; you will use them so often in Lion that they will force their way into your memory without too much effort on your part.

NOTE: The **Fn** key allows you to open up and use the extra functionality provided by the keyboard. Pressing the **Fn** key activates the "F" (function) keys located at the top of your keyboard (see Figure Q–7). Using **Fn** in conjunction with these keys lets you control your computer's brightness, volume, media playback, and other functions.

Figure Q–7. Lion's "F" (function) keys

Navigating Lion

Navigation in Lion is pretty straightforward. In fact, it is so simple that it doesn't really require any explanation. Apple designed its OS to be intuitive, even to novice users, so that you can gradually learn where everything is simply by using the OS. Things in Lion are located logically and somewhat ergonomically, so you have a grand view of what is going on at all times. We cover this in-depth in succeeding chapters, so this Quick Start Guide will just touch on some of the basics.

Figure Q–8 shows the overall layout of Lion when you first log onto the OS. You will need to familiarize yourself with a few basic elements depicted in this screenshot because they are referred to throughout this book. Learning what these elements are and do will speed up your reading and increase your comprehension as you explore this book's chapters (see Table Q-1 for a brief description of the most important aspects of Lion's UI).

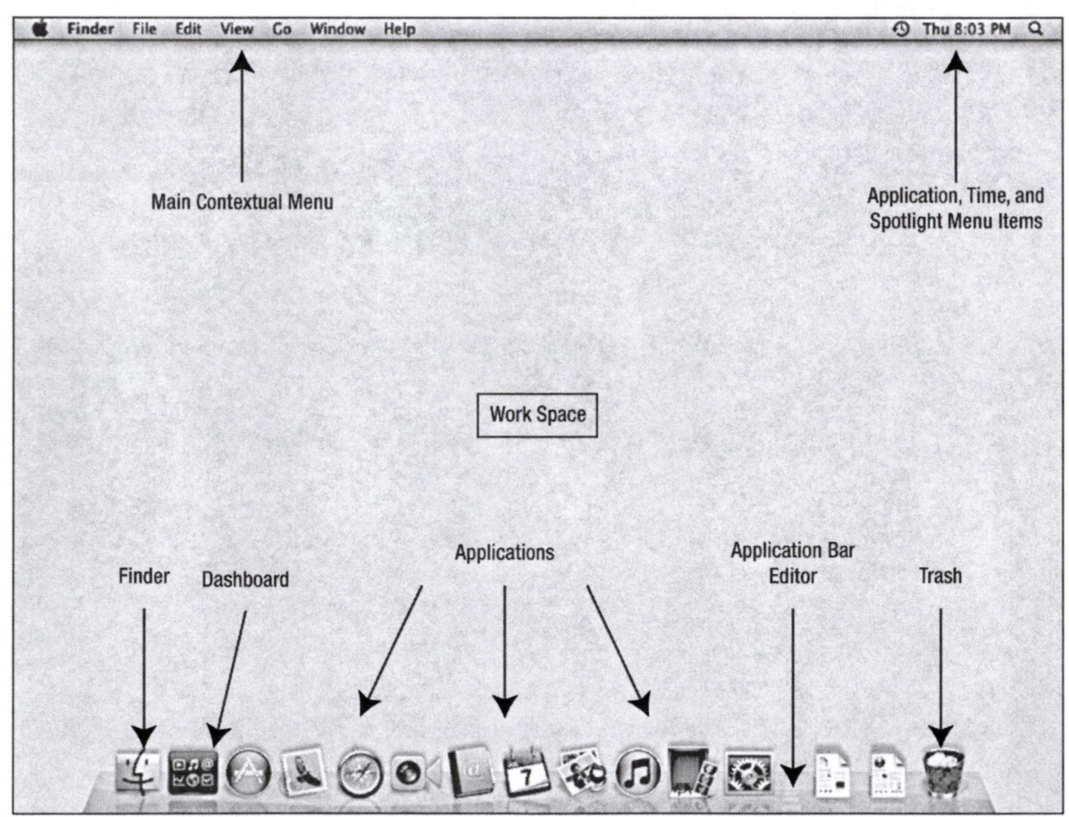

Figure Q–8. Lion's main interface

Table Q–1. Significant User Interface Elements in Lion

UI Element	Description
The main contextual menu	This menu changes depending on the application you are using; however, it always remains in the same place, and it is the core contextual menu for all applications.
Application, Time, and Spotlight menu items	This is where you can set your clock, search for files, and use applications that interact with the main contextual menu bar.
The Finder	You will use this app to navigate, locate, and use your files.
The Dashboard	The Dashboard contains widgets, which add extra but unobtrusive software layers of functionality to the Lion OS.
The applications menu	This is the main applications menu, which consists of icon-based shortcuts to your software applications.
The application bar editor	This small editor allows you to resize the main application menu.
The Trash Bin	After deleting a file, it is not deleted for good until you empty your Trash Bin. The Trash Bin allows you to restore documents you've accidently deleted or permanently remove documents you no longer need.

The Finder

The **Finder** is an application you will use over and over again. It may even become your most-used app because it enables you to locate and use the files and applications on your Lion OS (see Figure Q–9). You will learn about the **Finder** in detail in Chapter 1: "Getting Started with Lion."

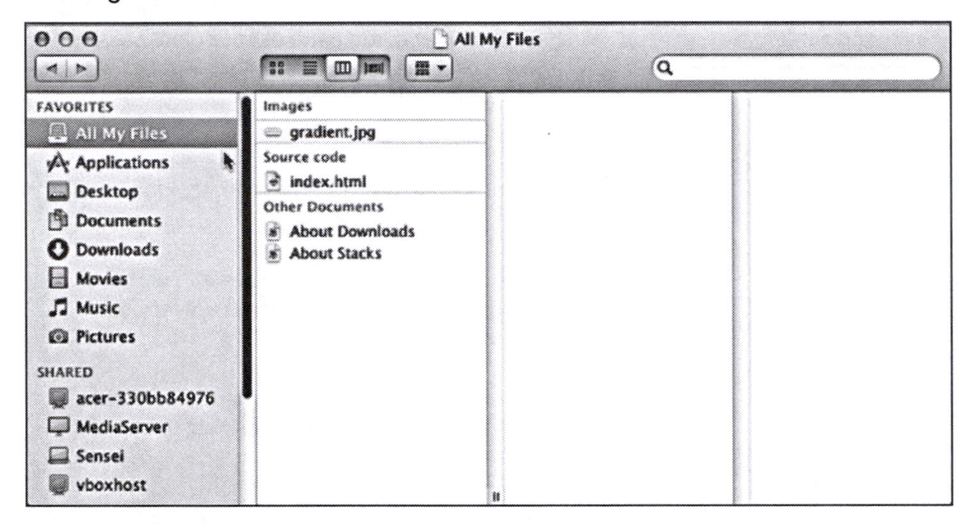

Figure Q–9. *The Finder*

One special menu item you will want to pay particular attention to is the **Apple** menu, which allows you to initiate actions such as software updates, access the Mac App Store, force-quit an application when it becomes unstable, and log out of Lion when you feel the need to. The **Apple** menu is also discussed in-depth in Chapter 1.

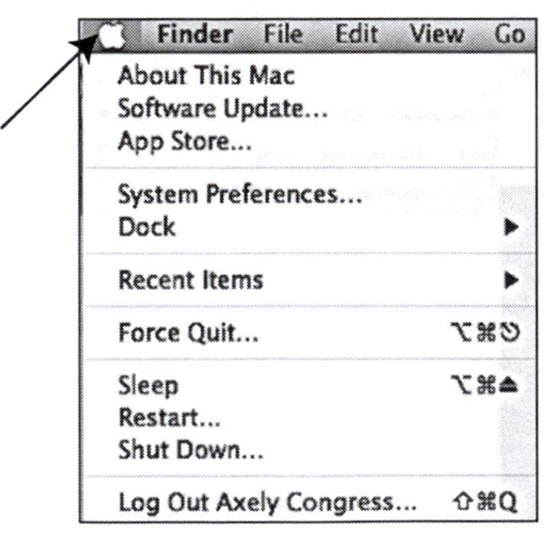

Figure Q–10. *The Apple menu*

Using the Trackpad

One of the most notable features of Lion is its uncanny ability to make computing easier. It even simplifies the way you physically interact with your Mac through what are known as *mouse gestures*. These gestures are motion-based shortcuts you can use in lieu of the actions people typically make when using computer mice today. For example, you can use these gestures to bypass old forms of input, cutting down on the amount of physical body movement required to accomplish certain computing actions.

To conclude this Quick Start Guide, I will briefly introduce you to the basics of using these gestures in conjunction with your Mac trackpad. As you go through this book, the gestures described in Table Q-2 will serve as a trackpad reference guide, enabling you to accomplish many tasks much more efficiently.

Table 2. *Trackpad Reference*

Trackpad Feature	Description
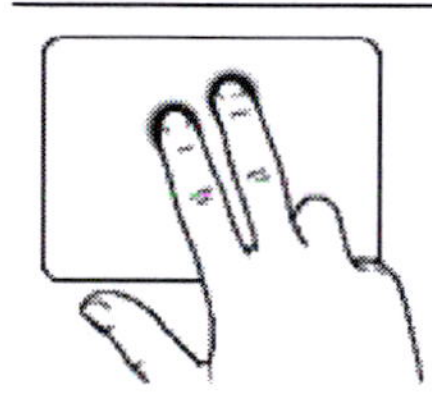	**Swipe:** This is equivalent to right-clicking a normal mouse. Just tap the trackpad with two fingers.
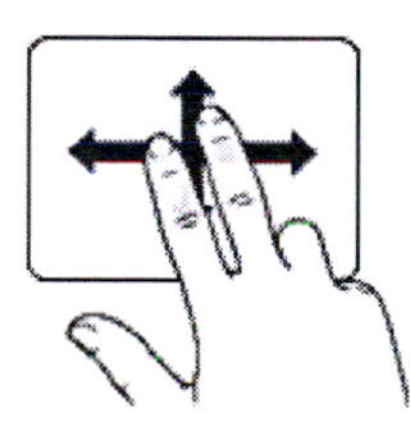	**Scrolling:** This is equivalent to using the scroll wheel on your mouse. Slightly press the trackpad with two fingers, and then move your fingers up or down to scroll.
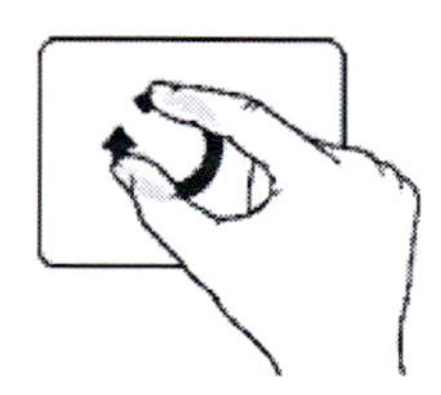	**Rotation:** This gesture allows you to rotate pictures and images; this gesture works well with **iPhoto** and other image-editing utilities.
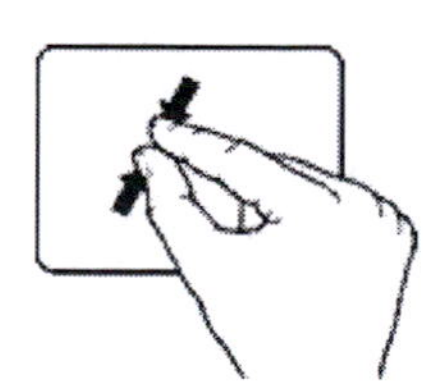	**Pinching:** This is equivalent to scaling and zooming. This gesture will allow you to zoom in and out using two fingers. Simply pinch your fingers in or out to use this feature.

Trackpad Feature	Description
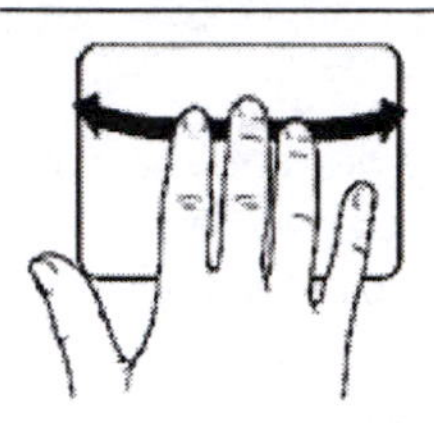	**Three Finger Swipe:** This feature lets you move between documents or images. **iPhoto** is also a good place to test this feature.
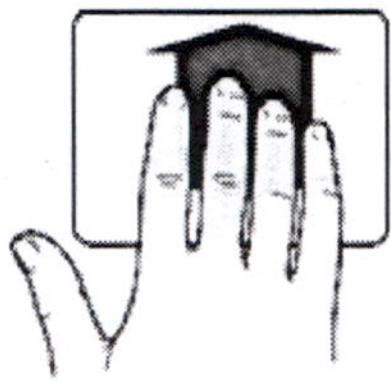	**Four Finger Swipe:** This feature lets you switch between applications and/or activate various features.

Part 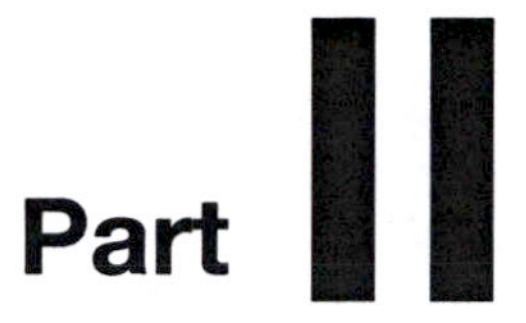

Introduction

Welcome to your new Mac OS X Lion operating system. This book will help you get the most out of Lion by teaching you how to leverage the power and flexibility of one of the most advanced operating systems in the world. This section will show you how the book is organized, providing you with a reference list for navigating its chapters. This reference list will help you find what you need to begin making the most out of your Lion OS!

Welcome to Mac OS X Lion!

There are many operating systems (OSes) in use today; however, the three most commonly used are Windows 7, Linux, and Mac OS X. In my opinion, Mac OS X Lion combines the best of both Windows 7 and Linux, marrying the ease of use of the former to the tremendous power inherent in the latter. Thus, Lion enables the most novice user to get his work done with ease, yet power users like myself can create programs and automation tools that take full advantage of the underlying software and hardware features of the UNIX operating system that underpins Mac OS X Lion.

Lion's combination of stability, usability, and reliability has no equal in any other operating system. It allows users to transparently take advantage of advanced computing technology in the form of built-in security, networking, communication, and file manipulation; yet does so in a way that doesn't expose the novice end user to the very complex beast that is UNIX. This is a big part of what makes Lion so attractive to developers and end users alike.

Lion gives developers the ability to deploy very sophisticated applications that rely on modern technologies in myriad powerful and novel ways. For example, the Lion OS enables users to take full advantage of technologies as diverse and powerful as voice and touch-screen communications. In this book, you will learn how to take advantage of this combination of ease of use and power to explore a world of computing that has no limits beyond those imposed by your own imagination. Simply put: if it can be done in the world of computing, Lion is capable of doing it—and a whole lot more!

Getting the Most Out of Lion Made Simple

This book covers the wide range of things that are possible using the Lion OS. It begins by walking you through the basics of getting started with Lion; moves on to discuss specific applications; and concludes by covering the importance of security and backing up your files. The chapters in this book are laid out as follows:

- **Chapters 1–3:** These chapters impart a basic understanding of the Lion operating system and how to use it. For example, you will learn about the core features that make up Lion's user interface; the different ways you can navigate around the OS; and some of the key attributes common to most Lion applications, including basic menu design and many useful keyboard shortcuts.

- **Chapters 4–6:** These chapters walk you through a handful of specific applications, including **iWork** and the apps that make up the **iLife** suite. These chapters cover what the apps do, where you can find them on your computer, where you can purchase them (if applicable), and how you update them. These chapters will help you become productive right away, explaining how to get the most out of your Lion OS out of the box.

- **Chapters 7–9:** These chapters cover how to use Lion's built-in utilities; how to use **Safari** to surf the Internet; and how to communicate with others using Lion's built-in communication features. Together, these chapters will help jumpstart your ability to communicate with the outside world quickly, easily, and securely.

- **Chapters 10–11:** This book's final two chapters cover how to back up your data, secure your information, and otherwise take advantage of some of Lion's more advanced features, including automation.

By the time you finish reading these chapters, you will have a great understanding of what you can do with the Lion OS, including how you can best make it work for you.

This book steers clear of "techy" verbiage, sticking to the basics. This means you can treat the book as a handy and easy-to-peruse resource. The best way to read this book is a chapter at a time, without skipping chapters. Even if you are a power user, you are sure to be rewarded in every chapter with hidden gems that will make you an even more powerful user. Take the time to digest every chapter thoroughly, and you will find this book an invaluable resource on Mac OS X Lion.

Lion, the Name

This book is meant for all users of the Mac OS X Lion operating system. It is a version-specific write-up; and while some of it is applicable to previous versions of Mac OS X, it is 100-percent compatible with Lion, the latest version of the Mac OS X operating system at the time of writing. Therefore, I recommended that you do not try to apply the lessons of this book to anything but the Lion OS.

Navigating this Book

This book consists of three main parts: "Part I: Quick Start Guide"; "Part II: Introduction"; and "Part III: Mac OS X Lion Made Simple." The sections that follow provide an overview of what you will find in these parts. In addition to these main sections, you will also find a handy "Day in the Life of a Lion User" reference. This reference is located inside the front and back covers, and it provides a general look into how I use the Lion OS throughout my workday and beyond.

Part I: Quick Start Guide

The Quick Start Guide covers two important subjects:

- **The Mac OS X Lion Interface**: Learning the basics of the Mac's hardware interface will help you navigate your Lion OS with ease.

- **Mouse Gestures and the Keyboard:** Learning how to use gestures on your trackpad will reduce the time and effort required to navigate your Lion OS, especially when compared to the time and effort required by a traditional mouse and keyboard approach.

Part II: Introduction

You are reading this part now.

Part III: Mac OS X Lion Made Simple

There are 11 chapters in this book, and each chapter after the first builds on the concepts that you read about in previous chapters. You will find that the material for each chapter is interconnected, and that each succeeding chapter is somewhat dependent on the chapter that precedes it. This part of the book is where you will get a good, in-depth look at the Mac OS X Lion operating system. It is also where you will learn to become proficient in using it.

Quickly Locating Tips and Notes

As you read this book, you will see specially formatted **NOTES** that discuss important things to consider when using your Lion OS to accomplish various tasks.

> **NOTES:** are formatted like this, with a gray background, to help you see them more easily. Pay special attention to them because they highlight special points of interest that can be critical to getting the most out of your lion os. I strongly recommend you do not skip or otherwise gloss over this important material.

Feedback!

Feel free to give me feedback, and let me know what you think of the book. You can also contact me if you have any questions pertaining to how to use the Mac OS X Lion operating system (relative to the contents of this book); time allowing, I will respond to inquiries you might have, helping you increase your understanding and comprehension of the Lion OS. I can be reached at `axely@macmoral.com`.

Part 

You and Your Lion...

This section represents the core of *Mac OS X Lion Made Simple*. The material in this section covers everything you will need to know to get started with the Lion OS. The chapters in this section focus on what Lion has to offer you as a user. It covers this topic from the standpoints of productivity, security, usability, and entertainment. In the final chapter of this book, you will even learn how to create your first Lion software program. This program will enable you to automate repetitive tasks on your system, saving you time and effort in your daily computing activities. This book will serve as an excellent resource if you are new to Lion, but it will serve as a great reference guide if you are a veteran Lion user. No matter how much prior experience you have with Macs or the Lion OS, you will find a wealth of information related to Mac OS X Lion that is sure to take you to the next level as a Lion user. Happy reading!

Chapter 1

Getting Started With Lion

Apple's OS X Lion (hereafter referred to as *Lion*) is the newest version of the Mac operating system. This chapter takes a look at some of the basic components of the operating system (OS) and explores some of the commonly used elements that you may find yourself using on a day-to-day basis.

The Lion operating system supports 64-bit processing and enables multi-user remote computing. Lion also ships with a wide selection of software, including apps for e-mail, web browsing, office productivity, multimedia interactivity, audio and video creation, printing, image creation and manipulation, web surfing, and videoconferencing. It also includes a host of other applications and system functions that can help you stay productive as you work—and play—with your computer. In short, Lion does a lot of things to make your computing experience a welcome and entertaining activity.

Navigating the Desktop

Navigating your way around Lion requires that you familiarize yourself with its menu system, icon layout, and other associated utilities. Becoming familiar with these features will help you move around Lion's environment with ease. It will also minimize the chances that you will become frustrated when using Lion because you will be able to find the applications and information you wish to use quickly and easily.

The first time you load Lion, you will see a menu at the top (see Figure 1–1). This is the Mac's unified menu for all its applications. All the application menus that you use on your Mac will be located at the top of the screen.

Figure 1–1. *The Lion Start-up screen and menu*

If you are used to working with Windows, there are several important differences you should be aware of when using Lion (or any other version of Mac OS X). First, there is no **Start** menu. Instead, you will want to become familiar with the **Apple** symbol located in the upper-left corner of your screen (see Figure 1–2).

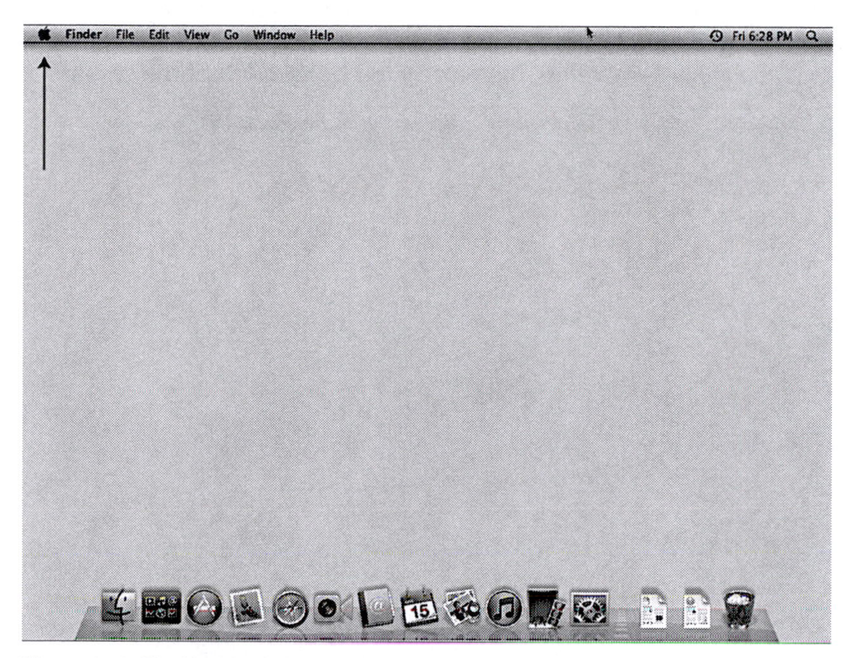

Figure 1–2. *The Lion Apple icon*

Second, the clock is in the upper-right corner of the screen (see Figure 1–3) instead of the lower-right corner.

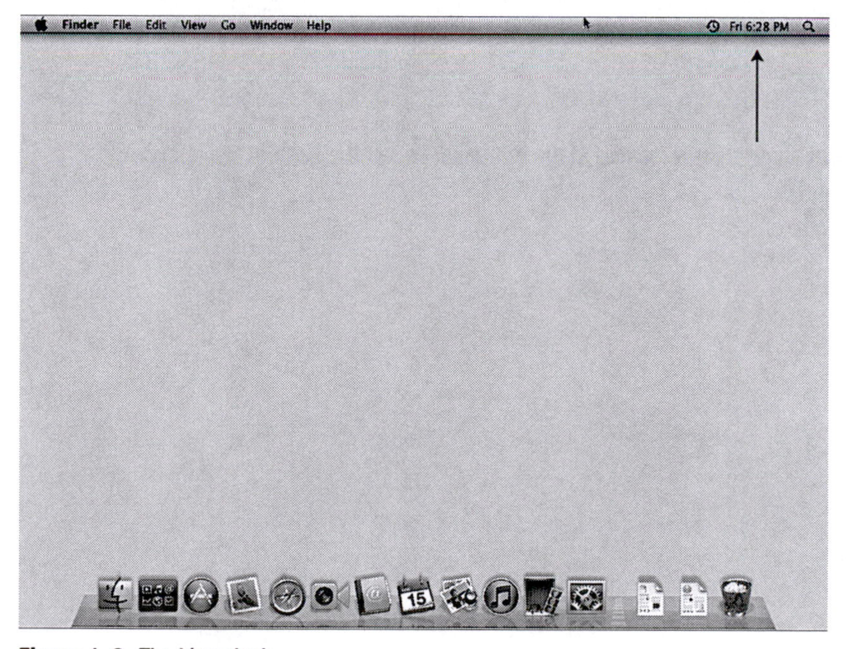

Figure 1–3. *The Lion clock*

Finally, your application shortcuts are located in the main menu bar, or *Dock*, along the bottom of your screen (see Figure 1–4), rather than along the bottom left of the screen.

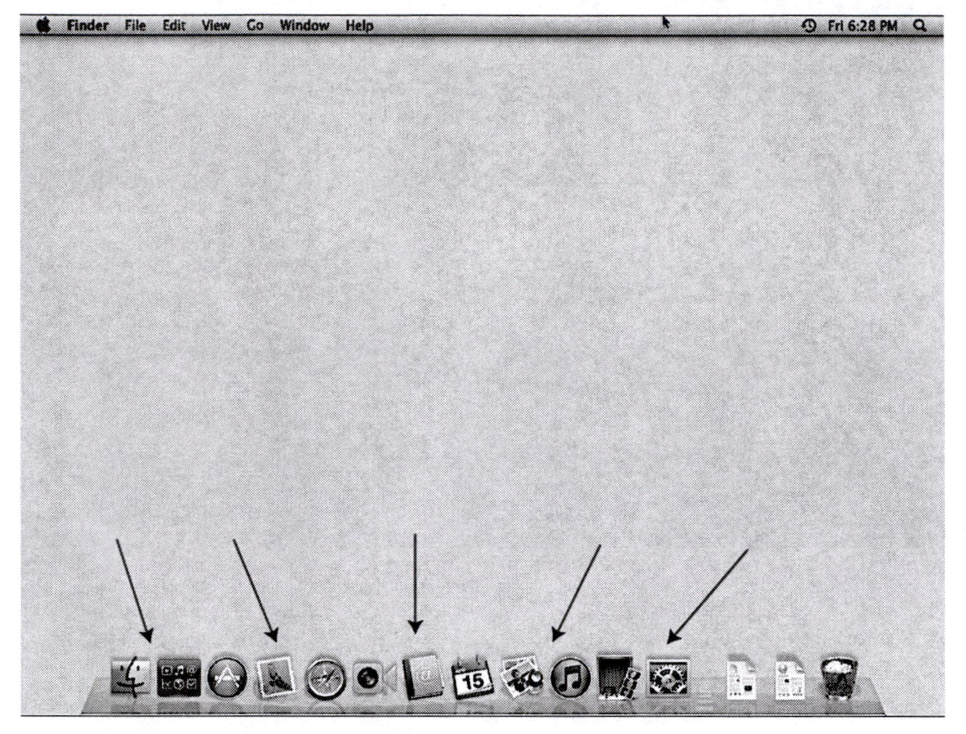

Figure 1–4. *The Lion Dock*

> **NOTE:** The **Trash Bin** application is located at the rightmost end of the Dock at the bottom of your screen (see Figure 1–5).

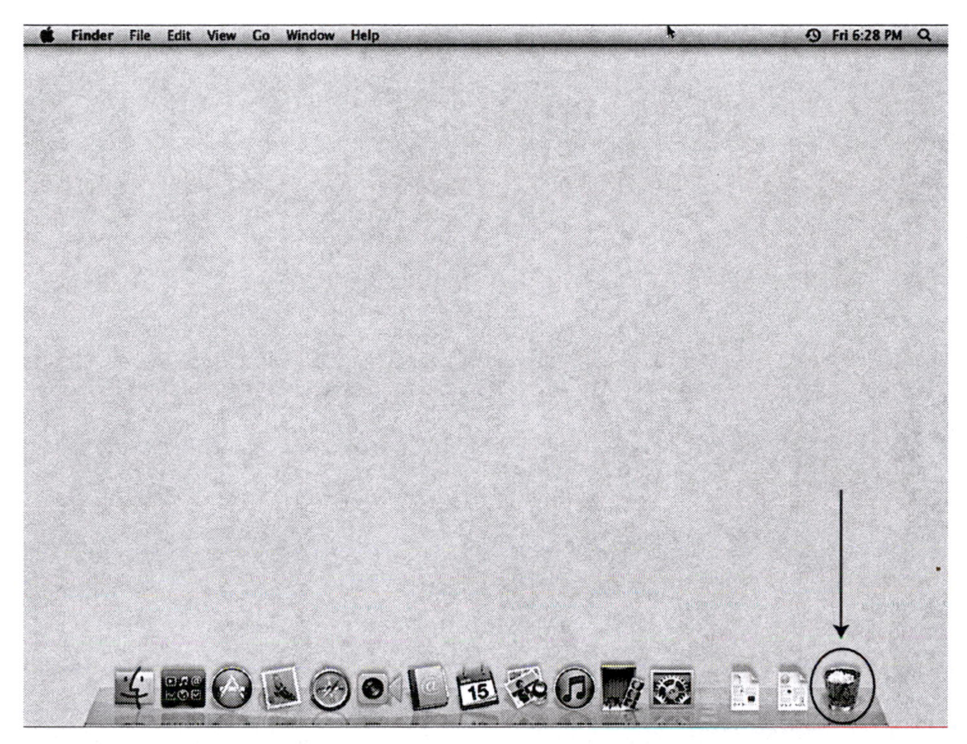

Figure 1–5. *The Lion Trash Bin icon*

In the next section, I will provide a snapshot of the applications you should pay particular attention to as you familiarize yourself with the Lion desktop.

Getting to Know Your Icons and Applications

An important aspect of learning to use Lion is getting to know where to find your application icons and what apps are launched when you click them. Mac OS X Lion comes with a useful set of applications; it displays the icons for several of these applications by default. These icons are located in the Dock along the bottom of your screen. You can launch any app in the Dock by clicking its associated icon. Table 1–1 shows a picture of the default icons in Lion's Dock and provides a brief description of what each app does. Note that there are many more apps (and associated icons) than the ones Lion displays by default; however, they will only show up as you change and manipulate your system to meet your needs or install new applications.

Table 1–1. *The Common Icons in **Mac OS X 10.7 Lion***

The Finder icon: This app opens to the default folder that houses all of your files. Use this app to navigate your system, as well as to find files that you need to open, delete, copy, or move. The **Finder** app also allows you to search for a file by its name or its contents, so that you can find the exact file that you are looking for quickly and easily. Later chapters—especially Chapter 2: "Getting Around in Lion"—will cover this app in greater depth.

The Launchpad icon: This application allows you to see and navigate all of your applications at once, so that you can choose an application without having to navigate through the Applications folder. **Launchpad** also provides easy access to your most important applications, and it can save you time when you're trying to find applications that you use on a daily basis, such as **iTunes**, **Safari**, and **Mail**.

The Mission Control icon: This app gives you a bird's-eye view of your active windows, so that you can see what is going on without needing to switch between different windows or any of your virtual workspaces. **Mission Control** also allows you switch between your virtual desktops within a single window, dramatically reducing the confusion often seen when working with multiple workspaces.

The Mac App Store icon: This app lets you access the Mac App Store, your ticket to buying and downloading some of the most popular and useful applications for Mac OS X Lion. Note that you must have an iTunes account with Apple before you can purchase apps from this store. You will learn more about this store in Chapter 5: "Using the Mac App Store."

The Mail icon: This application allows you to send, receive, and forward e-mails from other users. It also lets you subscribe to news feeds, such as those found on sites that allow you to subscribe to indexes of information using RSS. This app is tightly integrated with both the **Address** application and **iCal**, Apple's calendaring application. You will learn more about the **Mail** application in Chapter 9: "Mail and Other Ways to Say Hello."

The Safari icon: This application is the default web browser that ships with Lion. As such, it is one of the applications you will find yourself using most frequently on your Mac. Your gateway to the world, **Safari** lets you leverage all that the Internet allows. You will dive into some of the more intricate aspects of using **Safari** in Chapter 8: "It's a Jungle in Here:

Safari and the Internet."

The FaceTime icon: This video conferencing application enables you to communicate with other Apple users in real time using video and audio. Specifically, **FaceTime** allows you to interact with other people who use **FaceTime**–compatible computing devices. Such devices include the iPhone 4, the iPad 2, the iPod touch, **FaceTime**–enabled Macs, and so on. You will learn more about this application in later chapters.

The Address book icon: This application enables you to keep track of people by helping you manage important information. For example, you can use this app's menu and search system to retrieve e-mail addresses, phone numbers, addresses, and other personal information. This app is especially useful in conjunction with things like e-mail and office-productivity tasks. You will learn more about this application in later chapters.

The iCal icon: This calendaring application allows you to keep track of events using custom alarms, event management, and recurring tasks. This application is useful for organizing your day-to-day activities. It is closely integrated with several other applications, including **Mail**. **iCal** is another application you may find yourself using every day.

The Preview icon: This is a simple image preview and editing application that can be used to quickly open and lightly edit image files. This is also a great application for taking a quick look at your image files without having to open a heavy application such as **Photoshop**. The image editing utilities included in this app allow you to gracefully change attributes with ease (e.g., the size and color of an image). The functionality of this application will be explored in later chapters.

The iTunes icon: This app serves as the hub of entertainment and media on your Mac. It is Lion's default music and video player, allowing you to listen to and view various types of media, including video and music that you have either downloaded from iTunes or uploaded from another source. The **iTunes** application is also used to interact with other Apple devices, such as your iPhone and iPad. This app also allows you to transfer and sync your music and audio collection with other devices. This application will also be discussed in detail in later chapters.

The Photo Booth icon: This application really shows off some of the more advanced, functional features of the Lion operating system. A treat to use, **Photo Booth** allows you to shoot photos and videos, and then forward them to other people or save them to your hard drive for later viewing. We will discuss the details of this application in later chapters.

The System Preferences icon: This application lets you alter and edit the functional and aesthetic aspects of the Lion operating system to suit your particular needs or desires. For example, you can use it to adjust things like your mouse speed, desktop background, and other things related to the functionality and look of Lion. This application also allows you to specify different levels of functionality that the operating system will have, as well as to specify how those functions will affect the user when interacting with the operating system. You will learn more about this application in Chapter 11: "Automating Tasks and Customizing Lion."

The Trash Bin icon: This application allows you to archive, retrieve (i.e., undelete), or permanently remove files that you have previously deleted. Monitoring this app carefully is a good idea because you can run out of hard drive space quickly if you delete a lot of files. The **Trash Bin** is an important application that will be discussed in later chapters.

NOTE: This sounds counterintuitive on the surface—how can *deleting* files fill up your hard drive? It's important to understand that "deleting" a file does not remove it from your computer, but instead moves it to a special directory. A file is not actually removed from your computer until you use the **Trash Bin** app to permanently remove it from this special directory, thereby freeing up the disk space taken by that file.

Summary

This chapter covered some of the most basic aspects of using Mac OS X Lion. It began by explaining what elements you see on a typical Lion desktop screen, and covered some of the more important apps that ship with the OS, including their uses. It is essential that you understand the subjects covered in this chapter, so that you can navigate the Lion operating system with ease and use it effectively. It would be a good idea to re-read this chapter before you proceed to the chapters that follow. Doing so will help ensure that you are familiar with many of the basic elements of the Lion environment that you will be working with on a day-to-day basis. It will also help you become comfortable using the basic skills required to use Lion effectively.

Chapter 2

Getting Around in Lion

This chapter shows you how to get around the Lion OS, walking you through how to use Lion's built-in utilities to make navigating the operating system a lot easier. To that end, we will cover the basics of using the **Finder** file application, the Dock (which serves as Lion's main menu), and a few application tricks that make using Lion a more pleasurable experience. We will also cover how to use the Stacks feature, which gives you an alternative to the **Finder** for manipulating files on your system. Finally, we will cover Airdrop and Bluetooth, which enable you to share the files on your system with other Mac users.

The **Finder** is Lion's most important app because it lets you reference and retrieve the files that you create. Without a proper understanding of the **Finder**, you may find it difficult to use Lion effectively.

The most obvious way to navigate the Lion OS is to use the combination of a keyboard and mouse (or possibly, a trackpad). Using these effectively can help you increase how quickly you find and access what you are looking for, whether it's a file, application, or device. When combined with shortcut keys, a keyboard and mouse make navigating Lion simple and enjoyable.

> **CAUTION:** If you haven't already read the Quick Start Guide in Part 1 of this book, please take a few minutes to do so now. You should do this before you read any further, use the **Setup** app, or do anything else. This guide tells you how to find lots of useful things in this book, and it provides some great beginning and advanced time-saving tips and tricks that will help you get up and running quickly.

Using the Finder

The most commonly used utility in Lion is the **Finder**. This application allows you to explore your Mac's file system, which contains all of the files that are created by both the system (e.g., when applications are installed) and by you (e.g., when you decide to create a word processing document and save it to your hard disk).

> **NOTE:** The **Finder** icon, like all icons, can be both left- and right-clicked. This section of the chapter assumes that you are using the left-click button of your mouse.

By default, the **Finder** icon is the leftmost icon in the Dock at the bottom of your screen (see Figure 2–1).

Figure 2–1. *The Finder icon*

Clicking the **Finder** icon launches the **Finder** application, which presents a window that lets you quickly navigate to a handful of places on your system that you are likely to use frequently. The folders you see are set up so that you can access and organize your files quickly and easily. For example, the folder setup separates different types of files from one another. Word processing documents are separated from your photos, which are separated from your music, and so on (see Figure 2-2).

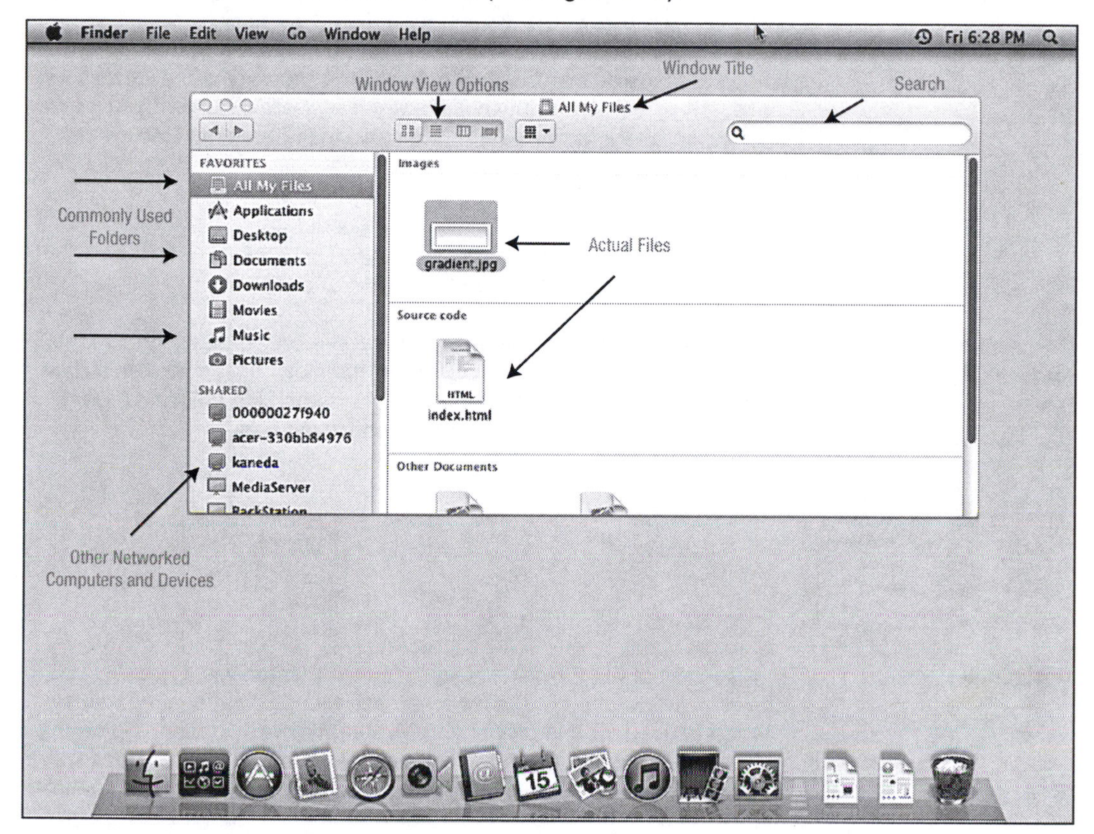

Figure 2-2. *The Finder's window layout*

Table 2-1 provides a complete description of the **Finder** window and the menu items it contains.

Table 2-1. *Commonly Used **Finder** Features and Items*

Feature	Description
Window view options 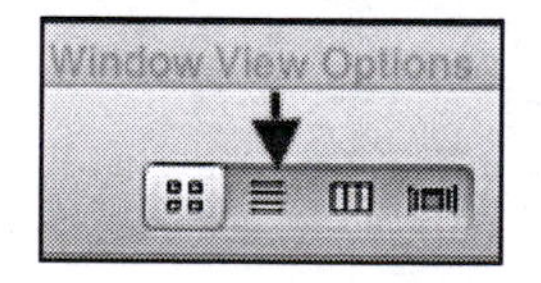	These options allow you to customize the look and feel of the **Finder** window based on your visual preferences. For a detailed description and view of each option, see Figures 2-3 through 2-7.
Window Title 	The Window Title displays the folder name of the current folder, so that there is no mistaking where you are in the folder hierarchy of your file system.

Feature	Description
Search 	This feature allows you to search for a file by name or by specific content within that file. To search by filename, enter a partial or complete filename into the **Search** box, and then press the **Return** key. To search by content within a file, enter the specific content you know the file contains into the **Search** box, and then press the **Return** key. The advantage of this feature is that you can use it to find a particular file without manually navigating to the folder that contains it. It's important that you get comfortable using this feature because it will save you a lot of time when you're trying to locate files and folders that may be buried deep within other folders.
Commonly used folders 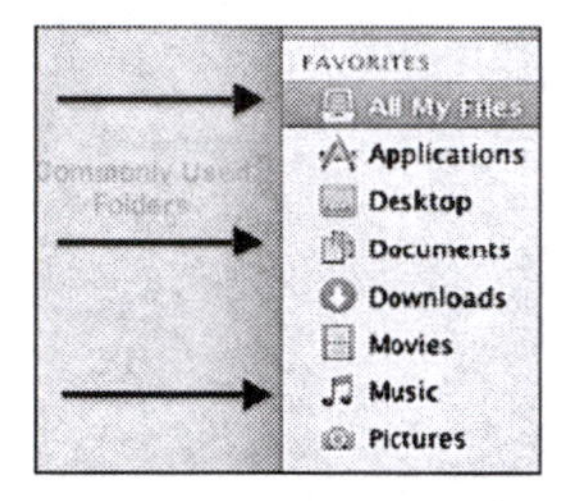 	Most people use these folders to store commonly created documents, such as important letters, music, and other files they access on a day-to-day basis. This is a convenient feature of the Lion OS, and it gives you quick access to your most commonly used files.
Actual files 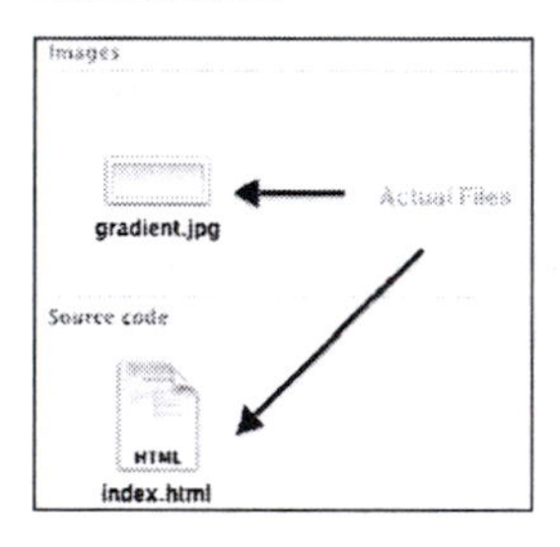 	This section of the **Finder** displays the files themselves; typically, you can click (or double-click) a file to access the information it contains. The icons used for this part of your system will vary, depending on the nature of the file and your user settings. No two application types share the same icons, so it's easy to distinguish the icon for one file type from another. If a file type exists that does not have an icon, a blank page icon will be used in its place. Also, you should be aware that the way icons for a file type are displayed can vary based on your preferred window views and other **Finder** settings. You'll learn more about these display options later in this chapter.
Other networked computers and devices 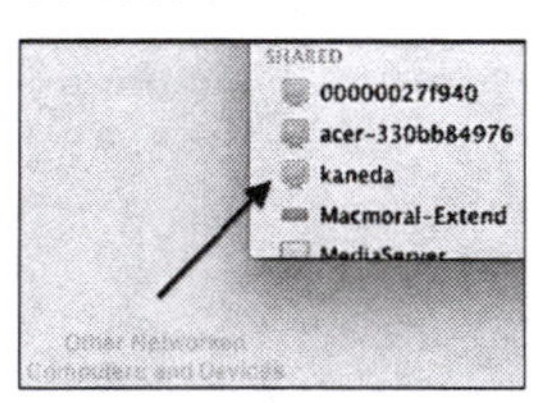 	In this section of the **Finder**, Lion visually depicts the other computers that are participating on your local area network. This section enables you to access shared resources such as files, printers, scanners, and digital media like music and video. This is also a good section to familiarize yourself with for a couple of reasons. First, it lets you see what is going on near you on the network. Second, it enables you to opt in or out of participating with various aspects of the network.

The Window View Options

In the upcoming sections, we'll take a closer look at what the **View Options** window can do for you, including how it can help you select the options that best fit your preferred style of navigation. You can choose from four basic view options for your windows: **Icon**, **List**, **Column**, and **Cover Flow**.

The Icon View

The **Icon** view displays the contents of your windows as icons. This is the best view to use if you're new to Lion or you're a visual person who prefers a more graphical approach to navigating your computer (see Figure 2–3).

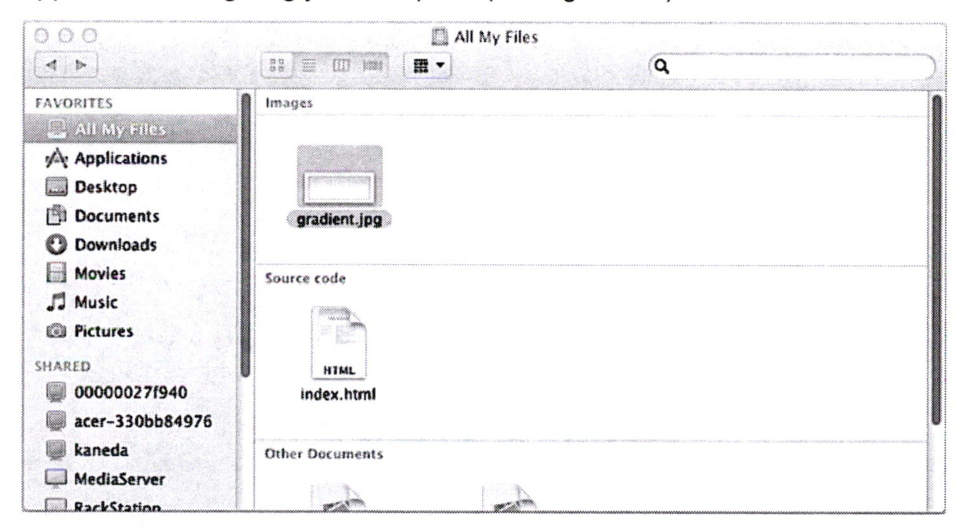

Figure 2–3. *The Icon view*

The List View

The **List** view displays files as a text-based list. While you can still see the icons to the left of the filename, they are much smaller in this view. This view is meant to give you a scrolling list of your content, and it allows you to see many more items at once. This view also displays important information about your files, including the file type, date, and other pertinent information. This is a good view to choose when you want to see a lot of files at a glance (see Figure 2–4).

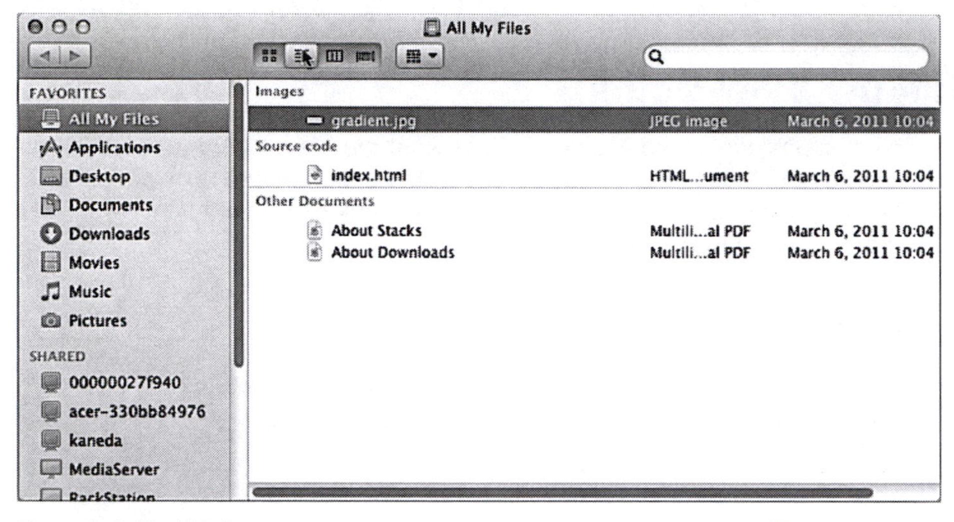

Figure 2–4. *The List view*

The Column View

The **Column** view displays your files in a column format (see Figure 2-5). The advantage to this view is that it lets you access multiple directories and files at once. This view is generally adopted by more advanced users; however, it can be useful if you want to compare the contents of two or more directories. It can also prove useful if you need to see a file's history (e.g., when it was created, last modified, or last opened), or you want to return quickly to where you were.

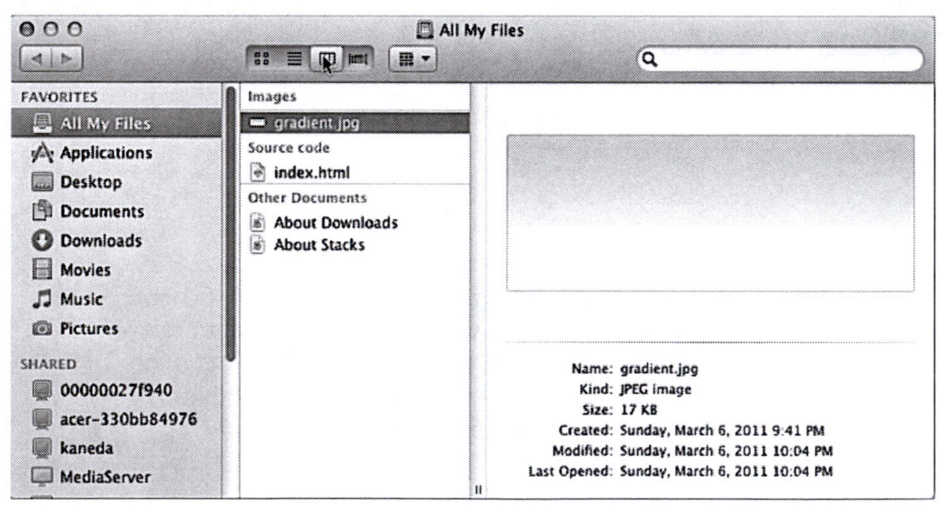

Figure 2–5. *The Column view*

The Cover Flow View

The **Cover Flow** view shows off some of the advanced graphical features for navigating the Lion operating system. This view allows you to interact with Lion's files and folders as though they were a on a carousel in a store. It provides a complete graphical preview of the file's contents; a detailed description of the file; and easy access to neighboring files, which can be seen without any extra effort on your part. This view takes some getting used to, but it also provides one of the easiest ways to get around Lion (see Figure 2-6).

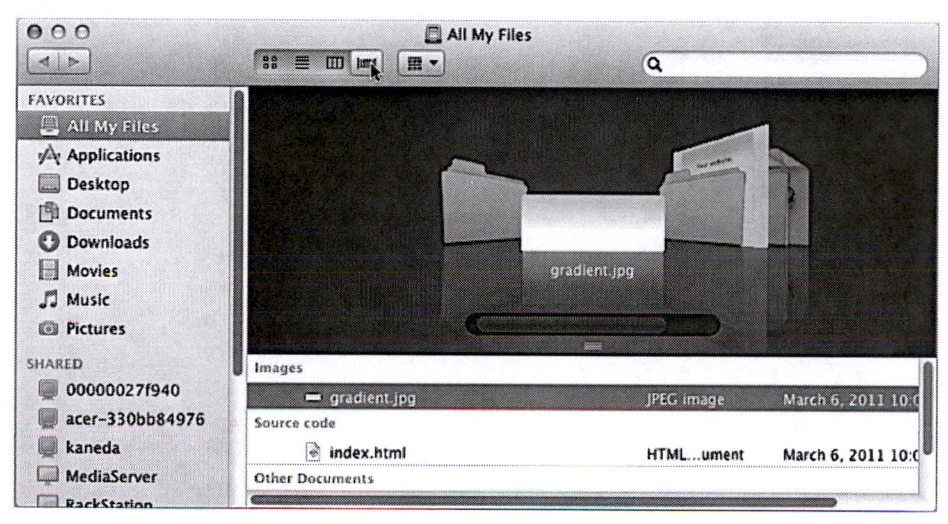

Figure 2-6. *The Cover Flow view*

Learning to use the different **Finder** views can help you quickly find your files in a manner that best matches your preferred style of using your computer. I recommend that you start with the **Icon** view because it is the easiest view to use, and it makes navigation much more manageable. Once you become comfortable with using the **Icon** view, I recommend that you gradually try out the other view styles. Knowing when and how to use the different view options is critical in getting the most out of the Lion operating system.

Finder Preferences

If you're a new Lion user who is accustomed to using Windows, you may find that one of the most difficult aspects of using Lion is that it behaves differently from Windows in almost every respect. These differences even extend to how files are displayed, stored, and accessed. Fortunately, Lion offers an intuitive way of helping you adjust to the layout of your files and folders. For example, the **Finder** includes a few important interface options that let you tailor the Lion operating system so that you can be more productive. These options help you control the way content is displayed as you navigate and use Lion. Specifically, these features allow you to customize the way the **Finder** works, so you can alter its behavior to suit your particular preferences. You can access the **Finder**'s **Preferences...** menu in one of two ways. First, you can hold down the **Command** key and then press the **Comma** key (,). Second, you can simply navigate to the **Preferences...** menu option under the **Finder** menu (see Figure 2–7).

Figure 2–7. *The Finder's Preferences... menu*

In the upcoming sections, you'll learn all about customizing the **Finder**'s various options.

The General Tab

Let's begin by looking at the **General** tab of the **Finder** app's **Preferences...** menu (see Figure 2–8). Knowing what you want displayed on your desktop is an important aspect of setting up your system. Choosing the right options enables you to keep your desktop environment as clean as possible. Table 2–2 describes the various features available for the **Finder** in the **General** tab.

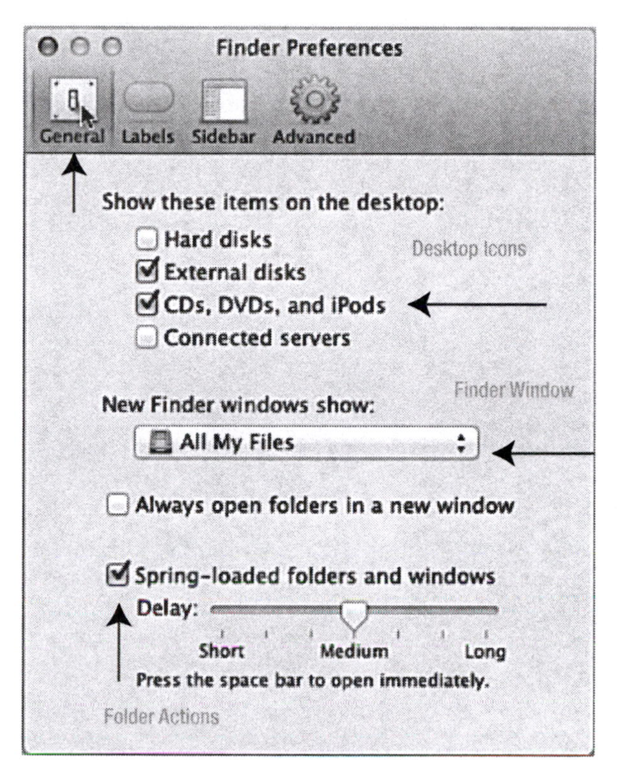

Figure 2–8. *The Finder app's General tab*

Table 2–2. *The Finder Options at a Glance*

The Finder's Options	Description
Options for desktop icons Show these items on the desktop: Hard disks External disks CDs, DVDs, and iPods Connected servers Desktop Icons	These options allow you to specify what icons are displayed on your desktop. Being selective about the icons shown can help you keep your desktop free of clutter. Users typically keep the default setup; however, if you wish to display more icons, this pane makes that possible.
Options for the Finder window 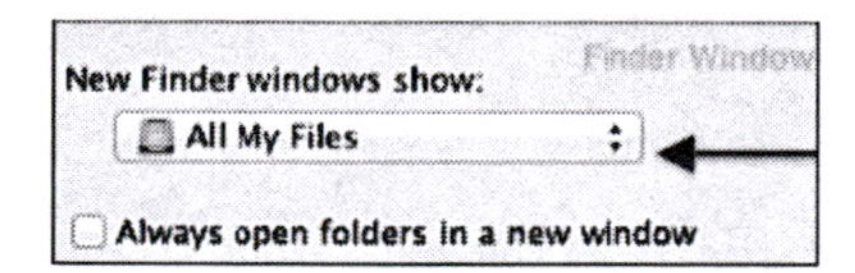 	This option allows you to specify the folder shown when you launch the **Finder**. It also allows you to specify whether folders should open in new windows when you navigate to different folders.

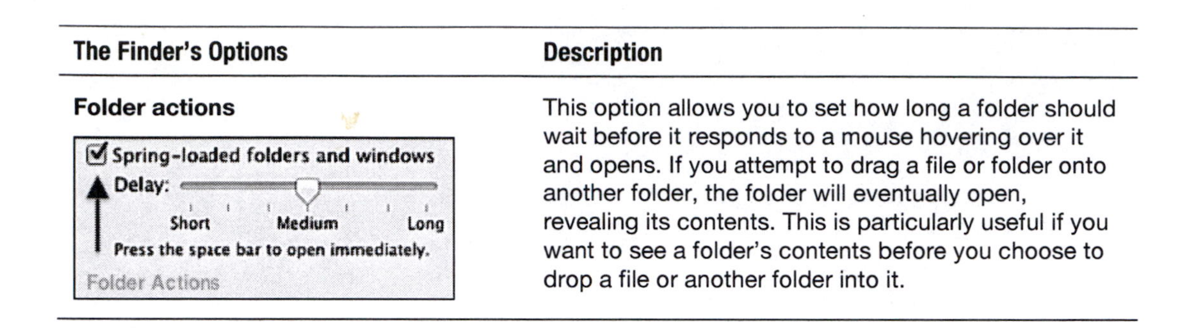

The Finder's Options	Description
Folder actions	This option allows you to set how long a folder should wait before it responds to a mouse hovering over it and opens. If you attempt to drag a file or folder onto another folder, the folder will eventually open, revealing its contents. This is particularly useful if you want to see a folder's contents before you choose to drop a file or another folder into it.

The Labels Tab

The **Labels** tab allows you to keep track of folders and files by assigning different color schemes to them. This allows you to easily identify and recognize folders and files without having to read their names or preview their contents. This feature simplifies the process of viewing and retrieving the correct files and folders you may be looking for (see Figure 2–9).

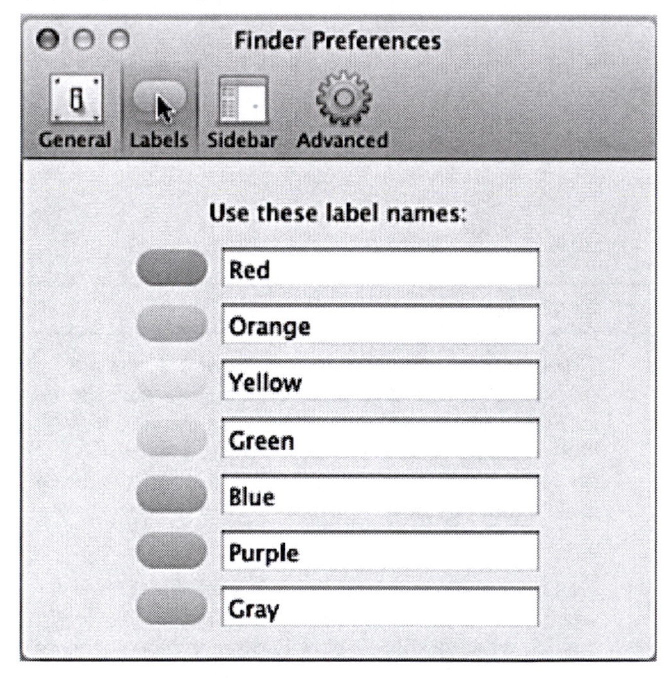

Figure 2–9. *The Finder app's Labels tab*

The Sidebar Tab

The **Sidebar** tab (see Figure 2–10) allows you to tweak the contents of the **Finder** app's **Sidebar** menu. This tab is great for minimizing the content seen when initially launching the **Finder**. Used appropriately, the options in this tab help you decrease the overall clutter seen in the **Finder**'s sidebar.

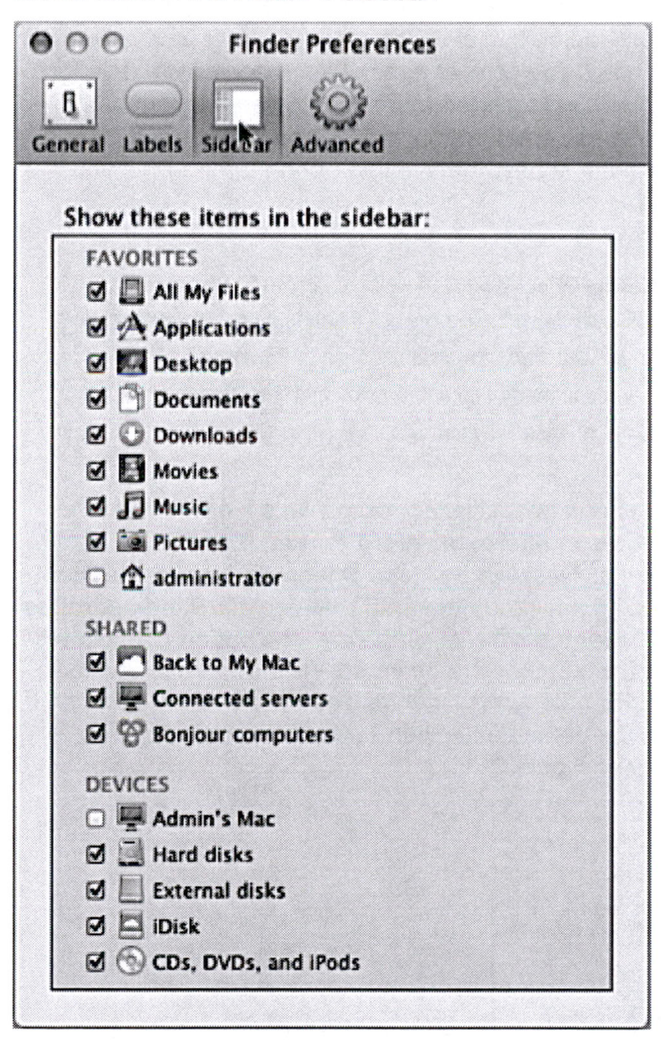

Figure 2–10. *The Finder app's Sidebar tab*

The Advanced Tab

Some of the more advanced options in the **Finder** app's **Preferences...** menu affect the way Lion functions. For example, the **Advanced** tab lets you change the way files are deleted. It is important to understand how functions like file deletion can affect your file management. A poor understanding of this essential function can lead to unwanted consequences, such as unintentionally deleting a file permanently. Lion's **Show warning before emptying the Trash** option helps you protect against such accidental deletions by prompting you to confirm that you do in fact want to delete a given file permanently. Further, you can use the **Empty Trash securely** option to make sure that the data is 100% unrecoverable once it is deleted. It is best to have this option turned on if you are in a place where security is an issue.

> **NOTE:** Selecting the **Empty Trash securely** option causes all deleted files to be completely unrecoverable. Selecting this option will slow down the process of deleting files, but you may find the extra couple of seconds required to be well worth the wait because of the security advantages this option provides. I highly recommend that you employ this feature to ensure that items you want deleted from your Mac are deleted irrevocably.

File extensions indicate the file format of a given file. For example, a file with the `.doc` extension indicates that the file is stored in **Microsoft Word** format. If you have **Microsoft Word** installed, it will open all files with the `.doc` extension. Lion is intelligent enough to create these associations, so it is recommended that you allow the operating system to manage these associations for the sake of simplicity. The option to show file extensions—and give warnings if and when they are changed—is a good option to use when you are dealing with a lot of similar file types, such as `.doc` and `.docx`. However, it is recommended that you stick with the default extension options if you do not fully understand what file extensions do (see Figure 2–11).

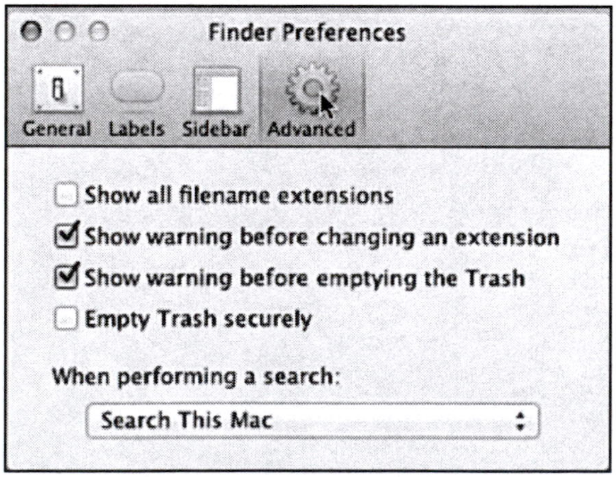

Figure 2–11. *The Finder app's Advanced tab*

The Finder App's Right-Click Options

Right-clicking a file or folder while using the **Finder** brings up a special menu that changes depending on the context (see Figure 2-12). The options exposed in this menu allow you to do several things with a folder, file, or group of files. Table 2-3 describes various menu options you will see when right-clicking a file or folder.

> **NOTE:** The options you see when you right-click a file or folder when using the **Finder** can vary significantly. The specific options displayed depend greatly on the nature of the folder or file you right-click.

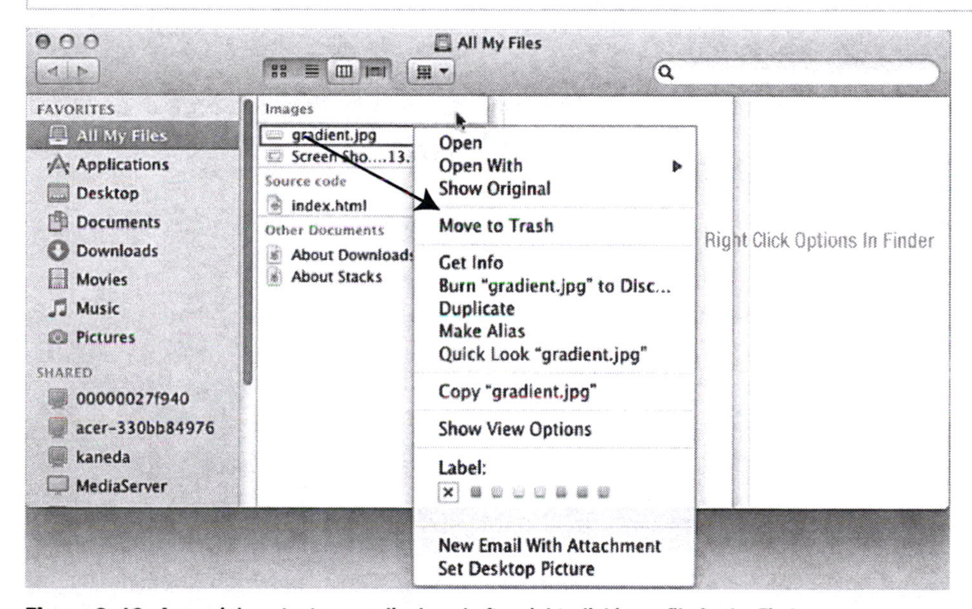

Figure 2-12. *A special context menu displayed after right-clicking a file in the Finder*

Table 2-3. *Drilling Down on the Finder App's Right-Click Menu Options*

Option	Description
Open	This option lets you to open a file using the default program associated with its file type.
Open With	This option allows you to open a file with the application of your choice. Use this option if you want to open a file with an application other than the default application set for that file type.
Show Original	If you right-click a copy or alias of a file, this option highlights the location of the original file.

Option	Description
Move to Trash	This option simply moves the item to your Trash Bin folder; you can then use the **Trash Bin** app to delete the file permanently.
Get Info	This option allows you to see the different attributes associated with a file or folder (see Figure 2–13).
Burn to Disc	If you have a blank CD-ROM or DVD capable of writing and storing data, you can use this option to *burn* (i.e., copy) a file or folder to your CD-ROM or DVD.
Duplicate	This option allows you to duplicate the current file with an exact copy. This option is useful for cases where you are working on a file, and you do not want to tamper with the original.
Make Alias	This allows you to create a shortcut to a file or folder. You can then place that shortcut in a location you find convenient to access (e.g., your desktop).
Quick Look	This option provides a partial or full-screen preview of the contents of the right-clicked file or folder.
Copy	This option allows you to copy the right-clicked item, which you can then paste to a new location.
Show View Options	This option allows you to access the **Finder** window options previously discussed in "The Window View Options" section of this chapter.
Label	This option allows you to associate a color with a file or folder. Labels help you organize and find files and folders more quickly and easily.
New Email Attachment	This option allows you to send the file directly to another person using the **Mail** application. This option saves you time and effort by creating the e-mail for you, and then inserting the file into the body of the e-mail.
Set Desktop Picture	This option appears in the right-click context menu for image files only. It lets you set the currently selected image as your desktop background.

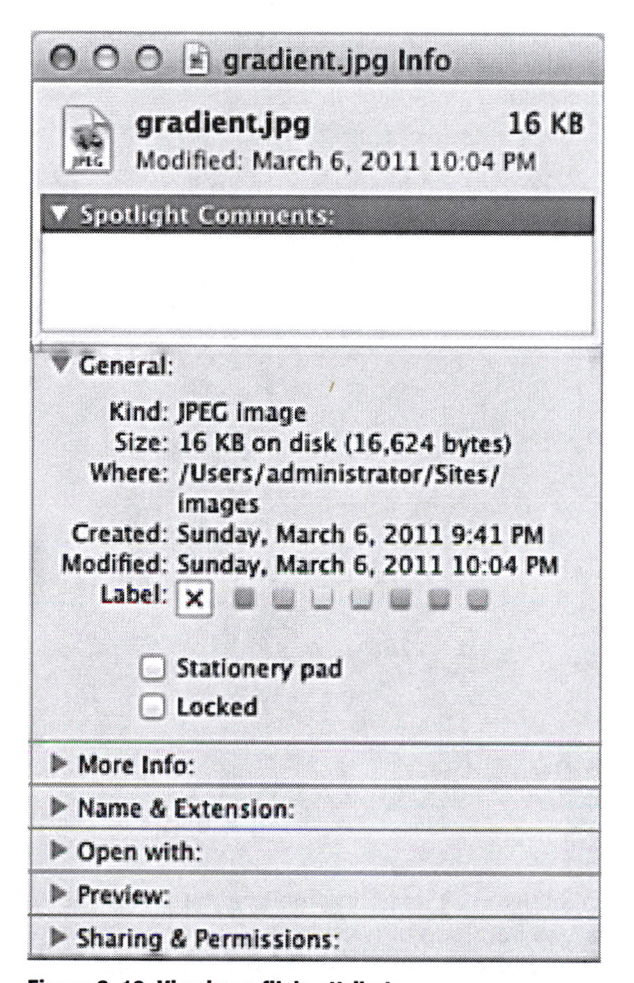

Figure 2–13. Viewing a file's attributes

Stacks

Mac OS X Lion was constructed around the basic premise that empowering users means giving them immediate access to the information on their system in an organized and easy-to-retrieve fashion. One way of achieving this is by ensuring that users have the flexibility to choose how they would like things to appear on their screen. Lion's Stacks feature provides users with an easy-to-use interface for accessing files. This approach for accessing files differs significantly from the approach provided by the **Finder**. For example, the Stacks feature overhauls accessibility on the Mac by letting you access files in a **Grid**, **List**, or **Fan** view. It is the content contained within the stacks that makes these views unique. Rather than seeing everything you have on your system, you get to specify exactly what shows up and how in a stack.

By default, the Stacks feature is located in the lower-right corner of your primary user window. It sits to the right of the Dock's divider line, which separates your application shortcuts from your stack items (see Figure 2-14).

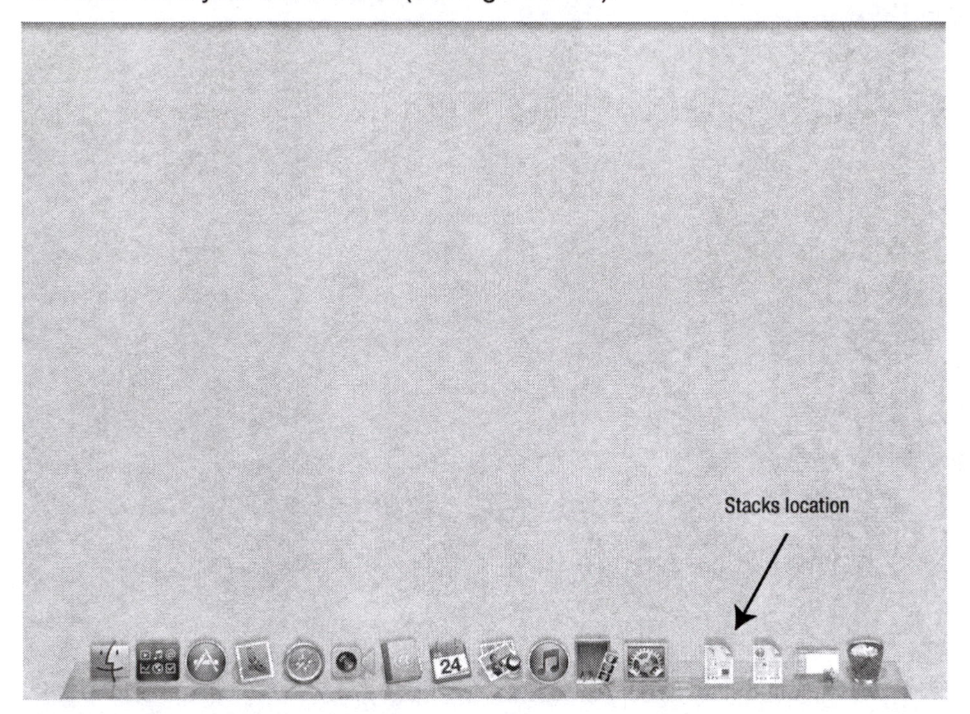

Figure 2–14. *The location of your stacks*

Using the Stacks feature is quite simple. You begin by selecting the icon type that you wish to use for a given stack. You can choose from one of two views: **Folder** or **Stack**. Selecting the **Folder** view will display a **Folder** icon that represents your stack; and selecting the **Stack** view will display a preview of the contents in a stack in icon form (see Figures 2–15 and 2–16 for a quick look at the differences).

Figure 2–15. *Folder views of stacks*

Figure 2–16. *Stack views of stacks*

Notice that one view displays the **Folder** icons, while the other displays a preview of the most recent document contained in a stack. Both views have their advantages. The **Folder** view simplifies the look and feel of the Stacks feature, blending it neatly into the desktop environment. On the other hand, the **Stack** view gives you a pictorial representation of the contents in a stack. This view enables you to examine a stack based on its contents, rather than its folder type. To choose your preferred view for a given stack, simply right-click that stack and select a view (see Figure 2–17).

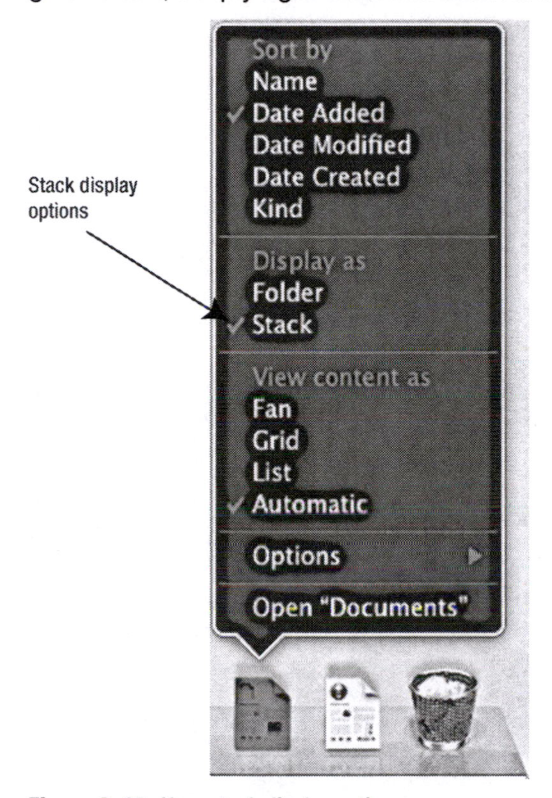

Figure 2–17. *Your stack display options*

Once you have chosen your display type, the icons for the items in that stack will change appropriately. After making these changes, you will want to configure how you view the files and folders contained within your stack.

Stack Viewing

The **Stack** view itself has three view modes: **Grid**, **List**, and **Fan**. Table 2–4 offers a quick rundown of the advantages of each view.

Table 2–4. *Stack Views*

View	Description
Fan View	This option displays your items in an elongated fashion that arcs as it extends to make better use of your screen space. This view provides very quick access to the information inside your stack. Use this view when there is not a lot of content in the stack. 
Grid View	This option provides you with a grid-like view of the contents of your stack. This is very similar to the view you would see if you were to view the same content in the **Finder**; and it provides a very clean and organized way of displaying your stack's contents. Use this view when you would prefer to have a spread-type layout, and you wish to get a closer view of the previews of the items contained in your stack. 
List View	This option is the simplest of your available views. It displays a text menu that lists of all the items contained in your stack. Use this view when you have a lot of items in your stack but limited screen real estate (such as when using a Macbook Air 11"). This view also has the advantage of being the fastest view; it brings the Stacks feature up almost immediately when accessed. 
Automatic	This is the default **Stack** view, and it will automatically select the most appropriate view for your stack, depending on the type and amount of content it contains. This setting has the advantage of offering what Lion believes is the most appropriate view of your stack, without requiring any input from you. Use this option when you want Lion to determine the best way to view your stack.

To create additional stacks, use the **Finder** to navigate to a folder you would like to have quick access to, and then drag that folder into the Stacks area to the right of the Dock's dividing line (see Figure 2–18 for more details).

Figure 2–18. *Creating a new stack*

The Stacks feature provides quick and simple access to your files—without requiring that you launch the **Finder**. Moreover, this feature can greatly reduce the need to rely on Lion's built-in search methods to find the files you want to retrieve.

Airdrop

The Airdrop feature is a new and truly innovative feature introduced by the Lion OS that makes sharing files extremely easy for Lion users. Airdrop solves the age-old problem of trading files between two Mac users who do not have an external storage device on hand, but who do not wish to go through the trouble of creating a folder, creating a user, and then configuring things to make that folder accessible to that user. The Airdrop approach also less cumbersome than sending files through e-mail.

By default, Lion sets up an ad-hoc Wi-Fi network between participating computers, enabling Mac users to exchange files wirelessly. Under this approach, sharing document-type files (which are typically quite small) occurs almost instantaneously. This approach can also make sharing files between office personnel safe and easy, while also allowing two strangers in a coffee shop to meet and exchange information securely.

Using Airdrop is extremely simple. You begin by accessing the Airdrop folder in the **Finder** (see Figure 2–19).

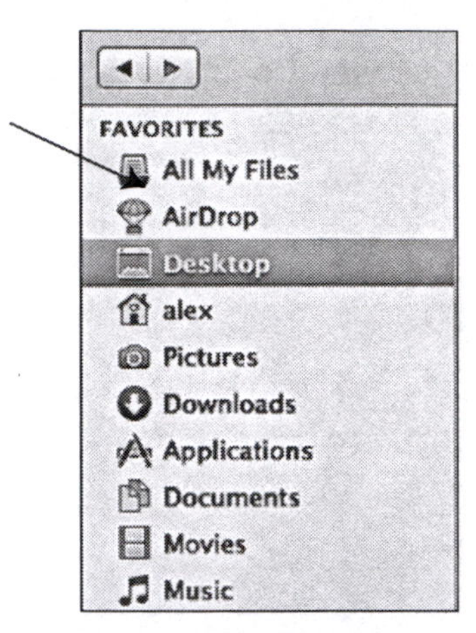

Figure 2–19. *Accessing Airdrop*

Upon accessing Airdrop, you will see the **Airdrop** icon change into an animated radar beacon, as shown in the image below.

Once the beacon is displayed and animated, you will notice that the bottom of the **Finder** window now displays the image of a fortune cookie (see Figure 2–20).

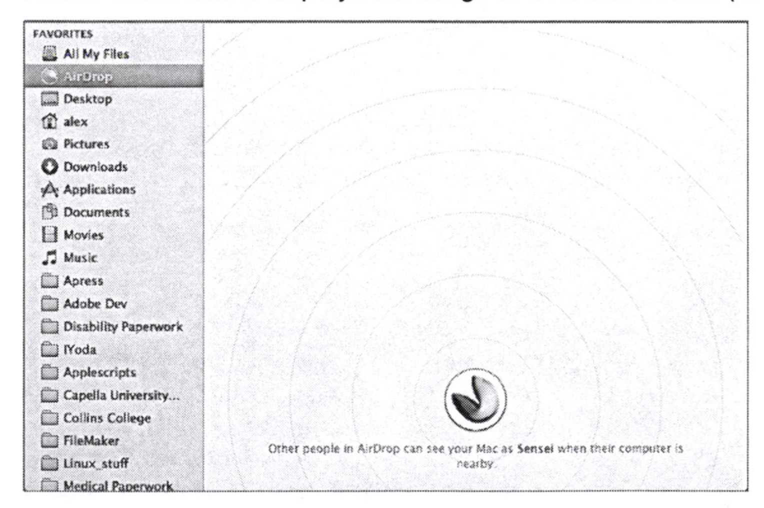

Figure 2–20. *Airdrop's Finder window*

You are now ready to begin sharing files with other Mac users who also have the Airdrop feature enabled. To share a file with another Airdrop user, simply drag and drop it into the Airdrop area on the image of the intended recipient. Doing so will present that user with a prompt that asks if she would like to accept the file exchange. If so, the fortune cookie will turn into an image icon that represents the recipient. If more than one Airdrop user is in the vicinity, then you will see multiple users in your Airdrop window. In that case, you can simply drag the file onto the image of the intended recipient.

Using Airdrop is just that simple. This feature was created to enable users to share specific files without giving access to the rest of the files on the Mac sharing the file. Another nice aspect of this feature: it easily bridges the gap between power users and novices when it comes to file sharing.

NOTE: Airdrop does not work on some older Mac models; and as a result, it may be unavailable to some users.

Bluetooth—the Airdrop Alternative

Fortunately, there is hope for Lion users who were hoping to use the Airdrop feature, only to discover they do not have the appropriate hardware. Almost all Macs made in 2006 or later ship with Bluetooth networking built into them. This file-sharing technology has the advantage of being compatible with any Bluetooth-capable device, not just other Macs. Thus, you could use this technology to transfer files to and from a Bluetooth-enabled phone, MP3 player, or video device. Bluetooth is slower than Wi-Fi, so don't expect blistering transfer speeds when moving your files. Still, it is a very usable and convenient option for exchanging files where one party can't use the Airdrop feature.

Transferring files with your Mac's Bluetooth capability is not difficult; however, it does require a few more steps than using Airdrop to accomplish the same task. Follow these steps to use Bluetooth to transfer a file between two Macs:

1. From the **Bluetooth** menu located on Lion's main menu at the top of the screen, select **Send File...** (see Figure 2-21).

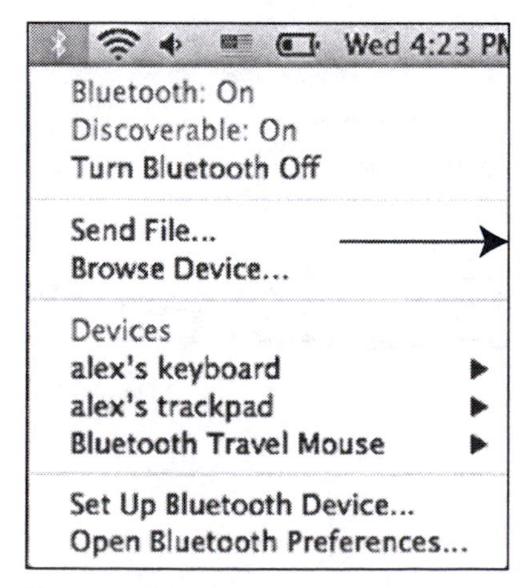

Figure 2-21. *Bluetooth's Send File... menu option*

2. Select the file(s) you wish to send.

3. Select the Bluetooth recipient you wish to send the file to (see Figure 2–22).

4. Click **Send** once you have selected the intended recipient.

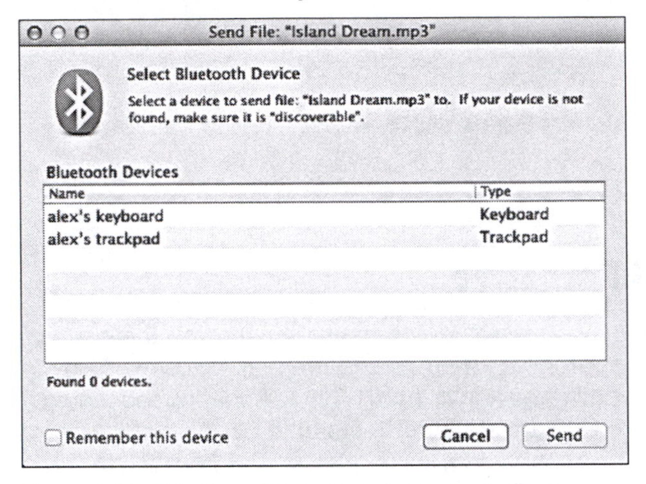

Figure 2–22. *Selecting a Bluetooth device to send a file to*

The rule here is that each recipient must have Bluetooth enabled before this type of file transfer will work. To enable Bluetooth on your Mac, go to your system preferences either by clicking the **System Preferences** icon in your Dock or by typing the words "System Preferences" into the **Spotlight** search box (see Figure 2–23).

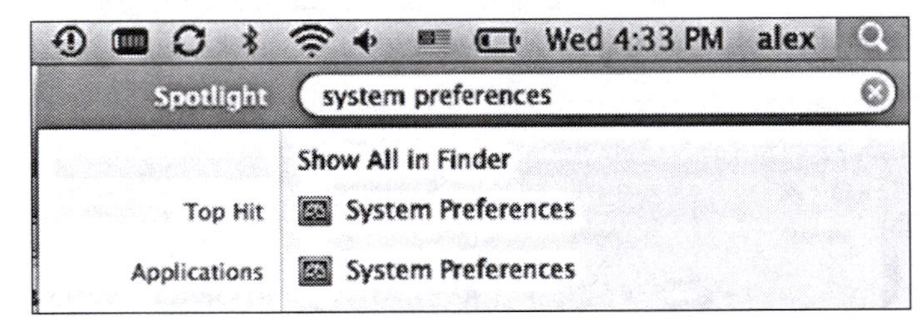

Figure 2–23. *Using the Spotlight search box to find the System Preferences folder*

Next, select the **Bluetooth** preferences option (see Figure 2–24).

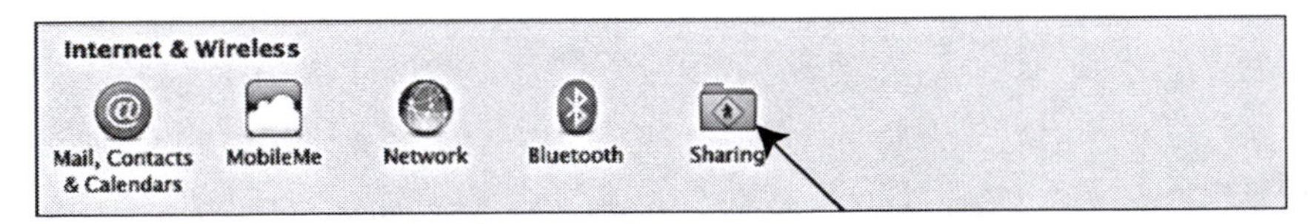

Figure 2–24. *The Bluetooth preferences icon*

At this point, you will see a dialog for setting that technology's options. Make sure that Bluetooth is turned on (see Figure 2–25).

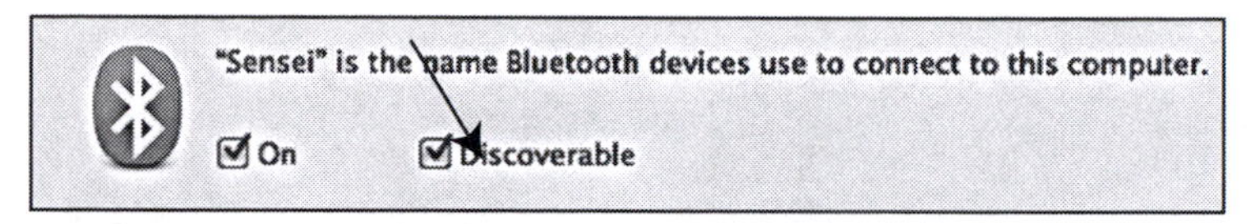

Figure 2–25. *Turning Bluetooth on*

After you turn Bluetooth on, you must enable sharing via Bluetooth. To do so, select the **Sharing Setup** option from the same window (see Figure 2–26).

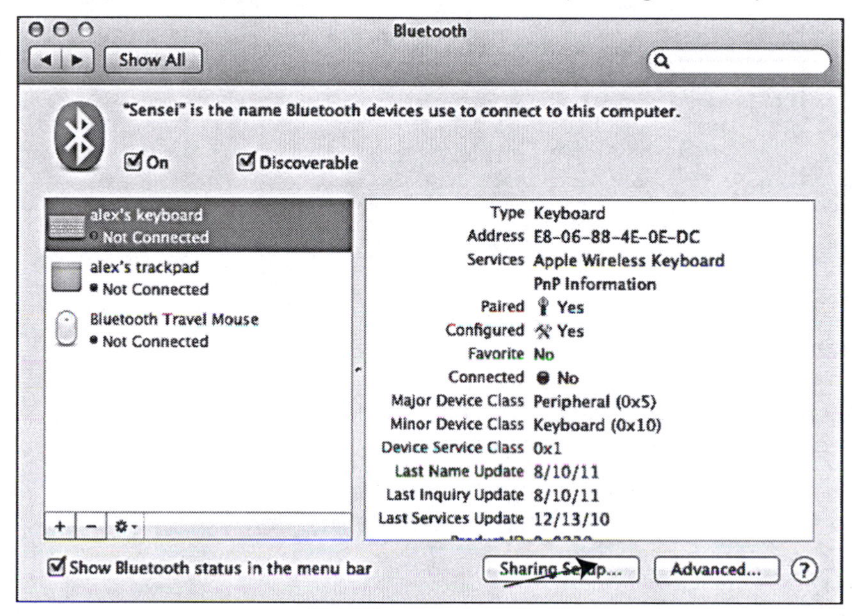

Figure 2–26. *The Bluetooth Sharing Setup options*

To complete this process, you need to enable Bluetooth sharing and configure the options you wish to use to transfer files between yourself and other Bluetooth users (see Figure 2–27).

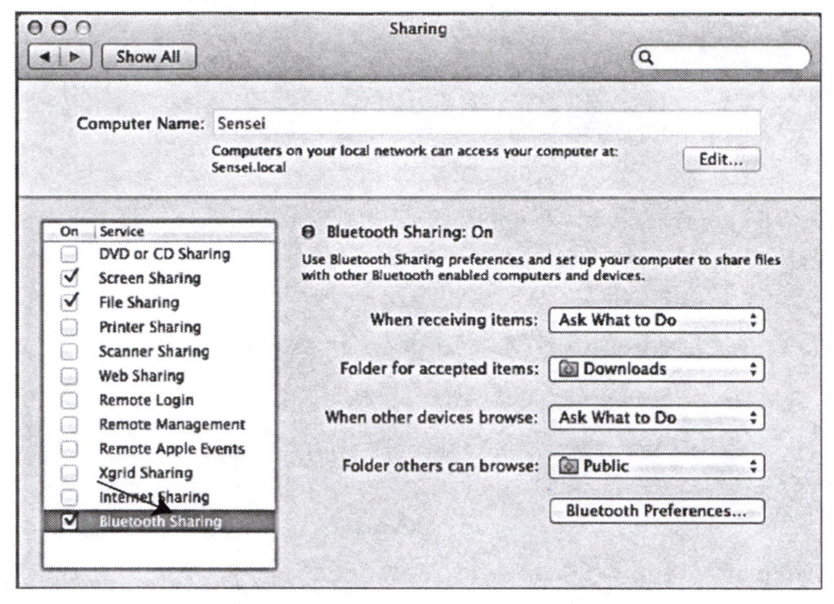

Figure 2–27. *Enabling Bluetooth sharing*

Once you are satisfied with the way your Bluetooth sharing preferences are arranged, you can proceed to share files using Bluetooth technology.

File sharing with Bluetooth isn't the ideal approach; however, it does provide an excellent alternative to the Airdrop feature, should you need one.

Using Launchpad

`Launchpad` lets you quickly access your favorite and most-used applications with one simple click. It also allows you to view your application list using the full screen of your Mac. This application works similarly to the `Launch Pad` app on an iPad or iPhone, allowing you to bundle and group similar files and folders (see Figure 2-28).

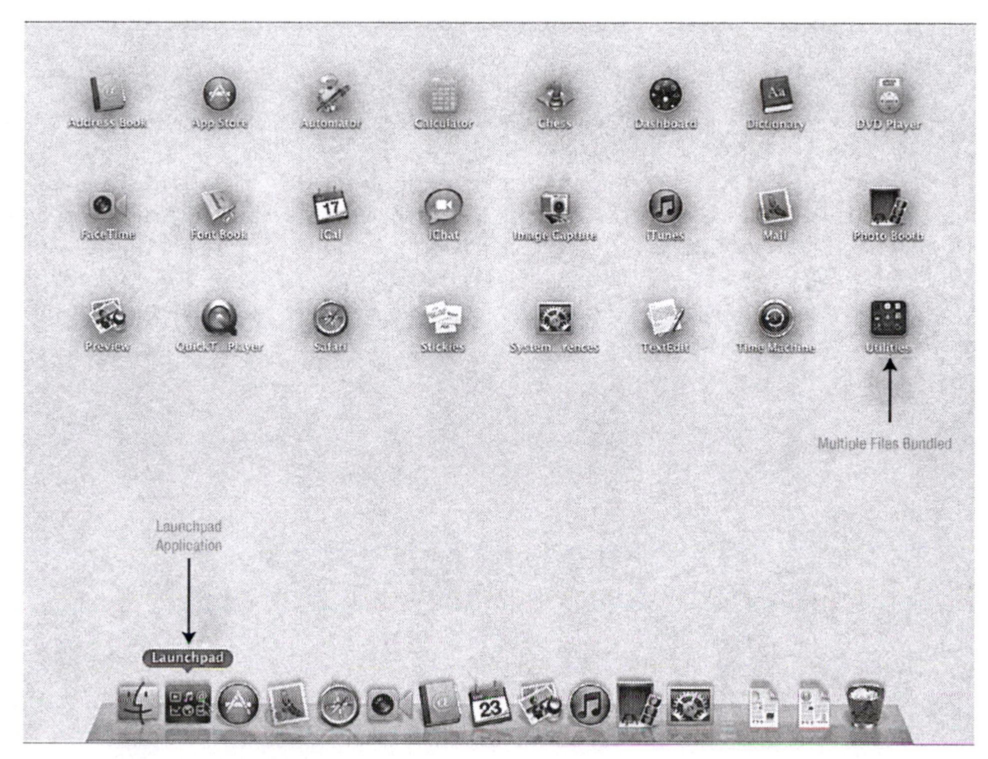

Figure 2–28. *The Lion Launchpad app*

Spotlight Searching

The **Finder**'s **Spotlight** box can greatly simplify your user experience and enhance your productivity. This box gives you a granular way to search for files, folders, e-mails, and even recently visited websites. You can use Spotlight searches to find anything associated with what you are looking for. For example, assume you type the words "my cat" into the **Spotlight** box. The **Finder** can find all of the files on your computer with names containing "my cat." But it does much more than that: it can also find any e-mails, documents, or images that have the words "my cat" located somewhere in them. This feature uses the index of your entire Mac, so there are virtually no limits on what it can find. Thus, a search for "Paul" will provide a link to his information in your address book. It will also find any documents you've created that contain his name. To conduct a Spotlight search, simply click the magnifying glass icon in the upper-right corner of your Mac's main menu. You can also bring up the **Spotlight** box by holding down the **Command** key and then pressing the **Spacebar** key (see Figure 2–29).

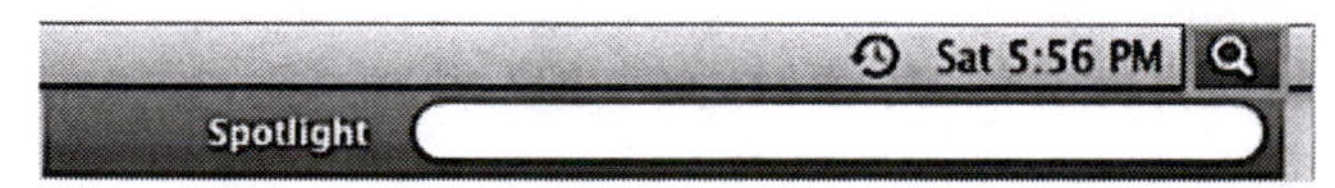

Figure 2–29. *The Spotlight box*

Summary

This chapter has covered some of the applications commonly used to navigate the Lion operating system. I have walked you through the various options available, explaining how these options work so you can get the most of out of your Lion desktop experience right out of the gate. I have also covered a couple different approaches for sharing your files with other Mac users. Remember to try out different options, so you can figure what approaches best suit your needs. There is no single right way to navigate the Lion OS; the best way to do this will be different for everyone. Your job is to experiment until you find the combination that works best for you.

Chapter 3

Understanding Lion Application Menus and Shortcuts

In this chapter, we will cover the menus and shortcuts included in a few of the more useful applications that ship with your Lion operating system: the **Finder**, **Safari**, and **iTunes**. Lion ships with many applications, but these three are the ones you'll use most often to enhance your overall desktop experience.

General Application Menus

Nearly all apps for your Mac—and that includes those that ship with Lion—include a menu system that allows you to navigate through their various features. Menu categories commonly included with most apps include **File**, **Edit**, **View**, **Go**, **Window**, and **Help**. To illustrate how you can use menus to get more out of the Lion OS, we'll begin by taking a look at the menu system of the **Finder** (see Figure 3–1).

The Finder

The **Finder**'s menus exhibit a lot of the traits you will see in just about every other program you will use on the Lion OS. Notice that the application's name—**Finder**—is shown in the leftmost menu category. All Lion applications follow this convention. All Lion applications also employ a common menu placement for some menu options. For example, the first few items that appear under the menu that contains the application's name generally provide similar functionality. Specifically, they provide information about the app; they let you tailor the program to suit your needs and preferences; or they let you adjust certain aspects of the program to improve its performance and functionality, based on the type of Mac that you have. In the case of the **Finder**, the first item listed under the **Finder** menu is **About Finder**; selecting this option reveals important information about the **Finder**.

NOTE: Remember that we are using the **Finder** because it nicely illustrates how to use menus in Lion. And while it does show many common features you should expect to see in other applications, the **Finder** may show more or fewer options than you'll see in those other applications. Let's take a look at some of the menu features commonly found in the leftmost menu that contains the application name (use Figure 3–1 as a guide for this section).

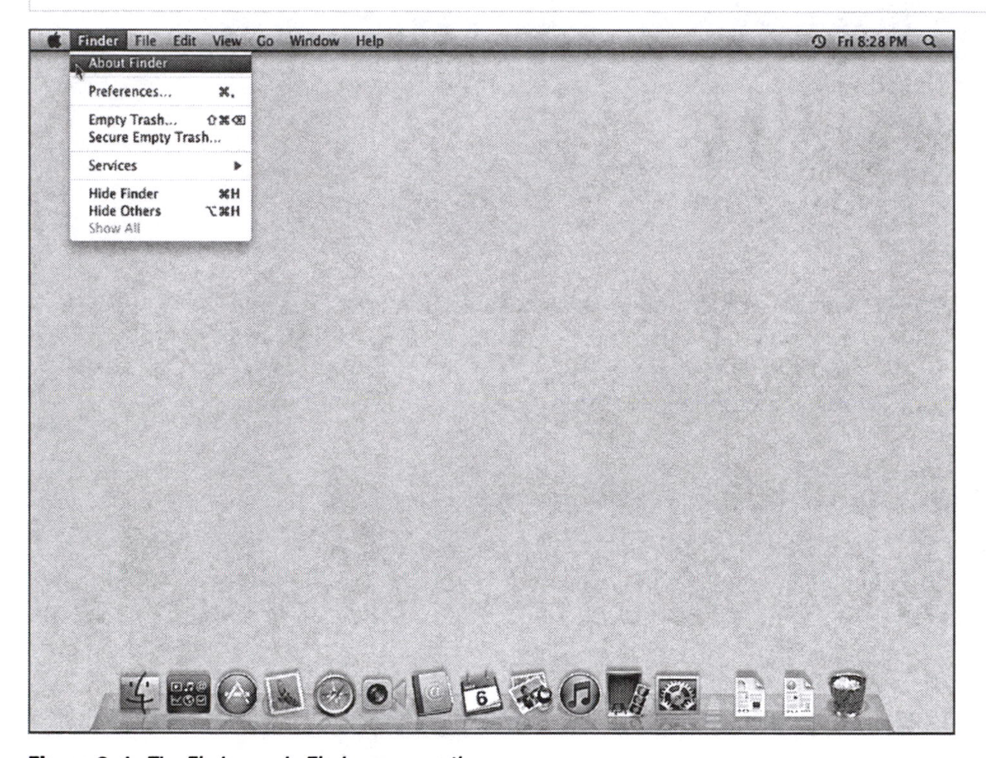

Figure 3–1. *The Finder app's Finder menu options*

You can see that there are several options available under the **Finder** menu (see Table 3–1 for a detailed explanation of each menu option).

Table 3–1. *What the **Finder** Menu Options Do*

Menu Option	Description
About Finder	Selecting the **About *[program name]*** option will let you know in detail what version of a program you are working with. This option will often list the authors of the program, copyright information, and where you can find support or contact information. Often, software authors will release updates and patches to improve the functionality of their software. For example, they might release a security patch to address the latest threats over the Internet. In many cases, the software developers will request that the user check the current version of the program that is running to determine whether the available patch or upgrade is necessary. Selecting the **About *[program name]*** option is where you go to figure out whether you have a version of the software that needs updating.
Preferences...	Almost all of the software that runs on Lion includes a **Preferences...** option. Selecting this option lets you turn various program features on or off, so you can change the way the program works to better suit your style of computing. The **Preferences...** option often provides a broad view of a program's options, telling you at a glance how changing the value of a particular option will affect the way the program runs or operates. This is a valuable submenu item, one that you will find yourself using time and time again. It is helpful to remember that, if you don't like the way a given program behaves, you might be able to use this menu option to change its behavior more to your liking.
Empty Trash...	You will not see this option in every application; however it is very common, and it does exactly what you would expect it to do. That is, it allows you to empty your computer's Trash Bin, thereby freeing up space on your hard disk. You will learn more about the **Secure Empty Trash...** option later in this book.
Services	Clicking the **Services** submenu item will reveal an entire list of options for you to choose from. This list can consist of application- and/or Lion-specific options. The particular options you see will depend greatly on the application you're using, so it is best that you simply explore what is available here as you use different programs. This is a good place to find hidden gems like *text to speech*, which allows you to highlight text in a word processing application and have your computer say that text aloud to you! Powerful options like these are often found only in the **Services** menu; keeping your eye on the functionality exposed here can significantly enhance your productivity.
Hide	The **Hide** submenus let you do one of three things: **Hide *[application name]*** (i.e., **Hide Finder** in this example): This menu item allows you to hide the application you are currently using completely from view. **Hide Others:** This menu item allows you to hide all other applications from view, so you can concentrate on the app you're using. This is a common feature, one that is available in almost every application. This feature works system-wide, allowing you to manipulate the position and appearance of the windows you are using to interact with various applications. **Show All:** This brings back all of the items you have previously chosen to hide.

Reviewing the File Menu

Most applications that run on Lion also include a **File** menu; the **Finder** app is no exception. This menu allows you to perform many basic actions, such as save files, open new files, and perform various other actions related to file maintenance (see Figure 3-2). The options in this menu will vary greatly from application to application; however, you will also see many similarities between the items listed here in most applications.

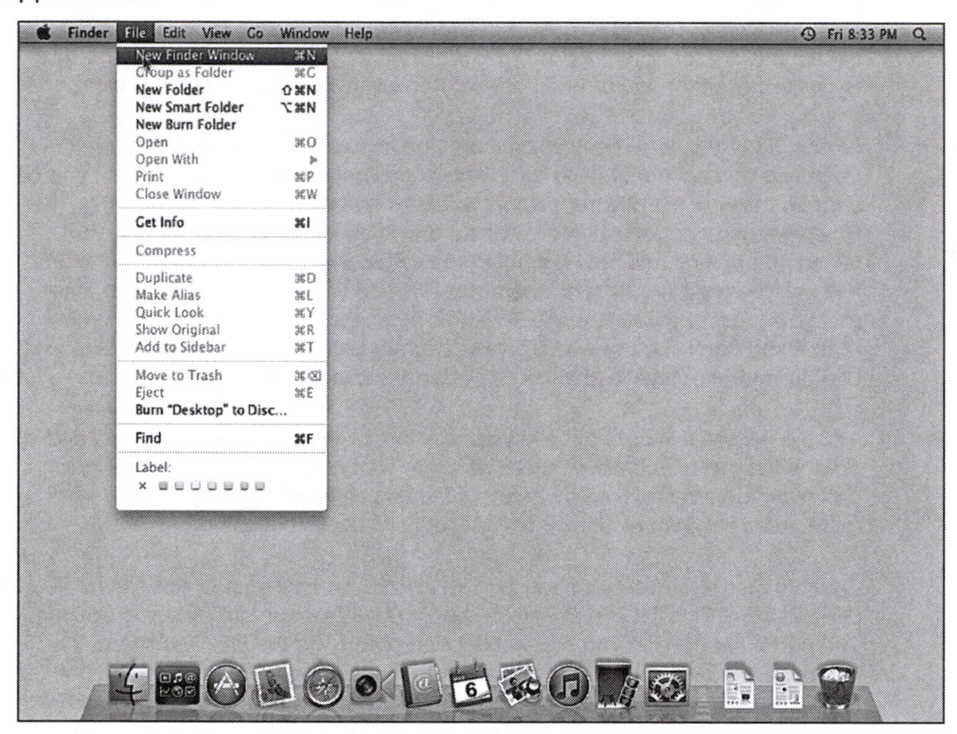

Figure 3–2. *The Finder's File menu options*

As is commonly the case, the **Finder** includes a wealth of items under its **File** menu. I recommend that you take the time to review an app's **File** menu before you begin to use the app in earnest; this will ensure that you know your options for manipulating an app's files from the outset.

Drilling Down on the Edit Menu

An app's **Edit** menu allows you to perform system actions such as **Cut**, **Copy**, and **Paste** (see Figure 3-3). Most applications allow you to do some type of copying and pasting, either within the application itself or between that application and other applications you might have open. This extremely useful feature can significantly increase your productivity because it allows you to share information between various, often unrelated applications. For example, assume you want to copy text from a **Microsoft Word** document to an **Adobe Photoshop** document. The **Copy** and **Paste** features exposed by the **Edit** menus in those apps enable you to accomplish that task.

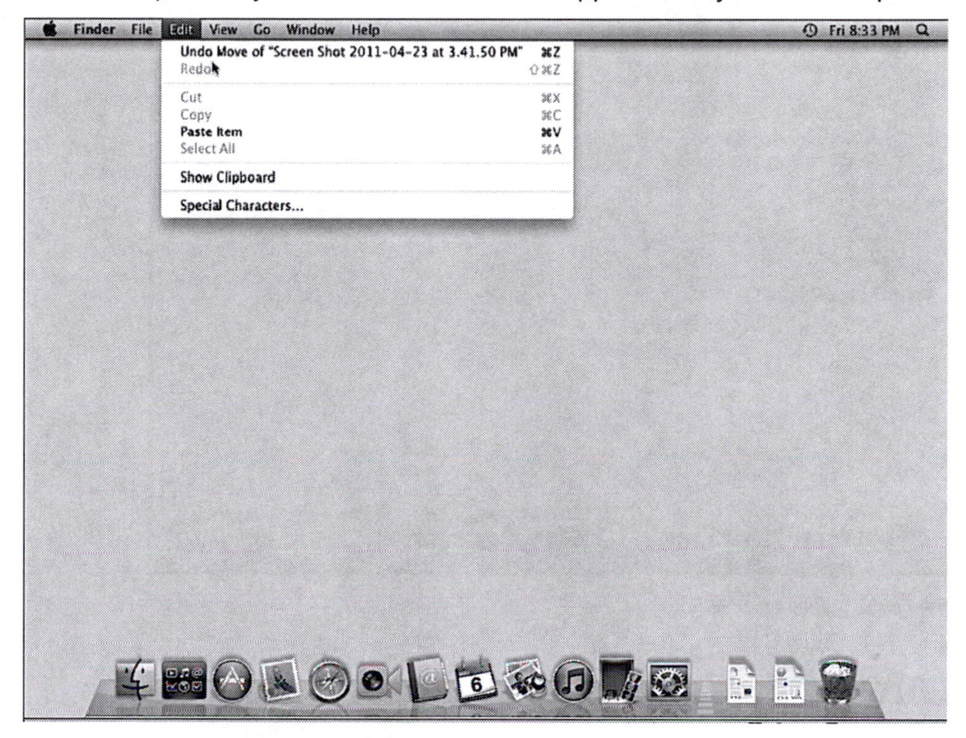

Figure 3–3. *The Finder's Edit menu options*

Exploring the View Menu

An application's **View** menu enables you to manipulate that app's visual options. For example, the **Finder**'s **View** menu lets you arrange the icons and file items you see in the **Finder** in various ways (see Figure 3–4). We covered a few of these options in Chapter 2: "Getting Around in Lion"; however, the **View** menu gives you an additional way of accessing the **Finder**'s visual options. The number and scope of the options you see in this menu can differ dramatically from application to application. For example, **Microsoft Word**'s **View** menu lets you select between different page-layout views, such as **Outline** and **Print Layout**.

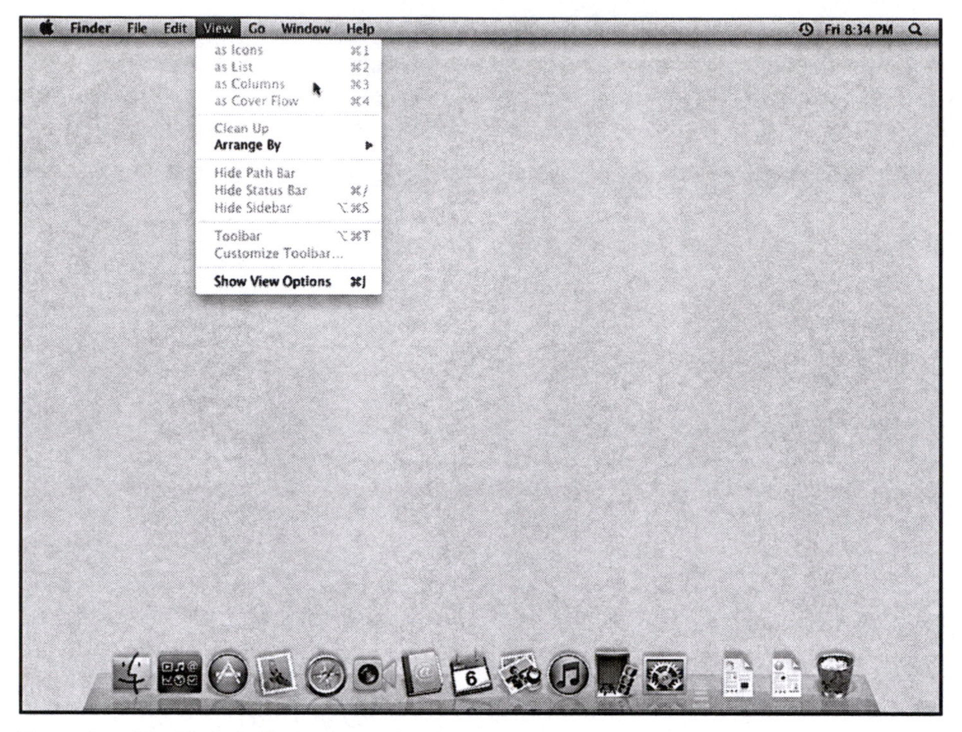

Figure 3–4. *The Finder's View menu options*

Zipping Around the Finder's Go Menu

The **Finder**'s **Go** menu provides the ultimate list of shortcuts. Note that the **Go** menu is only visible when you have the **Finder** application selected. This menu allows you to jump to many sections of your Mac quickly, reducing the time it takes to navigate from one part of your system to another. The options you see listed in this menu also serve as a great introduction to the idea of application shortcuts.

> **NOTE:** *Shortcuts* give you a fast, interactive way of navigating the Lion OS, letting you use your keyboard to access items and places on your system. This is a much faster way of navigating your system than relying solely on your mouse. For example, shortcuts let you jump from Point A to Point B instantly, whether Points A and B are applications or file areas on your computer.

There are thousands of available shortcuts; however, we will ease into the subject by concentrating on only a few, so you aren't overwhelmed by the sheer number of them available on Lion. Let's start with the shortcuts available from the **Finder**'s **Go** menu (see Figure 3–5).

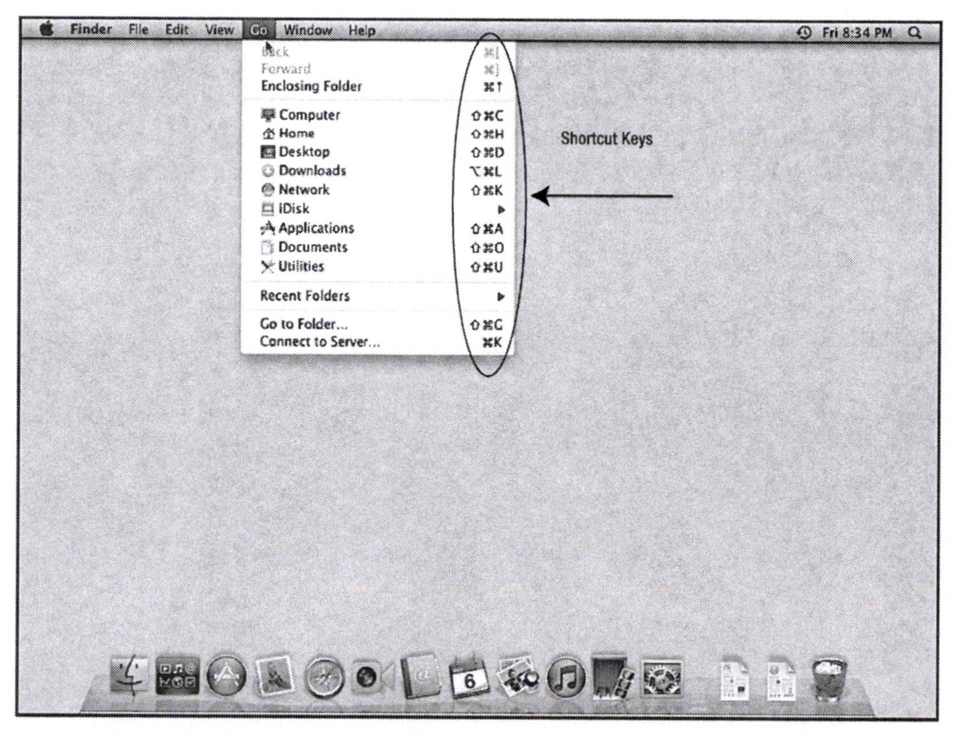

Figure 3–5. *The Finder app's Go menu options*

If you look closely at the circled area in Figure 3-6, you will notice that there are various symbols shown to the right of most menu options.

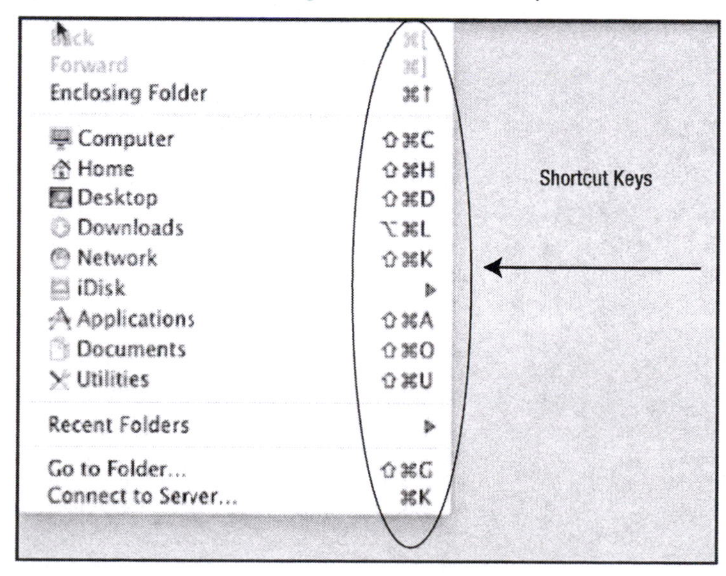

Figure 3–6. *The **Go** menu's shortcut key combinations*

The symbols shown in this figure indicate various key combinations you can press to execute the menu options. Of course, before you can use these shortcuts, you must first learn what each symbol represents and how it corresponds to the keys on your keyboard. Table 3–2 describes what each symbol is and how it maps to your keyboard.

Table 3–2. *The Mac Menu Symbols and How They Map to Your Keyboard*

Symbol	Description	Symbol	Description
⌘	The **Command/Apple** key (equivalent to the **Control** key on a PC)	⎋	The **Escape** key
⌥	The **Option** key (like **Alt** on a PC)	⇞	The **Page Up** key
⇧	The **Shift** key	⇟	The **Page Down** key
⌃	The **Control** key (Control-click = Right-click)	↖	The **Home** key
⇥	The **Tab** key	↘	The **End** key
↩	The **Return** key	←↑→↓	The **Left Arrow** , **Up Arrow**, **Right Arrow**, and **Down Arrow** keys
⌤	The **Enter** key (on the Number Pad)	⌫	The **Delete Left** key (like the **Backspace** key on a PC)
⏏	The **Eject** key	⌦	The **Delete Right** key (also called the **Forward Delete** key)

Using these keys in combination with the appropriate letters will yield some pretty interesting results. There are many other key shortcuts available; however, you will find yourself using the ones associated with the **Finde**r application more often than those of any other application. For this reason, I am providing you with the complete list of **Finder** shortcuts available for Lion (see Table 3–3 for a list of these shortcuts).

Table 3–3. *The Finder–Specific Shortcut Key Mappings*

Keystroke Combination	Action
Cmd-click the item	Open a Sidebar item in a new window
Cmd-1, **Cmd-2**, **Cmd-3**, **Cmd-4**	Switch **Finder** views (**Icon**, **List**, **Column**, and **Cover Flow**)
Right Arrow	In **List** view, expand a folder
Left Arrow	In **List** view, collapse a folder
Return (or **Enter**)	Rename the selected file/folder
Cmd-Down Arrow	Go into the selected folder or open the selected file
Cmd-Up Arrow	Go to the parent folder
Cmd-[(the left square bracket)	Go back
Cmd-] (the right square bracket)	Go forward
Tab (**Shift-Tab** reverses direction)	Select the next icon in **Icon** and **List** views
Tab (**Shift-Tab** reverses direction)	Alternate columns in **Column** view
Hold down the **Option** key while mousing over long filenames	Instantly show the long file name (for names condensed with a "...")
Double-click the column **Resize** widget	Resize the current column to fit the longest file name
Option-double-click the **Resize** widget	Resize all columns to fit their longest file names
Cmd-C, then **Cmd-V**	Copy, then paste a file
Cmd-drag file to disk	Move a file instead of copying it (i.e., this copies the file to the destination, and then removes it from the original location)
Cmd-Delete	Move the selected files to the Trash Bin
Cmd-Shift-Delete	Empty the Trash Bin (with a warning dialog)
Cmd-Opt-Shift-Delete	Empty the Trash Bin (without a warning dialog)

Keystroke Combination	Action
Esc	Cancel a drag-and-drop action while dragging
Cmd-Opt-I	Show the Inspector (a single, live refreshing information window)
Cmd-Z	Undo the last action (e.g., rename file, copy file, and so on)
Cmd-Opt-T	Hide/show the Sidebar (on the left)
Cmd-drag	Move or remove an item in the toolbar (at the top of the window). This works in most programs.
With a file selected, tap the **Spacebar** key (or **Cmd-Y**)	Open Quick Look
Cmd-+ (hold down the **Command** key and press the **Plus** key)	Zoom in on a Quick Look Preview
Cmd-- (hold down the **Command** key and press the **Minus** key)	Zoom out from a Quick Look Preview
Cmd-F	Find by file name

As you can see, there are a lot of options for getting around in the **Finder**. And believe it or not, there are even more general options, which we will touch on later in the chapter. For now, let's move onto the menu options in another important application: **Safari**.

Safari

You will find yourself using the **Safari** web browser constantly. For example, you will use **Safari** in conjunction with other applications to reference information or gather resources. **Safari** is Lion's primary web browser; and though there are others, such as **Firefox** and **Google Chrome**, you will find that **Safari** has the tightest integration with the Lion operating system. What does this mean? In practical terms, it means that many of the shortcuts and menu items you use in Lion will also be available to you in **Safari**. These shortcuts provide you with time-saving ways to get around in the application, simplifying the act of web browsing. We will explore **Safari** in depth in Chapter 8: "It's a Jungle in Here: Safari and the Internet"; for now, let's take a look at some **Safari** basics, like its primary menu (see Figure 3–7).

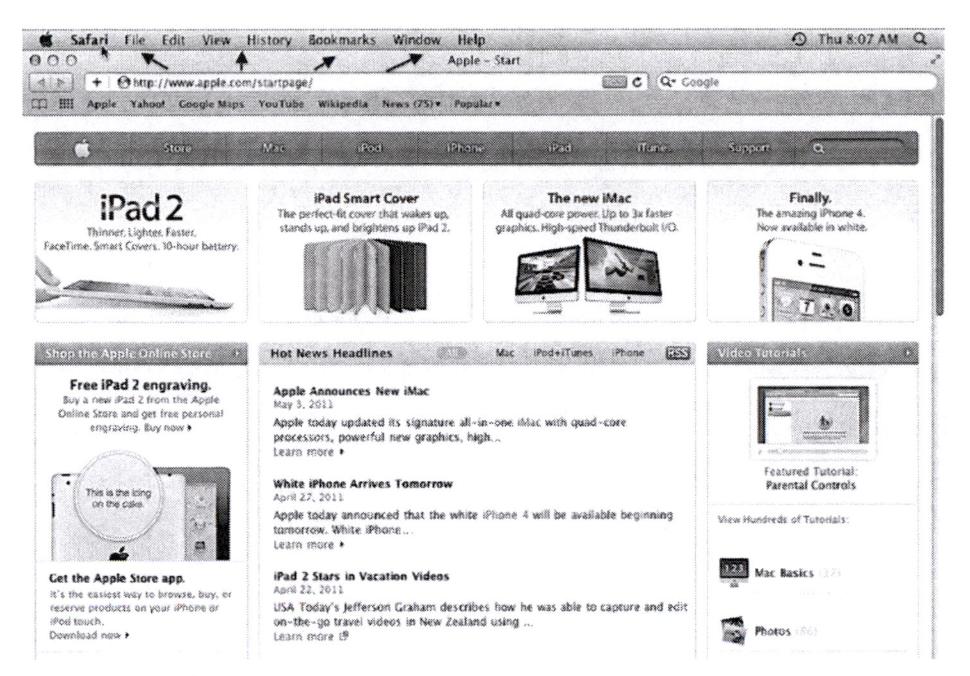

Figure 3–7. *Safari's primary menu options*

As you can see, many of **Safari**'s menu categories are identical to those of the **Finder**; however, you can also see a couple new menu categories (see Table 3–4).

Table 3–4. ***Safari****'s menu categories not found in the* ***Finder***

Menu Item	Description
History	The **History** menu displays information about the web sites you have visited (see Figure 3–8). This menu allows you to control the degree to which **Safari** keeps track of your browsing habits, including how long records of the sites you visit should be retained. This menu makes it easy to keep track of where you have been on the Web; but it is also makes it easy to protect your privacy by restricting how much information about your browsing habits is retained.
Bookmarks	The **Bookmarks** menu allows you to *bookmark*, or save, locations for later viewing (see Figure 3–9). This is similar to the functionality provided by the **History** menu; however, there are also some notable differences. When you bookmark a website, you have the option to name and organize that bookmark according to your preferences. This is different from records of your browsing history, where items are automatically saved in chronological order. Bookmarks allow you to store and recall web links that you visit often, so that you do not have to type in the entire web address each time you visit. Bookmarks can save you a lot of time when using your web browser .

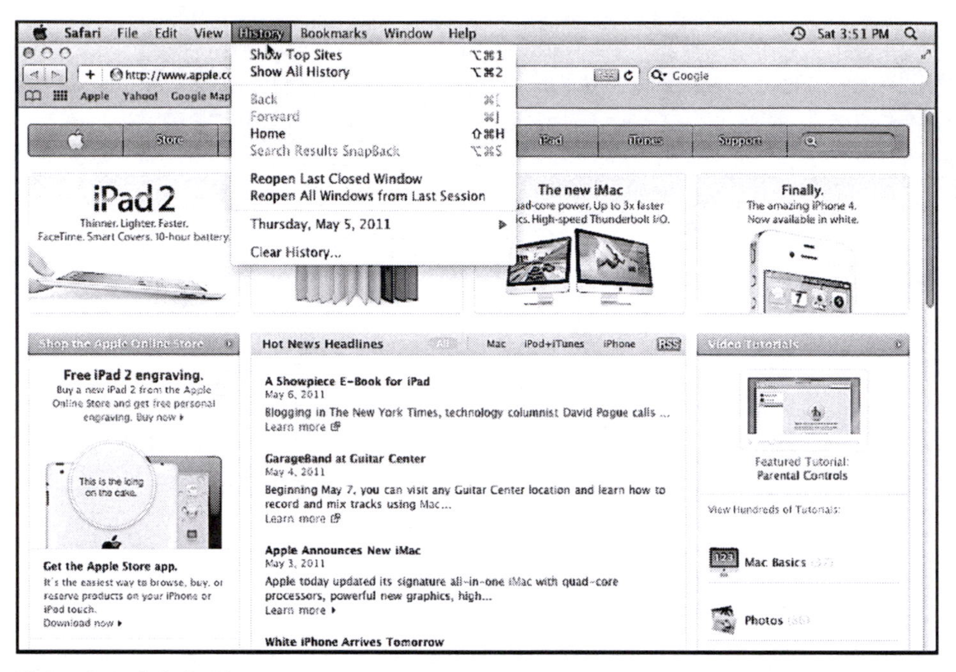

Figure 3–8. *Safari's History menu*

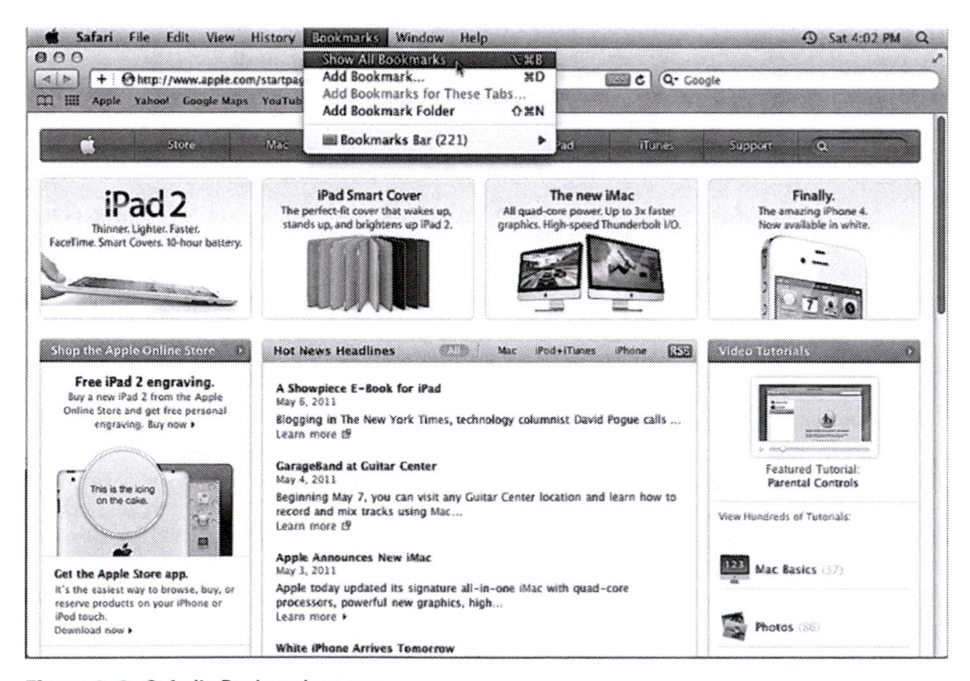

Figure 3–9. *Safari's Bookmarks menu*

Tables 3–5 through 3–7 list some shortcuts you may find useful when surfing the Web.

Table 3–5. *Some Useful Shortcuts While Surfing in Safari*

Keystroke Combination	Action
Up Arrow	Scroll up a page by a small amount
Down Arrow	Scroll down a page by a small amount
Left Arrow	Scroll left on a page by a small amount
Right Arrow	Scroll right on a page by a small amount
Option-Up Arrow	Scroll up a page by a full screen, minus a small overlap
Option-Down Arrow	Scroll down a page by a full screen, minus a small overlap
Cmd-Up Arrow	Scroll to the top-left corner of a web page
Cmd-Down Arrow	Scroll to the bottom-left corner of a web page
Spacebar	Scroll down a page by a full screen, minus a small overlap
Delete	Go back to the previous page in your browsing history
Shift-Delete	Go forward to the next page in your browsing history
Page Up	Scroll up a page by a full screen, minus a small overlap
Page Down	Scroll down a page by a full screen, minus a small overlap
Home	Scroll to the top-left corner of web page
Cmd-Home	Go to the **Home** page
End	Scroll to the bottom-left corner of the web page
Esc	If location field selected, restore viewed the URL
Cmd-click a link	Open a link in a new window
Cmd-Shift-click a link	Open a link in a new tab
Option-click a link to a file	Download a file
Shift-click the **Add Bookmark** button	Add a bookmark directly to the **Bookmarks** menu

Keystroke Combination	Action
Cmd-Return in an address field	Open a page in a new window
Cmd-Shift-Return in an address field	Open a page in a new tab
Cmd-Return in a search field	Show search results in a new window
Cmd-Shift-Return in a search field	Show search results in a new tab
Press and hold **Safari**'s **Back** button	Pop up a menu showing up to ten back entries by page title
Press and hold **Safari**'s **Forward** button	Pop up a menu showing up to ten forward entries by page title
Press and hold **Safari**'s **Back** button while holding down the **Option** key	Pop up a menu showing up to ten back entries by page URL
Press and hold **Safari**'s **Forward** button while holding down the **Option** key	Pop up a menu showing up to ten forward entries by page URL

Table 3–6. *Shortcuts in Safari's Bookmarks Menu*

Kestroke Combination	Action
Delete	Delete the selected bookmarks
Return	Start or finish editing the name of the selected bookmark
Tab	When editing, move to the next editable cell
Spacebar or **double-click**	Open the selected bookmark
Cmd-double-click	Open the selected bookmark in a new window
Option-click the **New Folder** button	Put the selected items in a new folder

Table 3–7. *Other Useful Shortcuts in Safari*

Keystroke Combination	Action
Cmd-A	Select All
Cmd-B	Show/Hide Favorites Bar
Cmd-C	Copy
Cmd-D	Add Bookmark...
Cmd-E	Use Selection for Find
Cmd-F	Find...
Cmd-G	Find Again
Cmd-H	Hide Safari
Cmd-J	Jump to Selection
Cmd-K	Block Pop-up Windows
Cmd-L	Open Location...
Cmd-M	Minimize
Cmd-N	New Window
Cmd-O	Open File...
Cmd-P	Print
Cmd-Q	Quit Safari
Cmd-R	Reload Page
Cmd-S	Save As
Cmd-T	New Tab
Cmd-V	Paste
Cmd-W	Close Window or Close Tab
Cmd-X	Cut

Keystroke Combination	Action
Cmd-Z	Undo
Cmd-Shift-A	AutoFill Form
Cmd-Shift-B	Send File To Bluetooth Device... or Bookmark this group of tabs
Cmd-Shift-D	Add Bookmark to Menu
Cmd-Shift-F	Full Screen
Cmd-Shift-G	Find Previous
Cmd-Shift-H	Go to the Home page
Cmd-Shift-L	Search with Google
Cmd-Shift-N	Add Bookmark Folder
Cmd-Shift-P	Page Setup...
Cmd-Shift-W	Close Window
Cmd-Shift-Z	Redo
Cmd-Option-A	Activity
Cmd-Option-B	Show All Bookmarks
Cmd-Option-E	Empty Cache…
Cmd-Option-F	Google Search…
Cmd-Option-H	Hide Others
Cmd-Option-K	Mark Page for SnapBack
Cmd-Option-L	Downloads
Cmd-Option-M	Minimize All
Cmd-Option-P	SnapBack to Page
Cmd-Option-S	SnapBack to Search

Keystroke Combination	Action
Cmd-Option-V	View Source
Cmd-Option-W or **Cmd-Option-Shift-W**	Close All Windows
Cmd-D	Add Safari Bookmark
Cmd-S	Save Browser Window...
Cmd-1 to Cmd-9	Jump to First Nine Bookmarks (Not Folders) in the Bookmarks Toolbar
Cmd-?	Safari Help
Cmd-[	Back
Cmd-]	Forward
Cmd-.	Stop
Cmd-,	Preferences...
Cmd-/	Show/Hide Status Bar
Cmd-|	Show/Hide Address Bar
Cmd-	Show Page Load Test Window
Cmd-;	Check Spelling
Cmd-Shift-:	Spelling...
Cmd--(Cmd-Minus key**)**	Make Text Smaller
Cmd-+	Make Text bigger
Cmd-Shift-*	Get Result of AppleScript
Cmd-Shift-Right Arrow	Select Next Tab
Cmd-Shift-Left Arrow	Select Previous Tab
Cmd-Option->	Send to...

As the preceding tables illustrate, **Safari** includes an almost endless number of shortcut options to enhance your browsing experience. It is not necessary to try to commit all of the shortcuts shown to memory. Instead, I advise you to begin by finding the shortcuts that you feel would benefit you the most in your day-to-day use of **Safari**. Once you feel proficient with the shortcuts that you have decided are most important to you, you can gradually pick up other shortcuts over time. One of the hallmarks of the Lion operating system is its flexibility, its ability to adapt to your computing style. The more you use the seemingly endless array of shortcut options in **Safari** and the **Finder**, the easier you will find it to do things like surf the web and navigate the your files on your system.

iTunes

iTunes will likely be your media application of choice. This application integrates nicely with the Lion OS, letting you shop for digital media, listen to music, and watch videos, among many other actions. Like **Safari** and the **Finder**, **iTunes** is easy to use, not least because its built-in shortcuts improve the user experience significantly. For example, you can **iTunes**' shortcuts to switch quickly from song to song or to begin watching a movie instantly. In this section, we'll take an in-depth look at the menus for **iTunes** and how they help make the already easy-to-use app even easier and more enjoyable to use (see Figure 3–10 for a detailed view of the contextual **File** menu for iTunes).

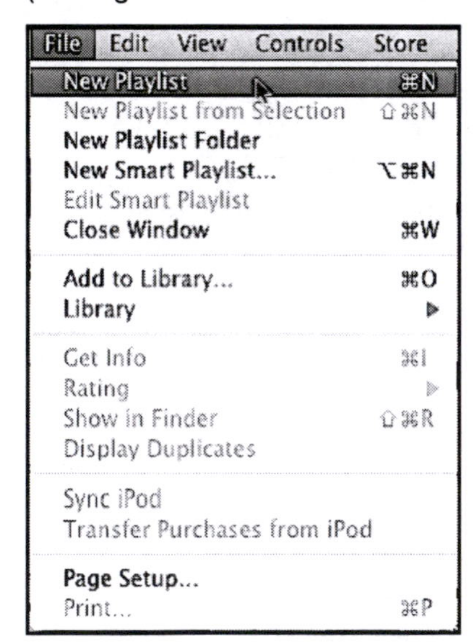

Figure 3–10. *iTunes' File menu options*

NOTE: iTunes' Edit and **View** menus contain exactly the options you'd expect, based on this chapter's earlier discussion of the **Finder** app's **Edit** and **View** menus. For this reason, I do not include them in my discussion of **iTunes**' menus.

Exploring iTunes' File Menu

iTunes' File menu includes several options for manipulating your playlists and media libraries. As mentioned previously, each Lion application has its own set of items listed under general menus like **File** and **Edit**. For example, comparing Figures 3-2 and 3-10 reveals that the options listed under the **File** menu for the **Finder** and **iTunes** differ significantly. **iTunes**' menus are very self-explanatory, but Table 3–8 provides some additional details for two of the most important items listed under **iTunes' File** menu.

Table 3–8. *Breaking Down a Couple Options in iTunes' File Menu*

Menu item	Description
New Playlist	This option allows you to create new playlists from various media items you have purchased or downloaded into **iTunes**. This is a great way to listen to music you would like to take with you on the go, and it can tremendously reduce media clutter when dealing with thousands of songs and videos.
Add to Library	**iTunes** maintains a media library database of all of your songs and videos. This database is constantly being updated, depending on whether you are adding or deleting media. This option lets you import media into your **iTunes** for playback. Selecting this option brings up a wizard that walks you through the steps required to put your new media where you would like it to be.

Using the Controls Menu

iTunes' Controls menu also includes some interesting options (see Figure 3–11).

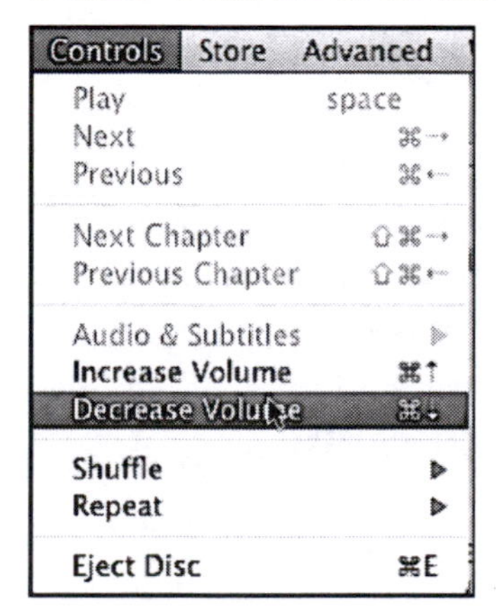

Figure 3–11. *iTunes' Controls menu options*

The **Controls** menu provides several options (with associated shortcuts) for manipulating and navigating the media you play with **iTunes**. For example, it includes options to increase or lower the volume, as well as to skip back and forth between the chapters of your videos and movies.

Accessing the iTunes Store via the Store Menu

As you might guess, the **Store** menu gives you access to the iTunes store (see Figure 3-12). The iTunes store is similar in spirit to the Mac App Store; however, the iTunes store only sells media like music and videos, not applications. You might visit the iTunes store to find your favorite song, rent or buy your favorite movie, watch an episode of your favorite television show, or view the various podcasts that you have subscribed to. In this section, we'll break down the most important option on the **Store** menu: **Authorize This Computer**.

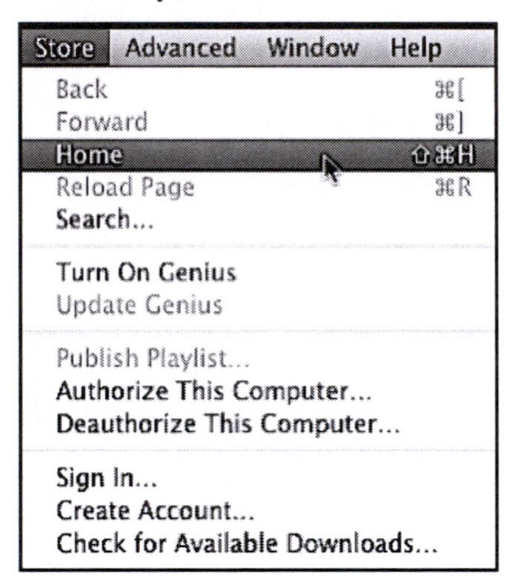

Figure 3–12. *iTunes' Store menu options*

The **Authorize This Computer** option enables your specific computer to download and play music and videos that you purchase from the iTunes store. The iTunes service allows you to authorize up to five other iTunes-compatible devices that you can use as playback devices for the media you have purchased. Authorizing a computer device indicates that you permit that device to use personal information like your credit card and iTunes user information. For this reason, you should be cautious when authorizing devices for friends or family, doing so only when trust is not an issue.

Manipulating Resources with the Advanced Menu

Finally, let's look at **iTunes' Advanced Menu**, which allows you to perform several tasks related to streaming and sharing resources with **iTunes** (see Figure 3–13).

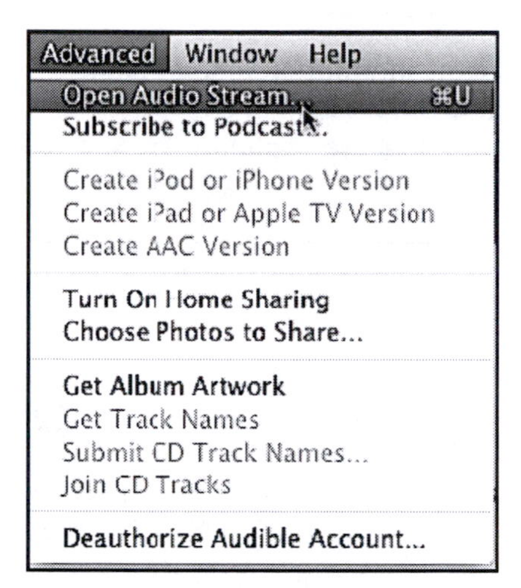

Figure 3–13. *iTunes' Advanced menu options*

Table 3–9 lists some of the more significant options in **iTunes**' **Advanced** menu and what they do.

Table 3–9. *Breaking Down Significant Options in iTunes' Advanced Menu*

Menu Option	Description
Open Audio Stream...	This option allows you to insert the web addresses used to stream Internet radio content. Doing so enables you to stream that content manually. Note you don't need to use this option unless you're trying to access a resource on the Web or your local computer that does not automatically launch **iTunes**.
Subscribe to Podcasts...	This option allows you to subscribe to a podcast of your choosing. Note that this option is only necessary when you're browsing the **iTunes** store or the Web, and clicking a podcast subscription link doesn't work. This isn't an option you'll use very often, but it's good to know where to find it.
Create	The **Create** options allow you to export your media into various formats, so that you can play them on different devices such as an iPhone or Apple TV.
Turn on Home Sharing	This option allows you to share your music and other media with other users on your network. Thus, users on your network can listen to or view the content you've purchased the rights to without having to download it themselves.
Deauthorize Audible Content...	This option is used in conjunction with your audible.com account. It allows you to deauthorize purchased audio books, so that they can be transferred from one device to another, and then reauthorized on that new device.

Like the **Finder** and **Safari, iTunes** comes with many useful shortcut commands that can significantly improve the overall app experience. Table 3–10 lists some general shortcuts for **iTunes**, while Table 3–11 lists some shortcuts that are useful for manipulating your libraries and playlists.

Table 3–10. *Significant General Shortcuts in iTunes*

Keystroke	Action
Return	Play the selected song immediately
Option-Right Arrow (or **Option-click** the **Skip Forward** button in the upper-left corner of the **iTunes** window)	Listen to the next album in a list
Option-Left Arrow (or **Option-click** the **Skip Backward** button in the upper-left corner of the **iTunes** window)	Listen to the previous album in a list
Cmd-Right Arrow (or click the **Skip Forward** button in the upper-left corner of the **iTunes** window)	Fast-forward to the next song in a list
Cmd-Left Arrow (or click the **Skip Backward** button in the upper-left corner of the **iTunes** window)	Rewind to the previous song in a list

Table 3–11. *iTunes' Library and Playlist Shortcuts*

Keystroke	Action
Shift-click the **Add** (+) button (you can also drag the songs to the white area of the source list)	Create a playlist from a selection of songs
Option-click the **Add** (+) button	Create a new Smart Playlist
Option-click the **Shuffle** button	Reshuffle the current playlist
Cmd-Delete	Delete the selected playlist from your source list without bringing up a confirmation dialog
Option-Delete a selected playlist	Delete the selected playlist and all the songs it contains from your library
Option-Delete a selected song	Delete the selected song from your library and all other playlists that contain the song

Summary

In this chapter, we covered how to use the menus and keyboard shortcuts built into most apps to get the most out of the Lion OS. We also looked at how to zip around your Lion OS by leveraging the shortcuts built into the **Finder**. This chapter looked specifically at the menu options and shortcuts available in three apps that ship with Lion: the **Finder**, **Safari**, and **iTunes**. However, the lessons learned are applicable to just about any Lion application you might use. There are literally thousands of shortcuts available for Lion, and these can be combined in an infinite number of ways to make using Lion both easier and more satisfying. I strongly recommend that you practice using the keyboard shortcuts described in this chapter; doing so will make you a much more productive user, not just when using the Lion OS and the apps that come with it, but when using any of the applications installed on your computing system.

Chapter 4

Making iWork '09 Work

There are a lot of office applications to choose from, but there is only one office suite made just for Lion: Apple's **iWork '09**. Apple made this office suite specifically to meet the needs of Mac users. It comes with all of the ease-of-use features that Mac users have become accustomed to, but it also includes all of the professional features found in other well-known office suites.

This chapter will walk you through the similarities and differences between **iWork '09** and those other office suites. For example, we'll cover how **iWork '09** offers Lion users easy-to-use navigation, automation, and file-sharing features that you won't find in competing office products. We'll also cover how **iWork '09** makes it easy to deliver high resolution, high definition office documents for distribution through all types of digital media. Let's get started!

> **NOTE:** You can get a free trial version of **iWork '09** from the App Store. Just search for "iWork" and download the 30-day trial version.

The iWork '09 Suite

The **iWork '09** suite consists of three core programs: **Pages**, **Numbers**, and **Keynote**. These programs work together seamlessly to give you a complete office experience.

We will start this chapter by exploring the inner workings of the most commonly used program in the **iWork '09** office suite: **Pages**. This word-processing program is very similar to other word-processing programs you may already be familiar with, such as **Microsoft Word 2010**. However, **Pages** also includes some important functionality you won't find in those other programs. So let's dive deeper into **iWork '09** and see what makes it different.

NOTE: As you look at the screenshots in this chapter, remember that some of the menu items you see may change when Apple releases future updates of this software.

Pages

Pages—like all of the programs contained in the **iWork '09** suite—are *native* to lion. This means that the software was made specifically to work on your Mac, and it is not meant to be installed or run on any other operating system. For example, **iWork '09** includes features that work only on the Lion operating system, making it easy to integrate **Pages** with the rest of the programs in the **iWork '09** office suite. Apple built **Pages** from the ground up to simplify the process of producing outstanding, feature-rich word-processing documents, such as those you would find in a popular magazine, newspaper, or brochure. It is great for producing resumes; reports; flyers; business cards; and even certificates for your home, school, or business. Let's explore some of the features that make this possible.

You should use **Pages** whether you need to do either small or extensive amounts of word processing. **Pages** can import and export just about any type of file, including those made using the current version of **Microsoft Office**. **Pages** also allows you to export to a variety of formats, including PDF and the now popular Epub format. The powerful word-processing features included in **Pages** make it ideal for both work and education. These features include spell checking, auto correction, and auto formatting—all of which allow you to focus on the content you are creating, rather than its formatting.

Using Pages

When you first start **Pages**, you will be presented with a template menu that allows you to select the type of document you would like to start working with. In this chapter, we will use the **Blank** portrait template located to the left of the **Blank Landscape** template (see Figure 4–1).

When deciding what type of template to begin working with, it is good practice to first decide what type of content you want to produce. This ensures that you do not interrupt the process of creating your document by wasting your time cycling through different template types. For example, if you intend to create a document to help you get a job, you should choose the **Resume** template. On the other hand, if you intend to create marketing materials for your business, you might choose the **Newsletters**, **Brochures**, or **Flyers** template.

Figure 4–1 shows three important sections of the template chooser that you should pay close attention to. The first area highlighted shows the template selection area (see the circled 1). This is where you select the specific type of template you want to use if you are going to start a new document. The second area highlighted gives you the option to open existing files, including files that you have recently worked on (see the circled 2). Finally, the third highlighted area shows you the scale option (see the circled 3). Adjusting the slider in this section will increase or decrease the size of the document previews, giving you a better look at what each template type has to offer.

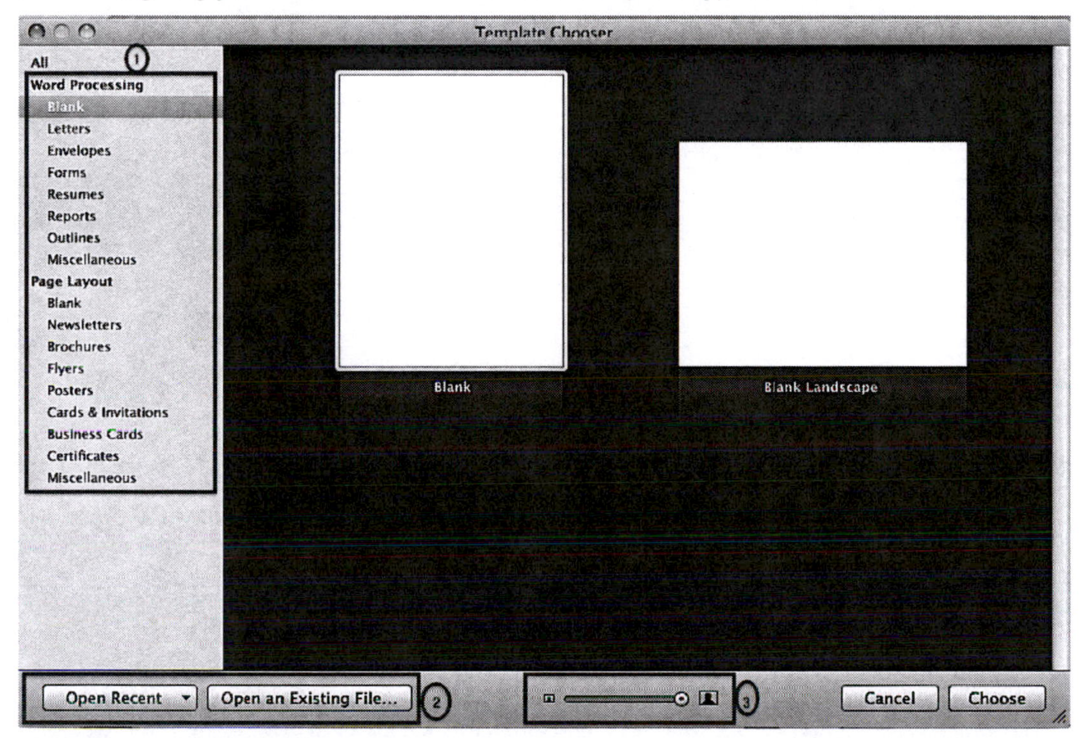

Figure 4–1. The ***Template Chooser in Pages***

Navigating Pages

Pages has a fairly standard menu system that contains all of the elements and options that you would expect see in a modern word processor (see Table 4–1 for a detailed description of these options). The layout has been simplified to give you access to the most important features first (see Figure 4–2).

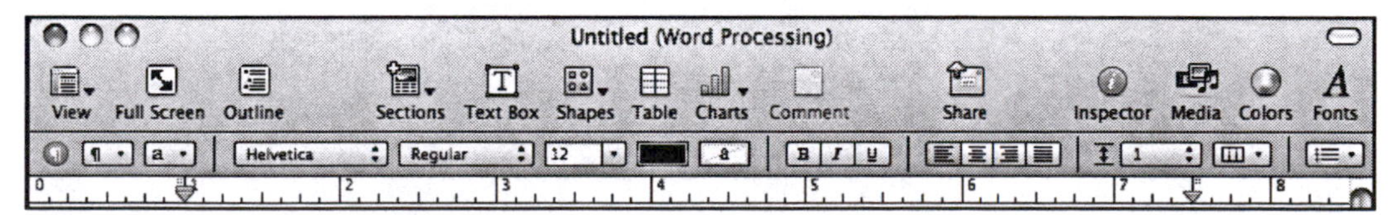

Figure 4–2. ***The main menu in Pages***

Table 4–1. *Exploring the Options in the Main Menu*

Menu Item	Description
View	Allows you to access a submenu from which you can manage your document's formatting. For example, you can use this option to change a document's styles, ruler settings, and layout. Page Thumbnails Search Show Styles Drawer Hide Format Bar Hide Rulers Show Layout Show Invisibles Show Comments
Full Screen	Allows you to view pages in full screen, so that your view of the application you're working with is not obscured by other applications.
Outline	Gives you a hierarchical view of your document according to the placement of your headers. This will allow you to view only the document's headers, so that you can see how it is organized and arranged. This option also enables you to rearrange your topics according to your needs.
Sections	Lets you separate your document pages into groups, so that you can edit, print, or delete entire sections separately. Sections differ from page breaks in one significant way: they do not bleed into one another when changes are made. Thus, changes can be made to sections of a document without affecting other pages in other sections of the same document. This is a great way to separate subjects or topics for something like a research paper. 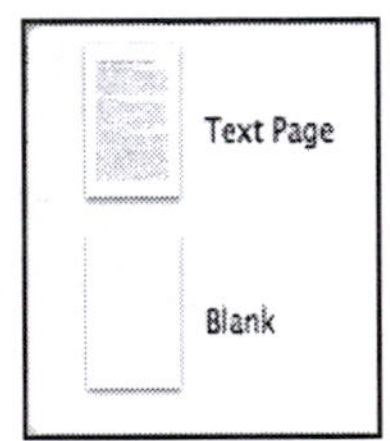
Text Box	Allows you to draw a text box of any size and place it anywhere on your document. This is great for placing text into places that are normally restricted by document formatting. You can use this method to put text anywhere you like on your document, without any restrictions. 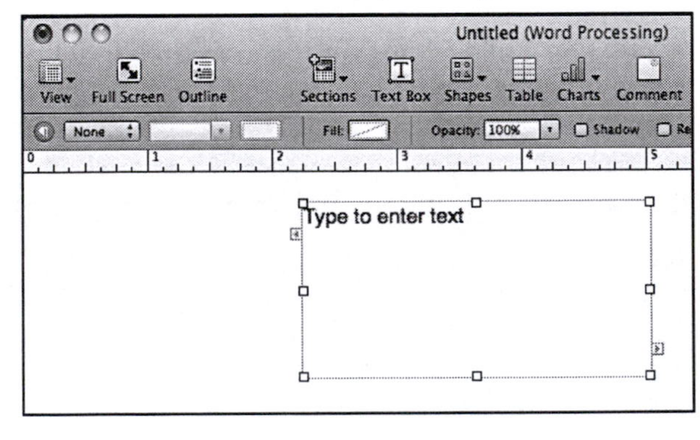

Menu Item	Description
Shapes	Allows for you to choose from many different shapes that you can place anywhere in your document. These shapes can be used as graphical assets to your document. 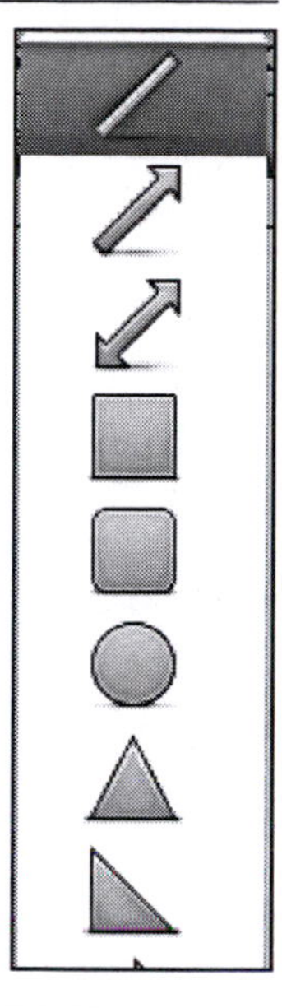
Table	Allows you to draw tables by both rows and columns. You should use this option when you want to insert an organized group of assets into your document that need to be aligned in rows and columns. The **Table** menu provides many options, including the ability to set the border color and thickness of your table. It also lets you set essential attributes, such as the formatting of the cells inside a table.

Menu Item	Description
Charts	Allows you to give a graphical view of value items contained in your document. **iWork '09** has a wide range of charts to choose from, including 3-D charts that allow you to rotate and skew the view of your graphs. Using charts can add a lot of flair to your presentation, as well as to simplify complex information. 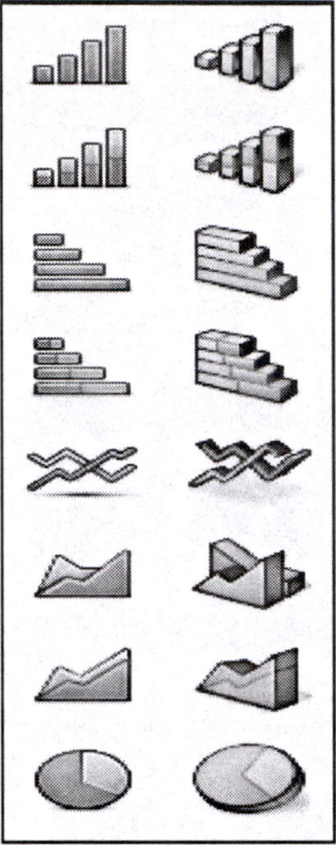
Comments	Allows you to mark sections of your document with annotations that describe observations or changes that need to be made to a specific object or at specific points in your document. Each comment is linked to an object or paragraph, and it saves with the document. This means that your comments remain intact—and associated with the right object or paragraph—when the document is shared or retrieved for later use. This is a great tool for making notes about specific things you would like to address in your document. 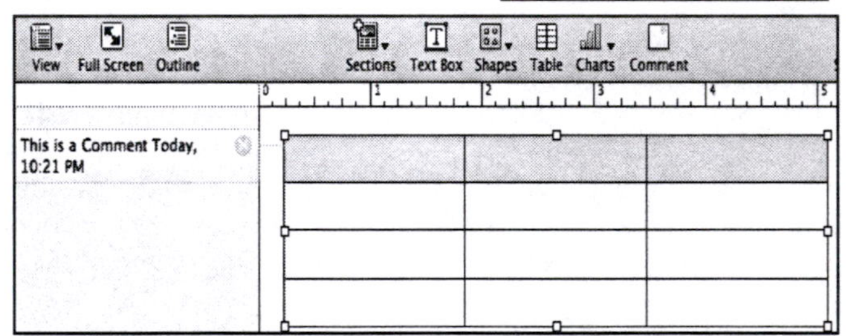
Sharing 	Allows you to use the `www.iwork.com` web site to share documents with other participating members. This site offers an easy way to make your documents accessible to other Mac users, as well as to provide secure and seamless access to your documents. Share Help Share via iWork.com... Show Shared Documents Sign In... Send via Mail Send to iWeb Export... Although iWork.com is the preferred way to share documents created by the applications in the **iWork '09** suite, you can also choose to send your documents to others

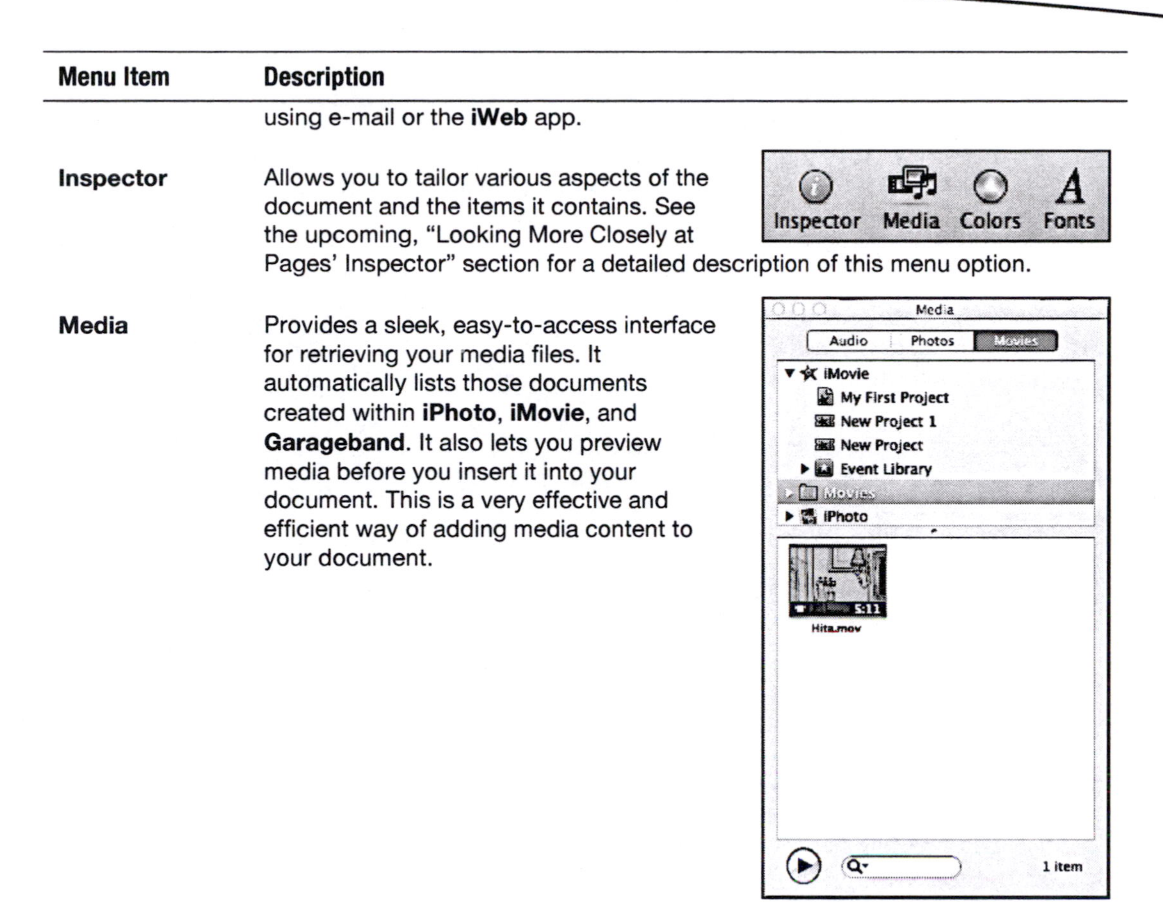

Menu Item	Description
	using e-mail or the **iWeb** app.
Inspector	Allows you to tailor various aspects of the document and the items it contains. See the upcoming, "Looking More Closely at Pages' Inspector" section for a detailed description of this menu option.
Media	Provides a sleek, easy-to-access interface for retrieving your media files. It automatically lists those documents created within **iPhoto**, **iMovie**, and **Garageband**. It also lets you preview media before you insert it into your document. This is a very effective and efficient way of adding media content to your document.

Menu Item	Description
Colors	Grants you a color swatch palette, which can be used to adjust the color of any object or text that you have selected. 
Font	Allows you to change the font of the selected text. This option also includes a **Search** box, so that you can find and use fonts without needing to perform the time-consuming task of scrolling through them. 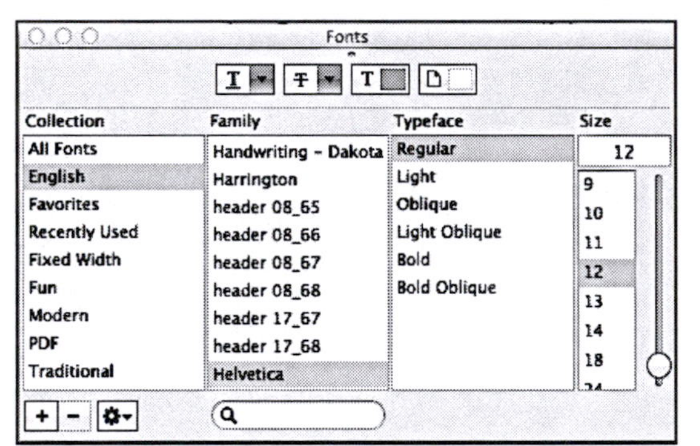

Looking More Closely at Pages' Inspector

The Inspector feature is used throughout the **iWork '09** suite to allow you to granularly tailor various aspects of the document and the items it contains. The fact that you will use it throughout **iWork 09** makes its worthy of a more thorough discussion. Table 4–2 dives deeper into its menu options and what they mean.

Table 4–2. *Inspector's Menu Options in Pages*

Inspector Menu Item	Description	
Documents	Allows you to tailor the general aspects of your document's information. Use this item to label your document and personalize author references.	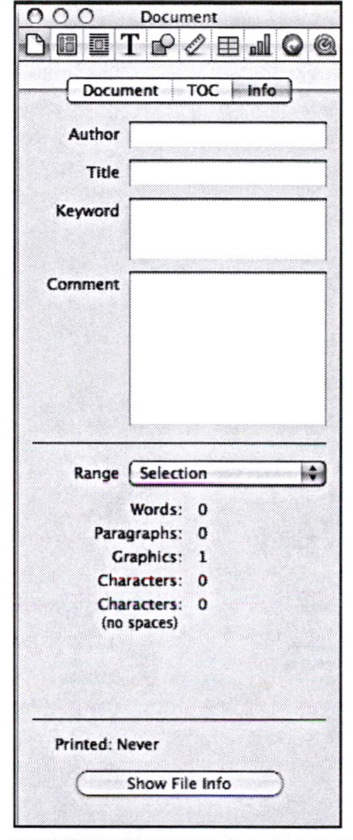
Layout	Allows you to change the way that your page is arranged. It also lets you add or remove columns to a page's décor. This is a great place to make changes to the margins of your document, as well.	

Inspector Menu Item	Description
Wrap	Allows you to determine how you would like to position images and other objects in relation to nearby text. This feature is great for formatting the parts of your document that need to include images or other media. 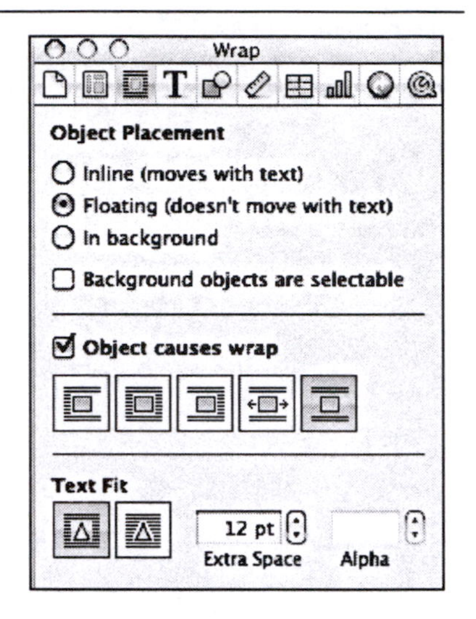
Text	Allows you to specify the text characteristics of your document, such as spacing, alignment, color, and listing preferences. This option also allows you to edit the appearance of your document in fine detail, so you can ensure that your text looks exactly the way you want it to. 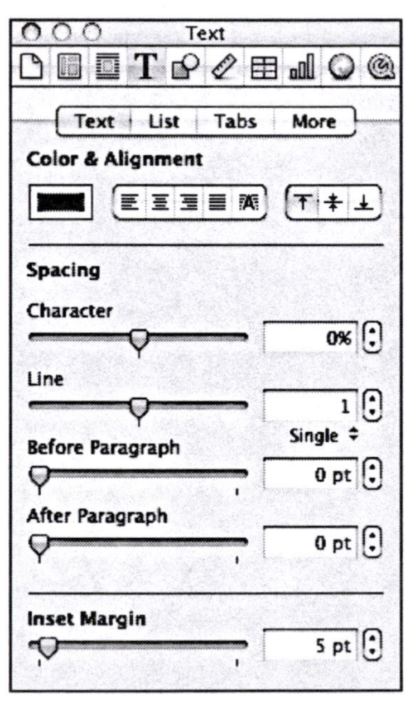

Inspector Menu Item	Description	
Graphics	Allows you to define the extra features you would like to add to the images in your document. For example, it lets you do things such as add shadows, reflections, borders, and fills to your images. This feature is great if you want you want to accentuate dull images or add some spice to your presentation.	
Link	Allows you to create hyperlinks and bookmarks within your document. You might use this cool feature to create a working table of contents that allows the user to interactively navigate your document. Similarly, you might use this feature to create hyperlinks that take viewers of your document to relevant places on the Web.	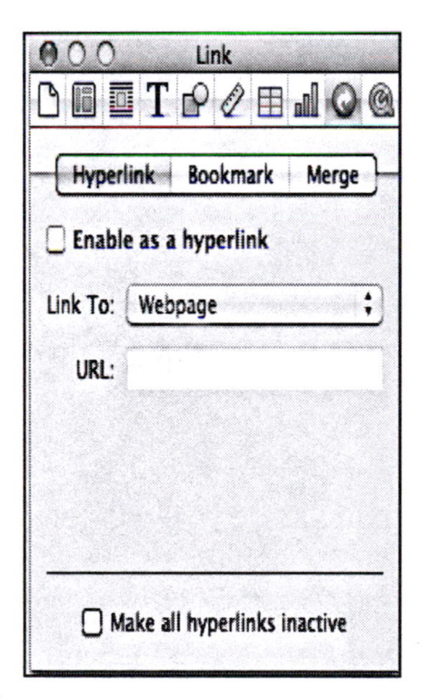

Inspector Menu Item	Description	
Metrics	Allows you to position and set the contours of images and other graphical objects that you might use in your document. This feature provides a granular control system for manipulating the graphics of your documents, so that you can have them displayed exactly as you would like them to be.	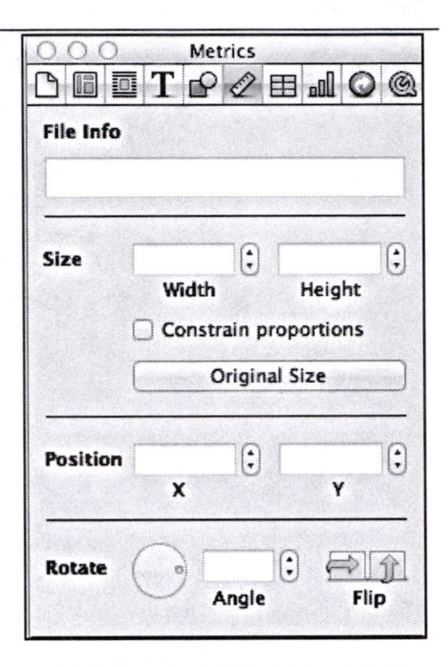
QuickTime	Allows you to set the start and stop times of any videos you may use in your documents. This feature also allows you to set the volume and create a poster frame for a video, which can be used as an image placeholder. This image will give readers of your document a good idea of the video's subject before they launch it.	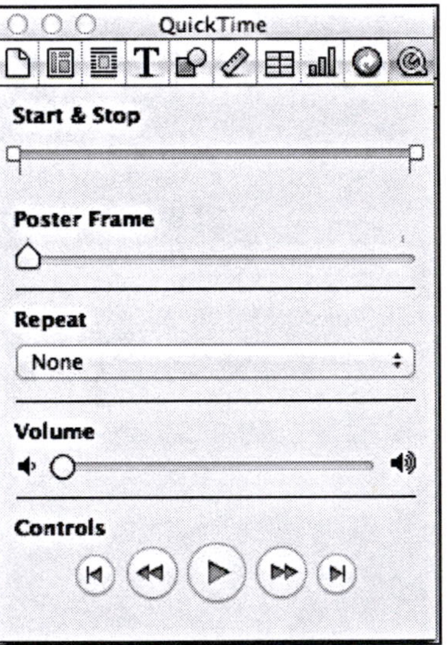

These are the most important features you need to know about to start using **Pages**—and **iWork '09** in general. Now let's take a look at another cool app in the **iWork '09** suite: **Numbers**.

Numbers

Numbers is a spreadsheet application that allows you to create sheets of information that you can use to keep track of any items that need organizing and sorting. This program is very similar to **Microsoft Excel**, and it includes many of the same features, as well as some Lion-specific ones. **Numbers** can enable a user to create complex graphs and perform various calculations. This makes it a great application for a wide range of uses, including business, home finance, education, and media organization. **Numbers** is also a great way to keep data clear and presentable as you automate the complex tasks required for sorting and calculating large pieces of information.

You should use **Numbers** whenever you need to do number crunching or to organize information in a form that can be easily read and understood by others. I personally use numbers to balance my budget, keep track of my customers, and for academic research. This app also gives you a great way to heuristically display information, so that trends relating to the information can be easily detected. **Numbers** can also be used as a phonebook, for keeping track of student grades, or even for keeping a detailed account of your expenses.

In this section, we'll drill down for a deeper look at **Numbers**. We'll begin by exploring the application's main menu. Part of what makes this app so powerful is its simplified menu, which gives you immediate access to the most commonly used functions of the application, but in a way that doesn't overwhelm you. **Numbers** takes an in-your-face approach to its menus. Its menu options make it very easy to create useful, working spreadsheets—and to do so without having you search through endless layers of navigational menus. Let's take a closer look at what makes the **Numbers** menu options so unique (see Figure 4–3)

Figure 4–3. *The main menu of Numbers*

The core menu items in **Numbers**' main menu are the most commonly used features in the application. Table 4–3 explains what these features are, what they do, and how they contribute to making **Numbers** easy to use.

Table 4–3. *The Key Options in Numbers' Main Menu*

Menu Item	Description	
View	Allows you to see how your worksheet will look when printed, as well as to see the full layout of your worksheets. This option gives you a great way to access the list of formulas being used within your spreadsheet. You can also use it to make quick adjustments to the algorithmic functions that are common to spreadsheets.	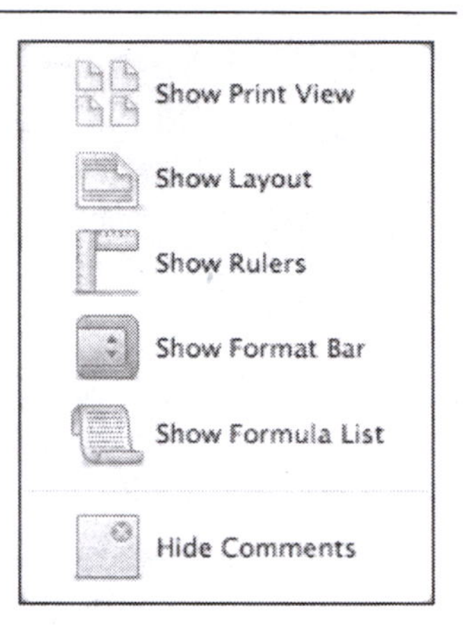
Sheet	Allows you to add extra sheets to your spreadsheet. This feature also allows you to separate the different sheets, so that you can improve the organization of your spreadsheet. Adding extra sheets will make your spreadsheet file larger; however, it will also give you the advantage of letting you view different elements of your spreadsheet separately—which is essential for keeping your spreadsheet organized. You might also add new sheets to your spreadsheet when you need to segment the variables you are attempting to sort, organize, or calculate in your document.	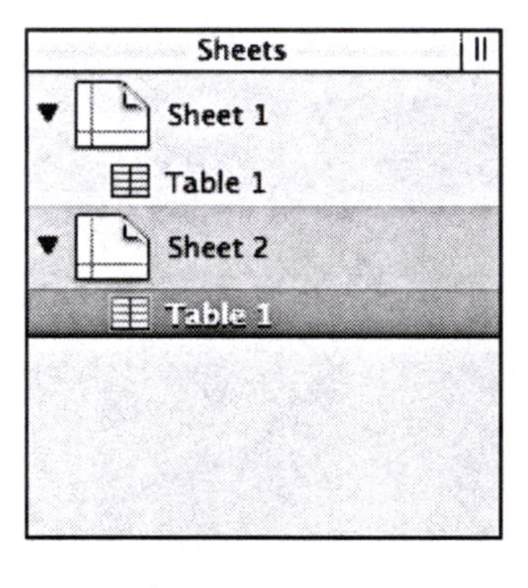
Tables	Allows you to insert prebuilt tables into your spreadsheet that contain built-in calculations and formatting. Using these prebuilt tables can greatly reduce the time it takes to create various sections of your spreadsheet because it spares you from having to build these sometimes complex items yourself.	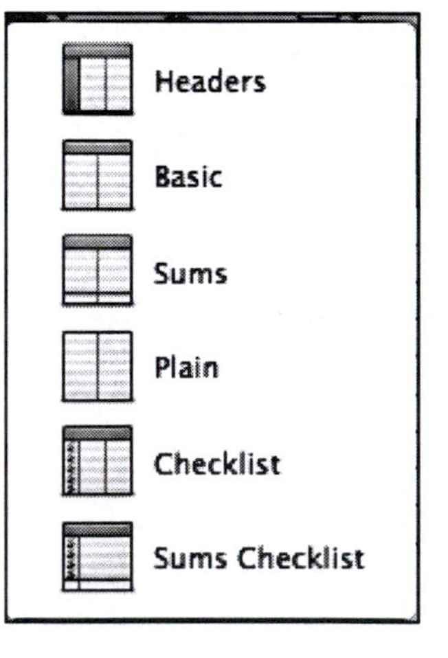

Menu Item	Description
Reorganize	Gives you access to a window that enables you to list your items alphabetically, numerically, or a combination of both. This feature is especially useful when you are using a spreadsheet to show trends. However it is also useful if you just need to list the data in a specific way for display, retrieval, or distribution. 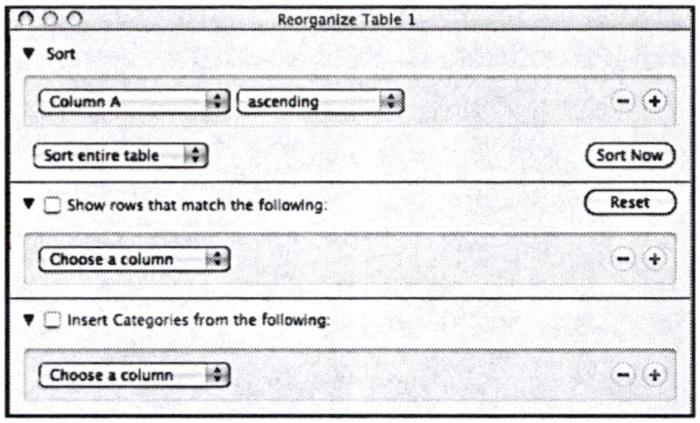
Functions	Allows you to place mathematical functions into the cells of your spreadsheet, so that calculations can be made between the cells. For example, let's say you plan on creating a spreadsheet that uses algorithms or computations that involve addition, division, multiplication, or subtraction. If so, this menu item will serve as a guide, walking you through the process of creating your functions. 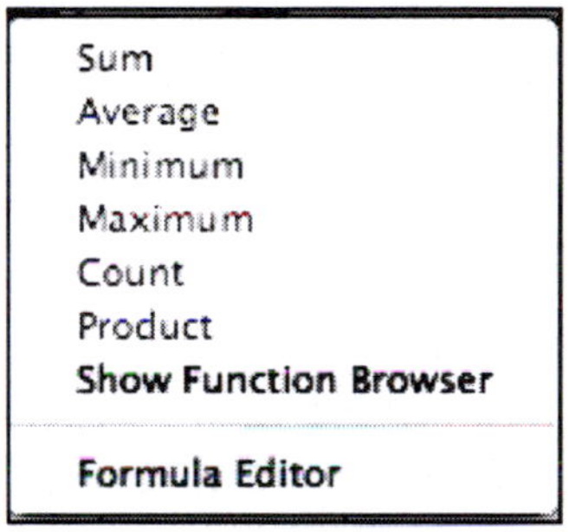
Formula List	Enables you to accomplish the essential task of tracking the functions you create in your spreadsheet. This feature gives you a great way to simplify the process organizing and modifying all of your spreadsheet's functions. 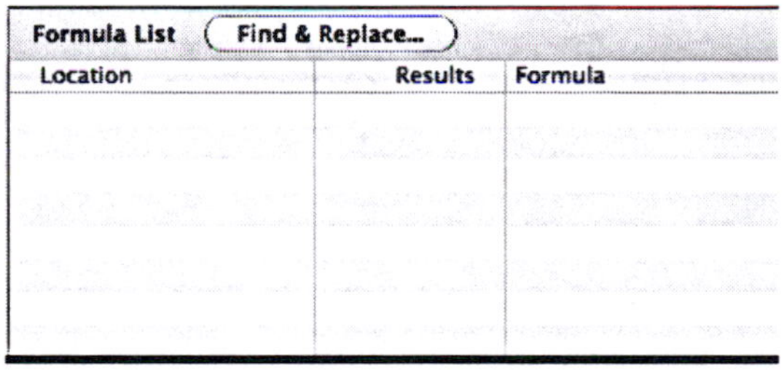

Numbers is meant to be easy to use. Referencing these few menu items will allow you to access the most common functions needed to build or maintain your spreadsheet—and do so in a way that doesn't introduce unneeded complexity. Learning the basics of **Numbers** is sufficient for creating rich, functional spreadsheets that you can use to better organize your life or business.

Word-processing and spreadsheet software can help create and manage most of the content that drives your business- or school-related tasks. However, sometimes you need to present that content in a visually sophisticated way to an audience. In the next section, we'll walk you through the **iWork '09** suite's presentation app: **Keynote**.

Keynote

The ability to create presentations is an inherent part of any modern-day office suite, and **iWork '09** delivers this functionality through its **Keynote** application. **Keynote** enables you to create visual presentations that are not limited by the media type or its delivery system. You can use this app to make your data easy for others to understand. You should use **Keynote** when you wish to provide an audience with a visual representation of the key points on a given subject, or you need to get an idea across to the widest audience possible.

When used correctly, **Keynote** can help you emphasize the important parts of a topic. It can also help an audience understand things that may otherwise be difficult to understand without a visual reference. I use **Keynote** for instruction, using it to create slideshows that deal with the content of my lectures.

Keynote includes many features and tools intended to help you get your presentation off the ground in front of an audience. Throughout the rest of this section, we'll look at some of the "key" features and other commonly used functions that you may find useful as you put together your first **Keynote** presentation. Let's begin by looking at the functionality of the app's main menu (see Figure 4–4 and Table 4–4).

Figure 4–4. *The main menu of Keynote*

Table 4–4. *The Key Options in Keynote's Main Menu*

Menu Item	Description
New	Allows you to create new slides to add to your presentation. You should use this option when you need to insert complementing information. Newly inserted slides get placed beneath the last slide already in place. This is good to know, so that you do not lose track of your slides.
Play	Displays your slideshow in full screen for playback. You should use this option when you want to get a real-world look at how your presentation will appear when you actually run it. This is a great way to preview your work and make necessary adjustments.

Menu Item	Description
View	The **View** menu option works slightly differently in **Keynote** than it does in **Pages** or **Numbers**. For example, it includes options that enable you to hide or expose specific aspects of your slides. 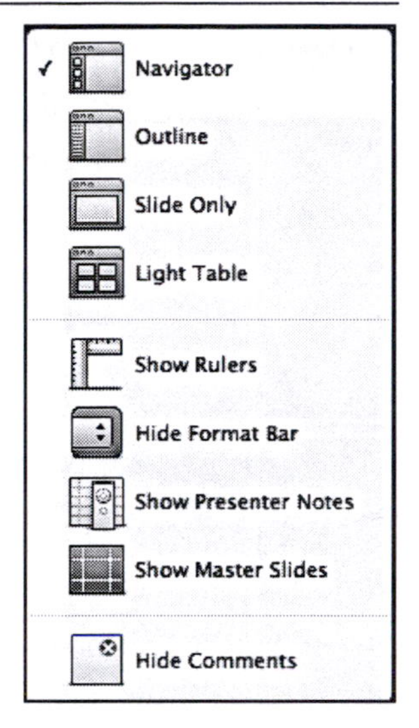
Guides	Allows you to expose where the objects in your slides sit relative to other objects. The more guides you use, the more definitive your view of relative object placement will be. This feature allows you to keep the icons organized and easy to access. Proper alignment of your application icons is not only visually appealing, but it also makes your computer much easier to use. 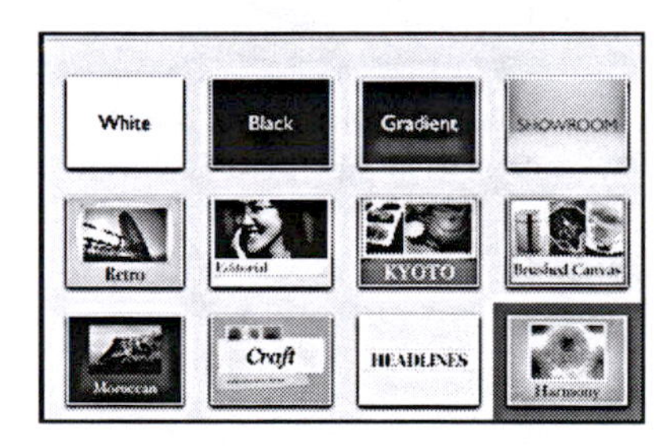
Themes	Allows you to select or change the theme of your current slide presentation. You should use this feature to alter the look and feel of your presentation, so it matches the information you're sharing.

Menu Item	Description	
Masters	Allows you to change the layout of each individual slide or any given selection of slides. Masters are slide templates, and they simplify the actions needed to create your presentation. Specifically, they provide a list of working slide layouts to choose from and apply to your slides. You should use this menu item when altering slides to fit a specific presentation schema.	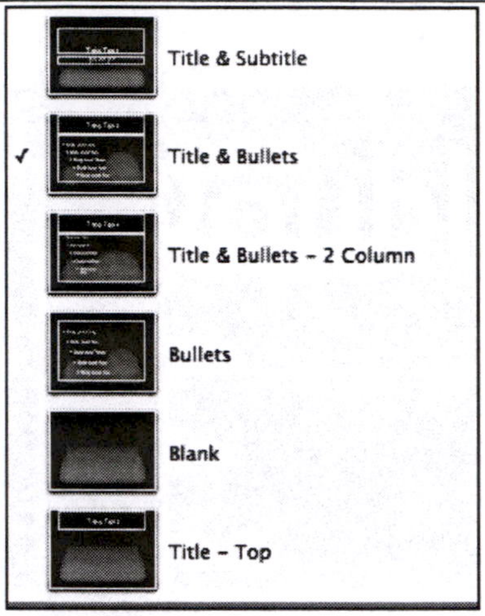 Title & Subtitle ✓ Title & Bullets Title & Bullets - 2 Column Bullets Blank Title - Top

Summary

In this chapter, we covered everything you need to know to get you up and running with the office suite of choice for OS X Lion users, **iWork '09**. For example, you're now ready to create that resume for your new job, to organize your financial life using spreadsheets, or to create presentations for marketing or information purposes.

iWork '09 contains all of the functionality you find in most modern day office suites, but it has been greatly simplified to meet the demanding needs of the growing numbers of Mac OS X Lion users around the world. However, using **iWork '09** effectively requires that you understand when to use which application. This means that you need to understand both what the various apps do, as well as the differences in their menus. Remember that good practice makes perfect.

Chapter 5

Using the Mac App Store

The Mac App Store hosts more than a million apps. Given how much content it lets you access, it's probably not suprising that it takes a little practice to get used to the the app that gives you access to this store. Sure, a lot of the app's features are obvious. But the app has other, less obvious features. And knowing what these are and how they work can help you get more out of the Mac App Store in significantly less time and with considerably less effort.

In this chapter, we will explore what makes the app to access the Mac App Store the most essential application in the Lion operating system. Specifically, we will walk you through the process of purchasing an application from the store. Along the way, we'll point out interesting aspects of using the Mac App Store, as well as different strategies you can employ to make more effective use of the store. Following these tips will help you get the most bang for your buck, saving you both time and money.

Applications are a huge part of an operating system's appeal. The types of applications available, their design, and their effectiveness are all part of what can make one operating system more desirable than another. The rest of this chapter will illustrate just how powerful it can be to have instant access to new applications and their subsequent updates.

> **NOTE:** The Mac App Store contains both free and paid applications. When using this store, remember to keep security in mind. Using the Mac App Store requires that you be responsible with your personal information. The store is a great asset, but it can quickly become a liability if you're not careful about securing items such as credit card information and other personal data. It is best to use only your own devices to purchase items, so that your account information does not reside on anyone else's iPhone, iPad, or Mac. Not confining your account information to your own devices could potentially leave you vulnerable to someone else using your account to make purchases without your permission.

The Mac App Store

The Mac App Store is only briefly mentioned in previous chapters, but it is an integral part of your Lion operating system. This store allows you to find software easily and cheaply, and without having to use Google or other search services to find the software you want. Another advantage to using the Mac App Store versus the Internet is that you are guaranteed a high level of quality and compatibility. Apple goes to great extremes to ensure that the software in the Mac App Store works with the Lion operating system. For example, Apple enforces a quality control standard for its software publishers, helping to ensure that you get high quality apps for your money. Now let's take a closer look at everything the Mac App Store has to offer.

> **NOTE:** The header section shown in Figure 5–1 is dynamic, and it will change as Apple updates its software product line. For example, note the portion of the image that reads, "Hidden Object Games." This is an advertisement, as is the menu to the left of it, which contains graphic objects that change daily. These frequently cycled advertisements promote the latest and most popular applications available.

The Mac App Store's menu consists of several icons (see Figure 5–1).

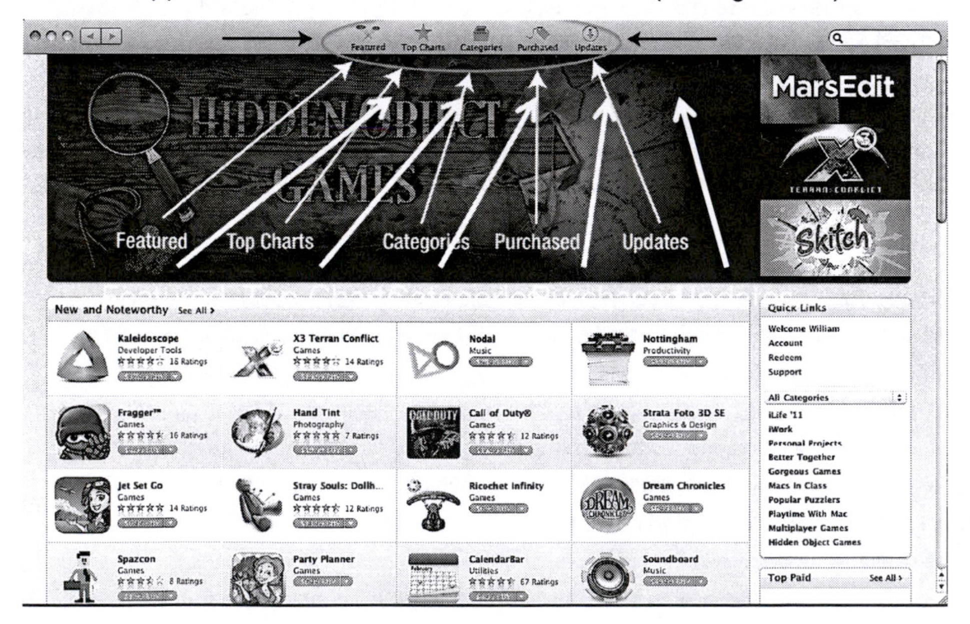

Figure 5–1. *The main menu of the Mac App Store*

These icons on the menu of the **Mac App Store** app enable you to navigate the store's various sections. Table 5–1 describes these sections.

Table 5–1. *The Mac App Store's Main Menu*

Icon	Description
Featured	Clicking this menu item takes you to the **Featured** section. This is where Apple displays those apps it feels might be of particular interest to its users. Reasons Apple might feature a given app include its quality, uniqueness, and/or newness. This feature provides a quick way to learn about the latest and greatest apps for your Mac.
Top Charts	Clicking this menu item takes you to the **Top Charts** section. This section of the Mac App Store allows you to see the most popular applications on the site, providing an easy way to gauge the quality of an app. It contains applications that have been downloaded thousands or even millions of times by users! If many Lion users are downloading an app, and you are looking for an app with similar functionality, then you might consider giving the app a try yourself, especially if it has good ratings. This is a section I recommend you visit frequently.
Categories	Clicking this menu item takes you to the **Categories** section, which lets you search for and view applications by category. Categories include **Games**, **Productivity**, **Health**, and many others. This section was designed to help users shorten the time that it takes to find a given piece of software. This section can save you hours of searching through the applications available in the Mac App Store.
Purchased	Clicking this menu item takes you to the **Purchased** section, which lets you view your application download and purchase history. This can help you ensure that you do not download the same application twice. It also makes it easy to track the money you have spent previously at the Mac App Store, as well as your store activity in general.
Updates	Clicking this menu item takes you to the **Updates** section. This section displays application updates for the software you have purchased previously. These updates address security issues, fix bugs, and generally improve the functionality of your software. It behooves you to visit this section of the Mac App Store frequently.

NOTE: You don't need to visit the **Updates** section to learn whether there are updates available for apps you've purchased from the Mac App Store. If updates are available, then the icon for the Mac App Store will have a number superimposed on it. This number represents the number of updates available from the store.

There are also several other sections in the Mac App Store that you might find useful (see Figure 5–2).

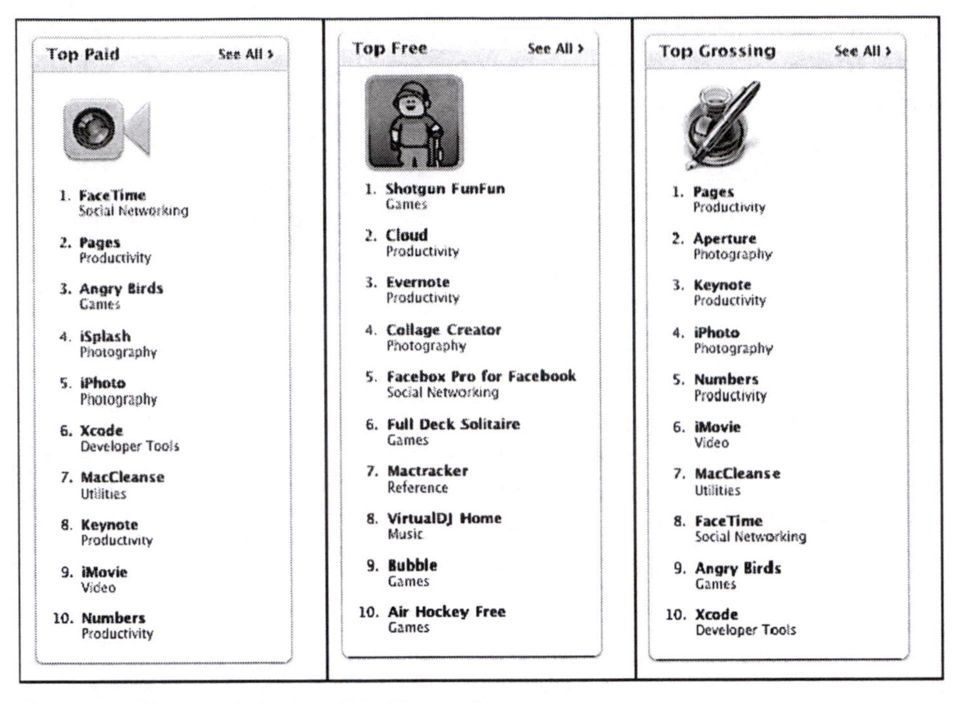

Figure 5–2. *The extended menu of the Mac App Store*

The Mac App Store lists items by **Top Paid**, **Top Free**, and **Top Grossing**. These sections give you a bird's eye view of what applications are doing well. Applications found in any of these three sections might be worth considering for purchase because they've earned their way onto these charts, much like an album on a music chart. Apple designed the Mac App Store to be simple, accessible, and effective at delivering the software you want, when you want it. And it does so with an elegant, sophisticated, and easy-to-navigate interface. I recommend that you give the Mac App Store a try, using it to feed your Lion OS the applications it craves!

Keeping Your Apps Up to Date

When installing applications, it is easy to overlook the fact that you may need to update them. Keeping your apps up to date is a very important part of properly maintaining your Lion operating system. Common reasons for issuing software updates include incorporating new features, addressing security vulnerabilities, and otherwise fixing functionality issues. Fortunately for you as a Lion user, maintaining the software you buy from the Mac App Store is as easy as, well, doing nothing!

What makes the Mac App Store so unique is its ability to simplify application management and maintenance. When you buy an app from the Mac App Store, you will update the application just by using it. Updating is done automatically by default, although you can alter the settings to perform such updates manually, at your convenience. If you wish to update your Mac applications manually, you only need to look for the icon that indicates you have updates waiting to execute, and then intervene by launching the **Mac App Store** app and selecting **Updates** (see Figure 5–3).

Figure 5–3. *The Mac App Store's Updates menu*

The number of pending updates is shown at the top of the **Updates** icon, which is located on the Mac App Store's main menu. If you feel like you need to perform an update before the Mac App Store does so on its own, simply click **Updates.** At this point, you will be able to update each application individually or all of them at once by clicking the **Update All** button (see Figure 5–4).

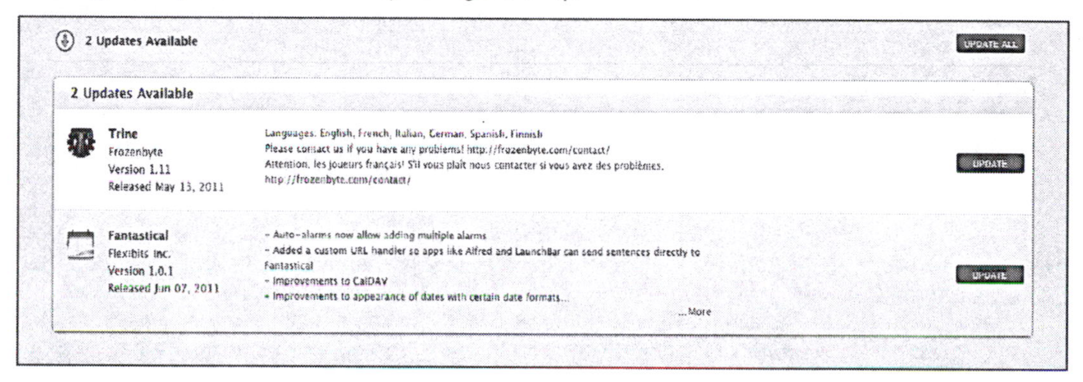

Figure 5–4. *Updating Apps*

Securing Your Identity

As previously mentioned, you need to be conscious of security when using the Mac App Store. The use of online digital media is growing, as is the number of people purchasing it; unfortunately, the number of would-be thieves trying to prey on those who buy such media is also growing. Following the guidelines described in Table 5–2 can reduce your online risk, helping you protect both your identity and your wallet.

Table 5–2. *Best Practices When Using the Mac App Store*

Proactive Tip	Description
Passwords 	When you create your passwords, be sure to do so in a way that they are difficult to bypass. It is important to create complex passwords that use numbers, letters, and special characters, so that would-be hackers will have a very tough time discovering them. The stronger your password, the more secure your Mac App Store account will be.
Sharing Accounts 	Your iTunes and App Store accounts will let you install purchased media on up to ten different devices. However, it behooves you to be selective when deciding which devices to enable content on, and to be especially careful when deciding whom you can trust to make purchases on your behalf using your Mac App Store account.
Monitor Your Account 	Keep track of your account and any emails that you get related to your account that come from Apple. You need to review purchases and your account information frequently. Doing so will help you spot suspicious charges or changes related to your account, enabling you to quickly to resolve the situation if you spot any irregularities.
Use the Reviews 	Apple has a way of finding criminals before they make it to the Mac App Store, but nothing is more powerful than word of mouth. Be sure to read the reviews of apps that interest you before you purchase them. This way, you can learn if anyone has noticed anything suspicious about a given application.

App Components and Purchasing

When you indicate you want to purchase an app, you will be taken to its information portal. This portal tells you more about the application, providing an in-depth explanation of what the application does. The portal also indicates the app's size and release date, and it includes reviews that indicate how well it is liked by others who have chosen to purchase it. Understanding the components that make up this section of the Mac App Store is a vital part of ensuring that you make the right decision when considering an application purchase.

In the following sections, you'll learn everything you need to know about the information portal, so you have all the information you need to make an informed decision about a potential purchase. For example, we'll walk you through everything you see on an information portal, so that you understand how each section relates to the application you are considering. To get started, simply click the **Mac App Store** icon located in the Dock, and then select the application that interests you (see Figure 5–5).

Figure 5–5. *The Mac App Store icon in the Dock*

Purchasing an App

Let's assume you want to purchase an application called *Civilization V: Campaign Edition*, an action-strategy game for the OS X operating system. The process is the same for any app you might want to purchase, so you can take the lessons described here and apply them to any app that interests you. This particular application was located in the **Featured** section on the first page of the Mac App Store (see Figure 5–6). Simply click the icon shown for this app to enter its particular information portal.

As you follow along, keep in mind that each subsection of this example is normally located on a single page. However, for the purposes of this discussion, I have broken out each section of the information portal for the *Civilization V* application. This will make it easier to understand what the different panels of information represent.

Figure 5–6. *The Civilization V portal link*

Application Information

When you enter an information portal, you are presented with a large page of information. The first thing you see is the **Information** section, which displays detailed information about the app, explaining both its purpose and content (see Figure 5–7). Clicking the ...**More** link will reveal more information about the product. Note that this section also shows the app's price beneath its icon.

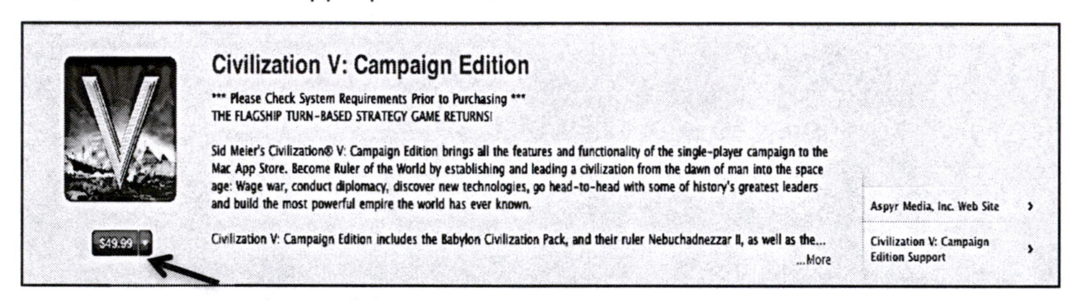

Figure 5–7. *The Civilization V Information section*

The Application's Origins

Clicking the application's icon, takes you to the **Information Bar** section, which shows a wealth of information related to the application's publisher and its creation (see Figure 5-8). Specifically, this section lists the publisher, version number, when the app was released, and so on. It also lists the app's requirements; it is essential that you compare these requirements against the specs of your computer system, so that you know for certain that your Mac can run the app *before* you purchase it.

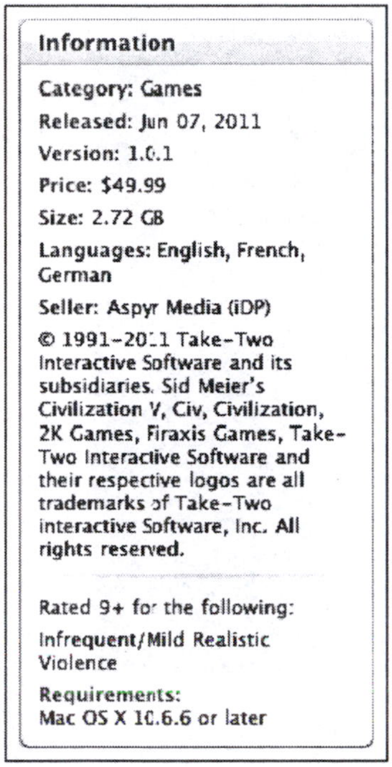

Information

Category: Games
Released: Jun 07, 2011
Version: 1.0.1
Price: $49.99
Size: 2.72 GB
Languages: English, French, German
Seller: Aspyr Media (iDP)
© 1991-2011 Take-Two Interactive Software and its subsidiaries. Sid Meier's Civilization V, Civ, Civilization, 2K Games, Firaxis Games, Take-Two Interactive Software and their respective logos are all trademarks of Take-Two Interactive Software, Inc. All rights reserved.

Rated 9+ for the following:
Infrequent/Mild Realistic Violence
Requirements:
Mac OS X 10.6.6 or later

Figure 5–8. *Information about Civilization V's origins*

Application Image Previews

Next, we'll look at the **Image Preview** section, which shows various screenshots of a given app (see Figure 5–9). Like the **Information Bar** section, the **Image Preview** section appears immediately after you click the application's icon. These images can give you a good idea of the app's basic interface, layout, graphics, and ergonomics (where applicable). Seeing these images can often make or break a purchase. They can entice you to buy the application, or they can leave you feeling that there may be other applications that fit your needs better. You can scroll through the images by manipulating the thumbnails at the bottom of the main image.

Figure 5–9. *The Civilization V Image Preview section*

Finding Similar Applications

Next, we'll look at the **Like Apps** section of the portal. This section shows you other, similar applications purchased by Mac App Store users who also purchased your app. This is a great way to shop for similar items, and it can decrease the time it takes for you to search for alternative apps (see Figure 5–10).

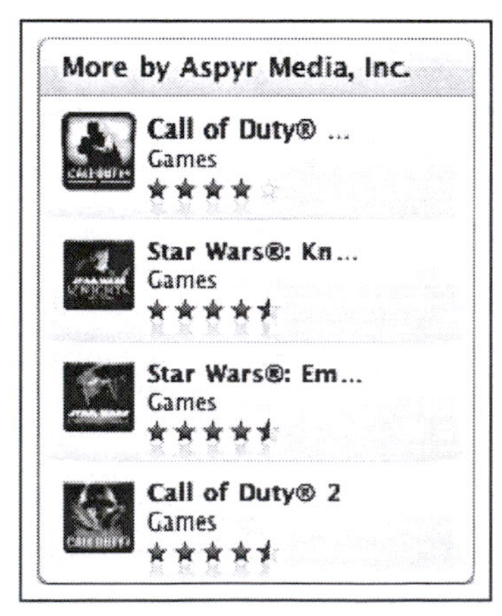

Figure 5–10. *The Civilization V Like Apps section*

Application Review

Last but not least, let's look at the **Customer Ratings** section (see Figure 5–11). You can see this section at the bottom of the application's **Information** section. It is revealed once you click the application's icon while browsing the Mac App Store. This is one of the most important sections of the portal because it shares the reactions of others who have purchased the application. Apps are rated on a five star scale; obviously, the more stars an app receives, the more its users liked it. Typically, you want to avoid an application with a large number of two star reviews (or less). Such an application may have functionality problems that keep it from delivering on its advertised promises.

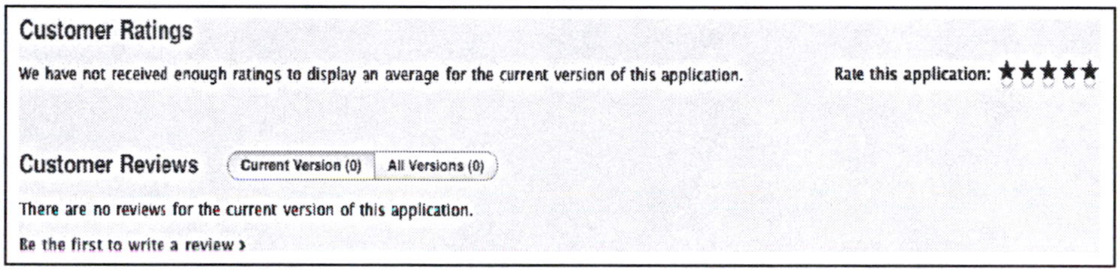

Customer Ratings
We have not received enough ratings to display an average for the current version of this application. Rate this application: ★★★★★

Customer Reviews Current Version (0) All Versions (0)
There are no reviews for the current version of this application.
Be the first to write a review ›

Figure 5–11. *The Civilization V Customer Ratings section*

It is important that you pay close attention to how the ratings for an application change over time. An app's ratings may go up or down, depending on what the authors are doing with it, and the ratings will reflect the buyers' opinions of the changes. Thus, an app with a two star rating today could have a five star rating at some future date. Be sure to monitor apps that catch your eye; this can help you determine whether an app has evolved into being exactly what you need.

Summary

This chapter provided in-depth information about the Mac App Store and how to get the most from it. This site is quite powerful; and with a little practice, you can use it to find just about any application you can think of. However, you should remember to use it responsibly. You need to keep your information safe from others, so that neither your account nor your financial information is compromised. You should also remember to keep watch on apps that interest you as they evolve over time—sometimes apps with rough edges today become extremely polished over time. And be sure to read the reviews for an app. These can help you gauge how others feel about the app and the company that makes it. The Mac App Store contains applications of every type and for every age level. Chances are, if you cannot find it in the App Store, it may not exist. You can use the Mac App Store to fill up your Mac with productive apps that suit your needs. And if you discover you have a new need, always remember: "There's an app for that."

Chapter 6

Finding Life in iLife

iLife consists of several applications, including **iPhoto**, **Garageband**, and **iMovie**. Each of these applications has a very distinct purpose; however, it is when you use them together to create multimedia projects that the power of **iLife** really shines through. For example, you can combine these apps to create entire movies, photo albums, or even soundtracks.

One thing that makes **iLife** so powerful is that its apps behave in similar, complementary ways. This also makes them easy to use. The interfaces of the apps in **iLife** have been simplified for proficiency, and their underlying code leverages every bit of your Mac's power. Let's take a closer look at exactly what the applications in the **iLife** suite do. Along the way, we'll examine some of the reasons you should consider making this suite among your most frequently used applications.

In this chapter, we will focus on the main and navigational menu items of each application. With **iLife**, no one can tell you what to do because the applications within it depend on *your* creativity and vision to get the most out of their rich features. Therefore, this chapter will focus mainly on how to use the simplified interfaces provided by the apps that make up the **iLife** suite.

NOTE: The Mac App Store sells all three of the applications discussed in this chapter, and each can be downloaded separately as either an upgrade or as a replacement for your existing **iLife** software applications. Your Lion operating system comes with **iLife**; however, future upgrades to this software must be purchased. As you might expect, you can be do so through the Mac App Store.

Those of you with earlier versions of **iLife** may also have the **iDVD** and **iWeb** applications. Both applications are being phased out, so I will not cover them here.

iMovie

One of the neatest things about owning a Mac is the limitless way it lets you create and distribute any kind of digital media that exists today. This includes video, which can be crafted into commercials, music videos, training simulations, and of course, movies. **iMovie** lets you create editable video reels that are full of special effects and sounds. Moreover, these videos can be professionally massaged to forge theater-worthy video productions. What makes **iMovie** stand on its own as a movie editor is the ease with which you can sit down and bring your ideas to fruition. As noted previously, the only limit to what you can accomplish is your imagination. Let's take a closer look at what you need to know to make **iMovie** work for you.

NOTE: What you see on your screen may vary from what is shown in this chapter, depending on which version of **iMovie** you have. I wrote this book using **iMovie** version 9.0.2, which comes free with the **iLife '11** suite. To check which version of **iLife** you have, simply click the **iLife** text title after opening the application, and then click the **About** option (see Figure 6–1).

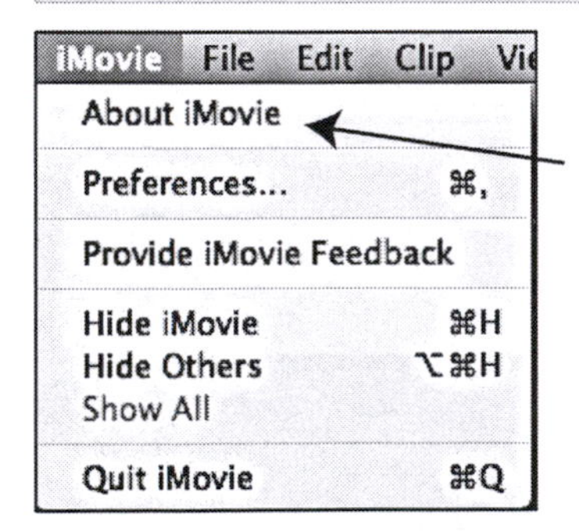

Figure 6–1. *The About iMovie menu option*

Clicking the **About *[application name]*** menu option for any application will bring up an information window that reveals the app's version and some licensing information. Figure 6–2 shows the information window that comes up when you select the **About iMovie** menu option.

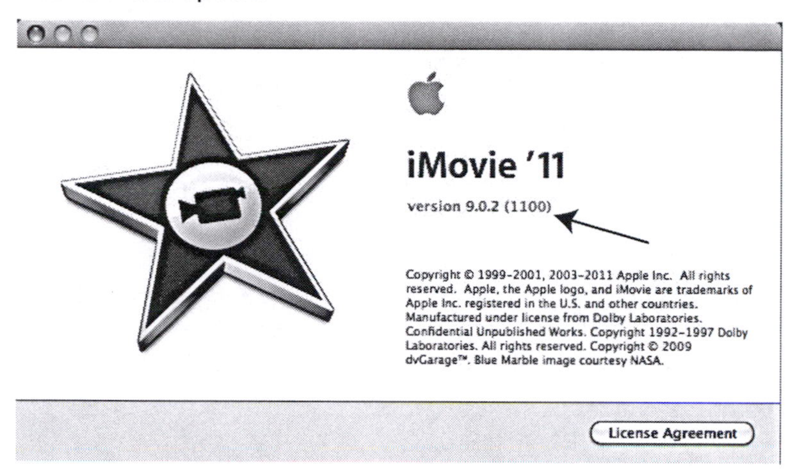

Figure 6–2. *About iMovie's information window*

After accepting the license agreement, you will immediately be taken to **iMovie**'s main menu, where you can either choose to get started or browse for help on specific topics. If this is your first time using **iMovie**, I recommend that you peruse the **Browse Help** section, so that you can make yourself comfortable with what the app has to offer.

The iMovie Menu

The first active window you see after accepting the license agreement is a menu that helps you get started. You have a couple options for doing so. First, you can take a guided video tutorial that walks you through the application. Alternatively, you can browse for help on various aspects of using **iMovie** (see Figure 6–3).

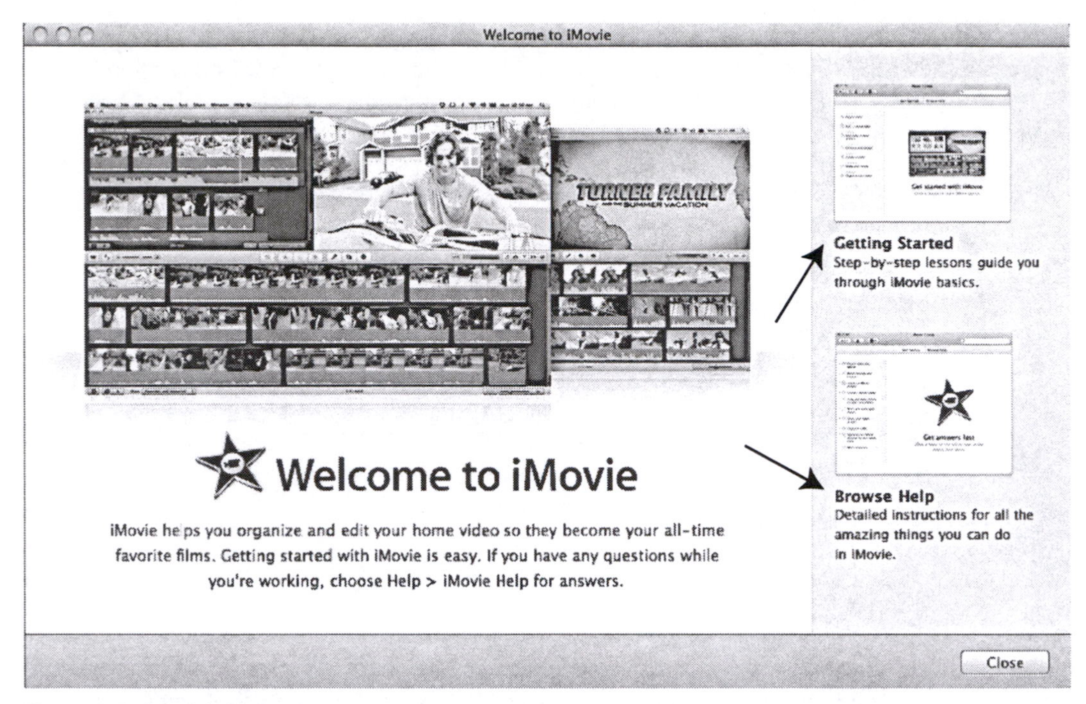

Figure 6–3. *iMovie's Welcome menu*

Depending on how seasoned you are as an **iMovie** user, you may want to take the time to go through the **Getting Started** tutorials. These tutorials give you step-by-step instructions on the basics of using **iMovie**. Experiencing these tutorials can quickly make you comfortable enough with the program to venture into other areas of the app that are not fully explained by these tutorials.

Like the tutorials, the **Browse Help** section allows you to learn about some **iMovie** topics that you may be initially curious about. This section can also serve as a handy reference guide if you forget one of the many shortcut combinations or how to use one of the tools included in the application.

I recommend that all users—from novice to expert—take the time to get to know this software before using it. Even an expert is likely to discover new tricks, services, and tools in newer versions of the software. In fact, I recommend doing this with all of the applications in the **iLife** suite, especially when you are attempting to use a new version of the software. It is always best not to assume that all of an app's features will continue to work in the exact same way.

The iMovie Interface

The interface for **iMovie** is simple enough that even someone who has never done any type of video editing can jump right in and get started, yet powerful enough that it can bridge the gap between professional movie-makers and video hobbyists. As simple as the **iMovie** interface is, however, it is still a good idea to know some of program's basics before you begin using it. For example, it behooves you to select the right template *before* you start working on a new **iMovie** project.

Selecting the Right Template

One thing that sets **iMovie** apart from other applications is that it requires a bit of planning to use it effectively. This planning might include creating a story or selecting the music you wish to include for certain scenes in your movie. Above all, this planning means selecting an applicable theme and trailer to complement your movie and accentuate your efforts.

Selecting the right theme can make a significant difference in how the content of your movie is both perceived and received. You definitely want to get this part right because doing so can make or break your idea. Fortunately, **iMovie** includes several templates in the form of themes and movie trailers that you can leverage to create and advertise your project. **iMovie** also offers several ways to customize its included templates, so that your movie can still be unique and authentic. Let's proceed with creating your first project and selecting a movie template.

You can create a new project by selecting **New Project...** from the **File** menu or by pressing the **Command** + **N** keys simultaneously (see Figure 6-4).

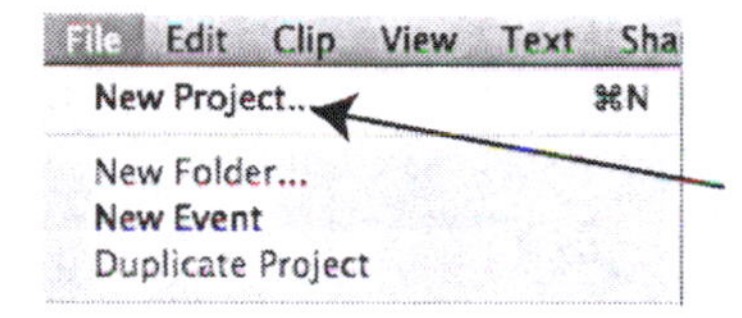

Figure 6–4. *iMovie's New Project... option*

After choosing to create a new project, you will be prompted to pick a template for it (see Figure 6-5). **iMovie**'s templates can be highly modified, so take your time here, and choose the template that bears the closest resemblance to what you want your movie to feel and look like. Be sure to choose a good name for your project, as well as the right aspect ratio and an appropriate frame rate. When you select a theme for a movie, you will be presented with a preview of that theme. This will help you determine whether you're choosing the most appropriate theme for your movie.

Project themes are templates that **iMovie** uses to create content for your project before you start. These themes are used throughout the initial and concluding stages of your project. Movie trailers are intended to be used to promote your project; as such, they should advertise and specify what your movie is about, as well as give proper credit to all the parties involved in your movie's creation.

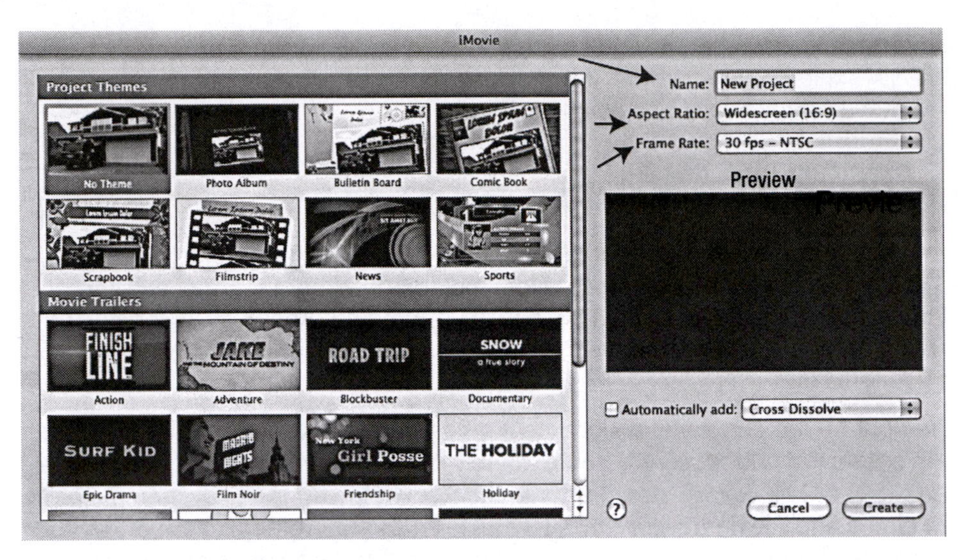

Figure 6–5. *iMovie's template chooser*

Once you choose your template, you will see **iMovie**'s primary interface (see Figure 6–6). For this chapter's example, I've chosen the **Supernatural** template located under the **Movie Trailers** section. To follow along, choose the same trailer (or any other trailer that you like).

Breaking Down iMovie's Interface

iMovie, like most software, requires that you understand its layout. This understanding will enable you to access the resources you need to create your movie quickly and easily. **iMovie**'s interface is balanced by the inclusion of four sections: the contextual editing region, the movie's **Preview** window, the **Information** window, and the **Media Browser** window (see Figure 6–6). Together, these window panes form the interface that you will use to create your movie. Let's take a look to see what each part does in detail.

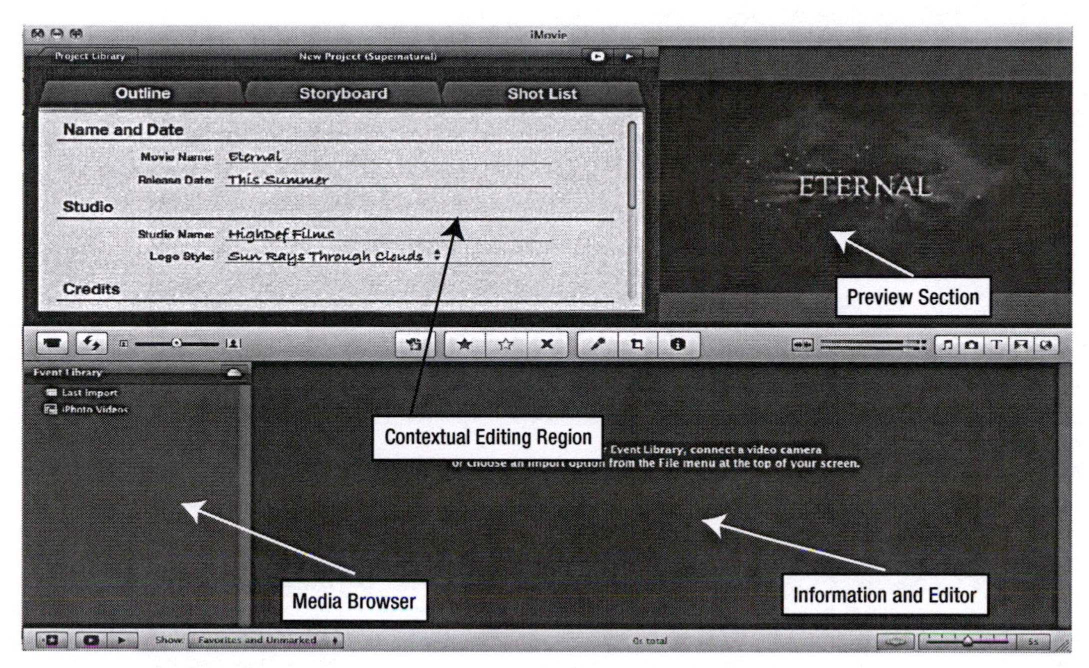

Figure 6–6. *iMovie's primary interface*

Each **iMovie** project is broken into three primary sections:

- **Outline**: This section holds all the information about those involved in making the film, such as the producer, studio, and other individuals like musicians (see Figure 6–7). This section is also where you place the title and release date for your movie.
- **Storyboard**: This section determines the contextual aspects of your **iMovie** project (see Figure 6–8). These aspects include the credits and storyboard; you will use these features to organize and align video clips in the preferred order.
- **Shotlist**: This section lets you fine-tune individual images and snippets of video you have taken (see Figure 6–9). For example, this section is where you can apply special effects to shots in your movie, such as slow motion and other enhancements.

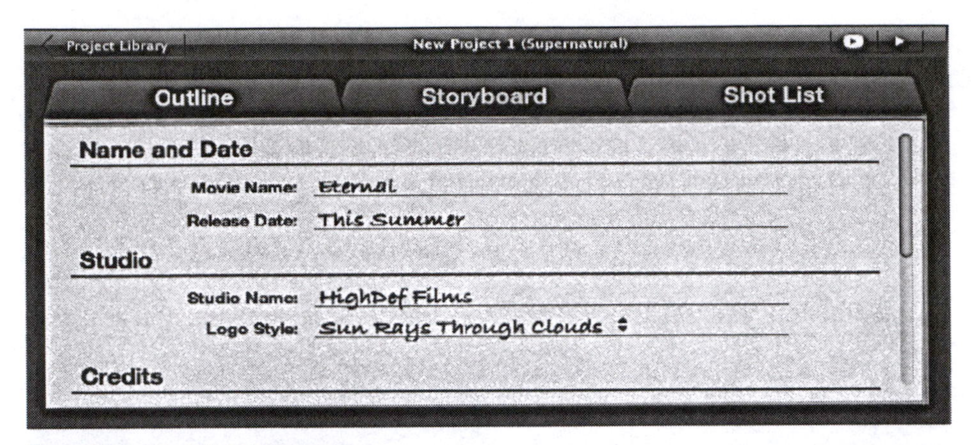

Figure 6–7. *iMovie's Outline interface*

Figure 6–8. *iMovie's Storyboard interface*

Figure 6–9. *iMovie's Shotlist interface*

Prepping Your Video Content for Editing

So far, we have taken a short peek into the basic interface segments required to edit your movie. Our next step is to look at what it takes to manage, organize, and prepare your video content for editing. When using **iMovie**, you will notice that there is a consistent menu bar that separates the pane for contextual editing from your **Media Browser** window (see Figure 6–10). This menu serves as a go-between for these two sections (see Figure 6–6).

Figure 6–10. *iMovie's primary editor toolbar*

To learn what each button in the menu does, systematically place your mouse over each button and read the descriptions that pop up (see Figure 6–11).

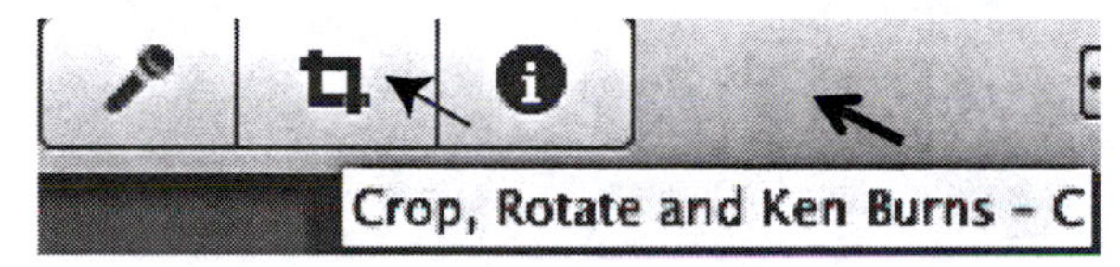

Figure 6–11. *iMovie's primary editing toolbar with pop-up notations*

Managing your project's events requires a keen focus on both the content you will provide for your project and what you will do with it. For example, you need to know what special effects and transitions you will want to apply to your content. Using the **Event Library** and the **Event Manager** together is what allows you to add content to your movie. You add this content either by using the **Import** menu option or by simply dragging and dropping movie, audio, and/or image files into the **Event Library** section. The **Media Browser** section immediately to the right of the **Event Library** section is what you will use to specify and manage timeline action items associated with your media objects (see Figure 6–12). Such objects might include images, movies, audio clips, and so on.

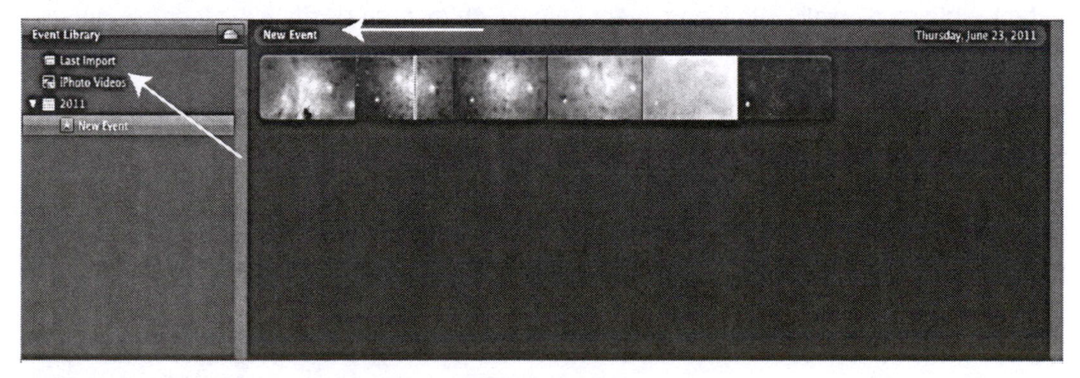

Figure 6–12. *iMovie's Media Browser and Event Library interfaces*

You can find **iMovie**'s **Footer** menu immediately below the **Events Layout** section of the primary interface. The **Footer** menu allows you to initiate playback and adjust the scale of the **Event Manager** window, which is located immediately to the right of the **Event Library** menu (see Figure 6–13).

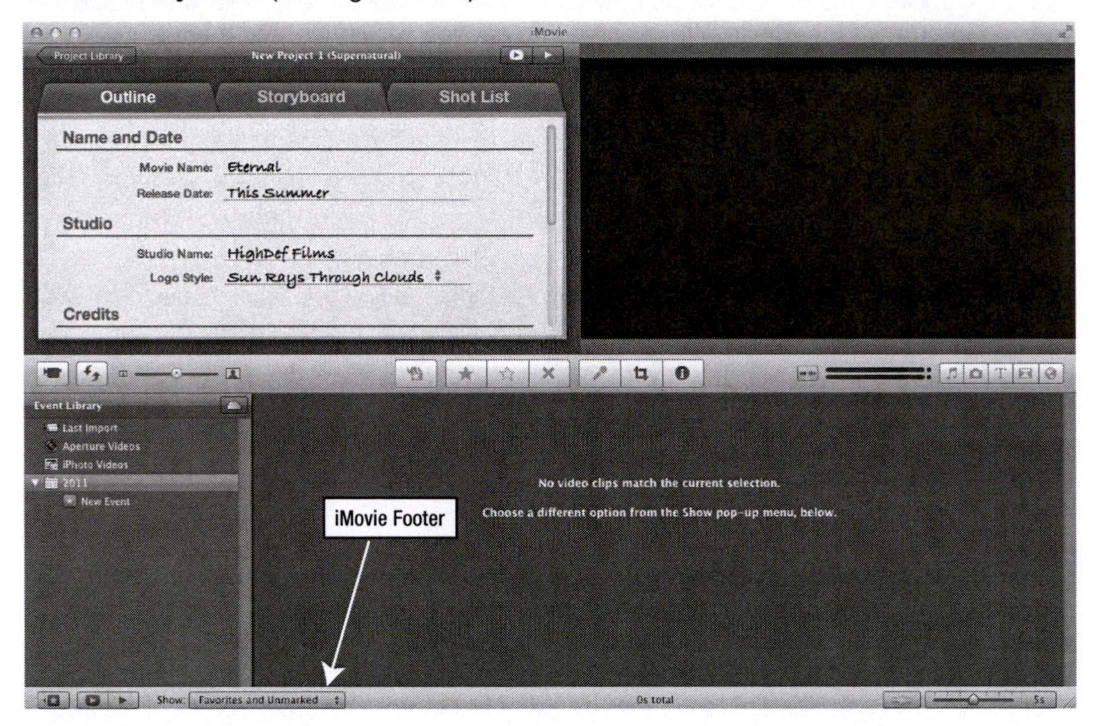

Figure 6–13. *iMovie's Footer menu*

When working with **iMovie,** there are two menus you will want to become very familiar with: **Clip** and **Share**. Together, these menus enable to you to share and granularly edit your project. The **Clip** menu allows you to implement things such as special effects and instant replays, as well as to insert event items such as *fade points*, which cause one scene to fade into another (see Figure 6-14).

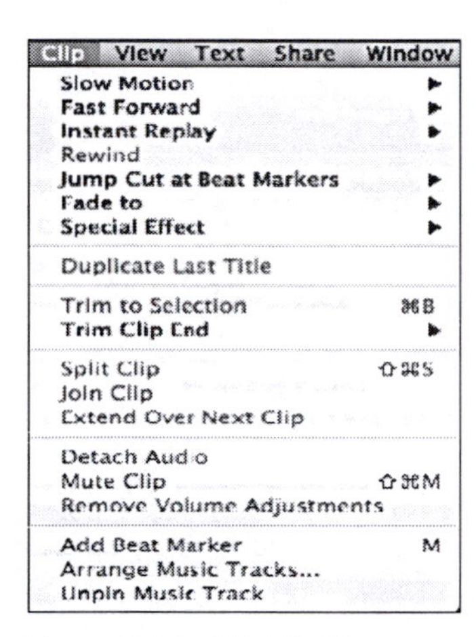

Figure 6–14. *iMovie's Clip menu*

The **Share** menu allows you to distribute your content in several ways (see Figure 6-15). For example, it lets you export your finished project to **iTunes**, from which you can upload it to the Internet to places like YouTube or Facebook. The **Share** menu also allows you to export your projects into third-party applications such as **Final Cut Pro**, a professional editing program. The latter program includes theater-quality effects and industry-standard editing tools that you can use to manipulate and edit your video further, giving it a higher level of polish.

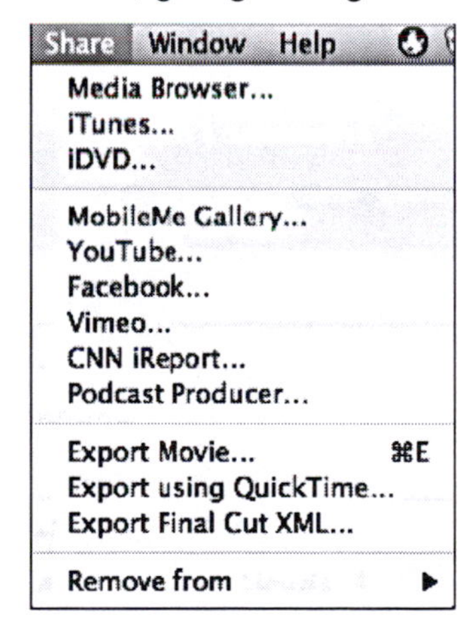

Figure 6–15. *iMovie's Share menu*

Using **iMovie** can be fun and entertaining. And with enough practice, you and your friends and family can enjoy movie-making at its finest. All it takes is a little bit of patience—and a lot of creativity.

iPhoto

Photo management is a part of computing life for almost everyone who owns a computer. Most mobile devices include photo-taking capabilities, and just about every modern consumer-oriented computing device can take photos in some capacity. Photos represent a large part of computing, and they serve as the foundation of communication for platforms such as marketing and web technologies. Photos allow us to store memorable moments and relive those great—and sometimes not so great—moments we want to look back at and sometimes share with others. **iPhoto** is the **iLife** application that makes all of this possible.

One of the most important aspects of leveraging digital images is finding tools that allow you to edit and organize your images in a way that fits the way you think. **iPhoto** provides a very simple way to access the features of a powerful image editor. For example, it includes a handful of utilities and tools that assist you in keeping your photos organized for later retrieval.

In the upcoming sections, I will describe some of the most commonly used features of **iPhoto**, so you can get the most out of the application right from the start. Along the way, we'll explore what it takes to organize, edit, and tag your photos for later retrieval.

Getting Started

Like **iMovie**, **iPhoto** does some initial hand-holding when you enter the program, getting you started with video tutorials and help files that can dramatically reduce the learning curve associated with using the software (see Figure 6–16).

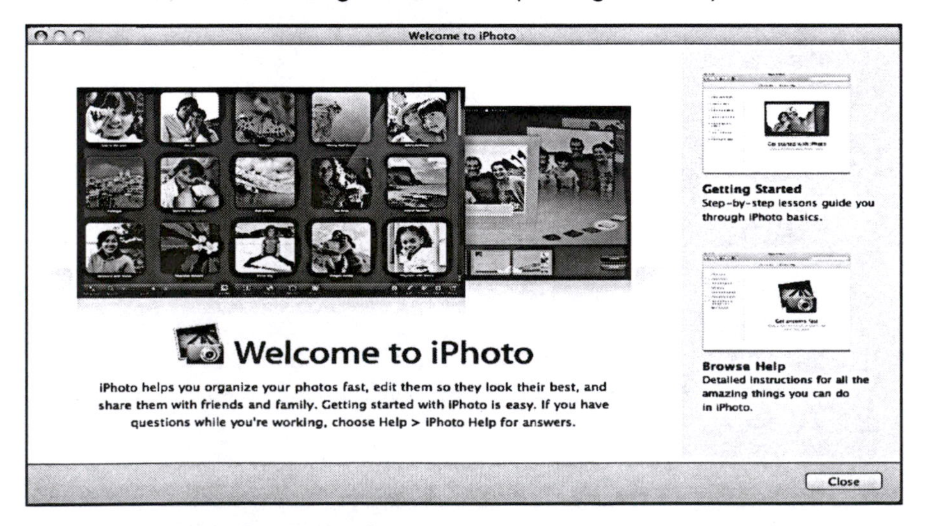

Figure 6–16. *iPhoto's Welcome interface*

When you launch **iPhoto**, you will be shown the **Welcome to iPhoto** screen, after which you will be taken to the **iPhoto**'s primary interface (see Figure 6–17).

Figure 6–17. ***iPhoto**'s primary interface*

iPhoto's primary interface includes a very simple set of menu options that let you navigate, edit, and organize your database of photos. You can access your library by event or photo entry, or even by face recognition or place. **iPhoto**'s primary interface includes the **Library** submenu, which lets you access your **Photos** library (see Figure 6–18).

Figure 6–18. *iPhoto's Library submenu*

iPhoto's Faces and Places

iPhoto is full of advanced technology that is presented to the user transparently. This technology enables Mac users to leverage advanced photo-image technology without difficulty. For example, **iPhoto**'s facial-recognition technology lets users access and organize photos based on the faces contained in the images. This is great for visually organizing your photos. This feature also makes it easy to access and manipulate photos in your library (see Figure 6–19).

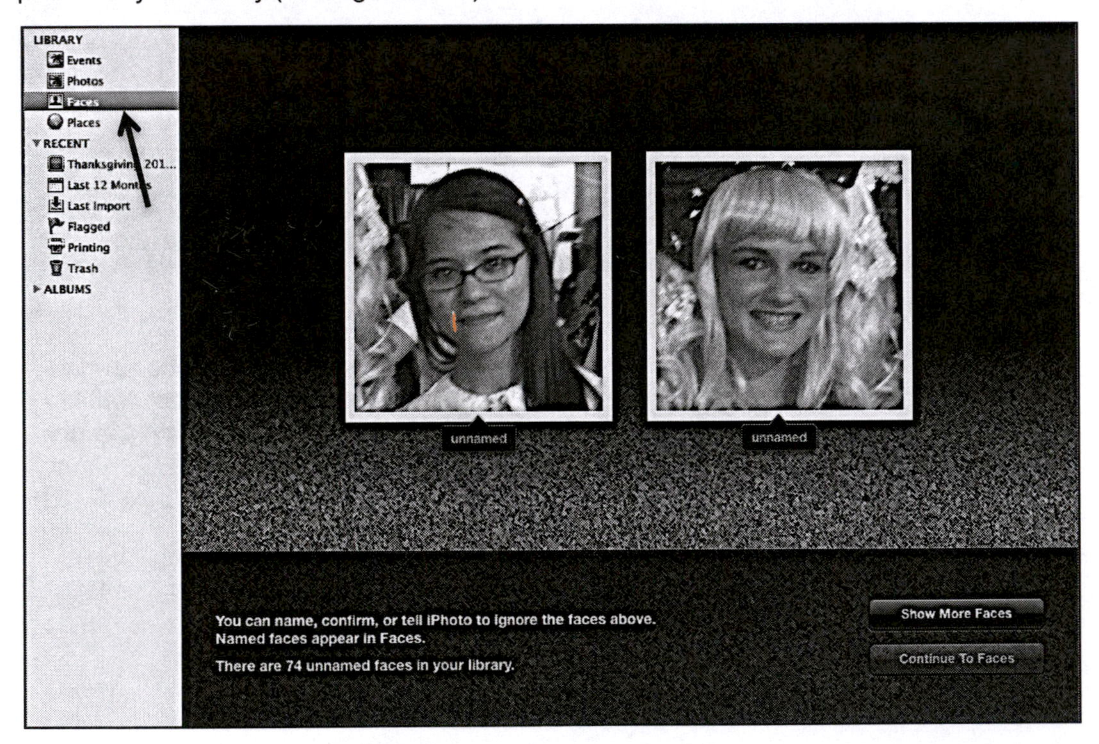

Figure 6–19. *Accessing iPhoto's Faces feature*

Geotagging with Places

Geotagging is another great feature built right into **iPhoto**. This feature places geographical location information inside your photos when taken with devices that support it. This allows each photo you take to be referenced by location, and it can assist you in pinpointing where the photo was taken. This feature is great for reliving events by location (see Figure 6-20).

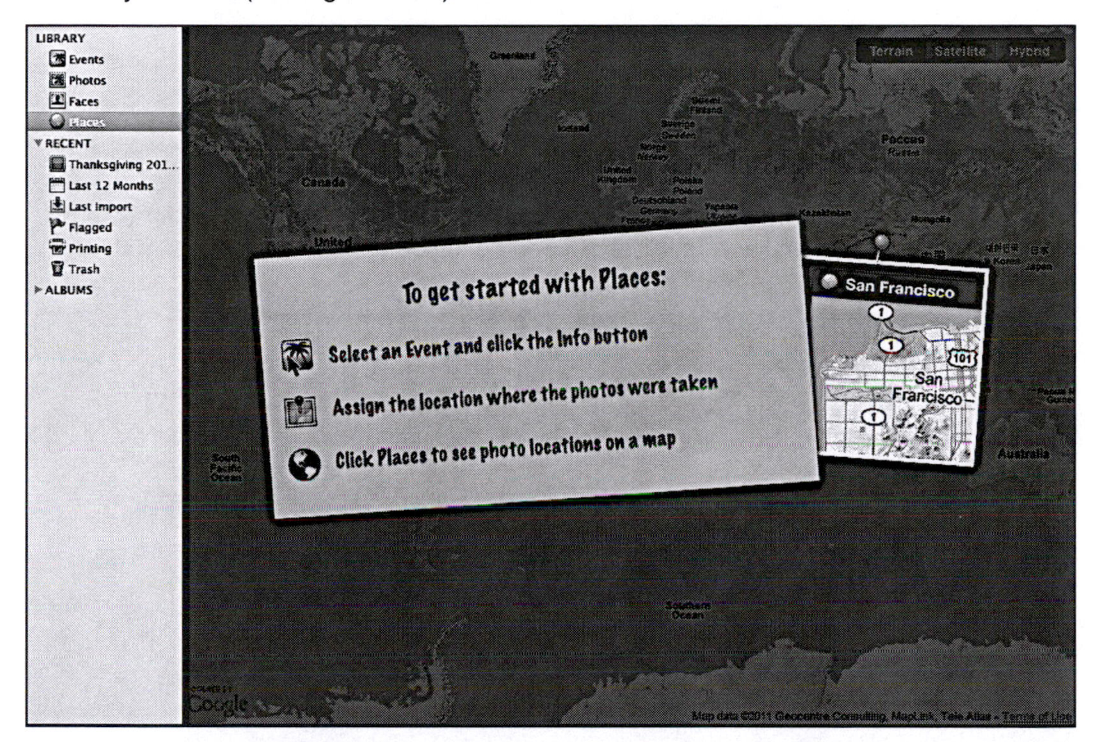

Figure 6–20. *iPhoto's Places feature*

Accessing images by face, place, or event is a very convenient; however, **iPhoto** gives you even quicker ways to find images in your library. For example, **iPhoto**'s **Recent** submenu lets you access your images by the time they were taken. And once you locate the photos you're looking for, you can use the **Flagged** option to mark them as important (see Figure 6–19). Marking photos as *flagged* makes it easier to find them later.

Figure 6–21. *Selecting iPhoto's Flagged option*

Additional Features in iPhoto

Locating information in your photos is very easy. For example, **iPhoto**'s **Information** utility exposes important information about each photo, such as its file name, date of creation, and a description (see Figure 6–22).

Figure 6–22. *iPhoto's Information utility*

Editing in iPhoto

A photo application without great editing capabilities is not a great photo application. Fortunately, **iPhoto** is very strong in the area of image editing, and it allows you to apply professional-grade filters and changes to your photos, helping you ensure that each picture comes out looking stunning. **iPhoto** raises the quality bar for photo-editing applications by placing powerful, simple-to-use controls at your fingertips. This makes it possible to dramatically enhance your photos with a few simple clicks (see Figure 6-23). For example, **iPhoto** makes it easy to crop or retouch your photos, or even to fix red-eye errors.

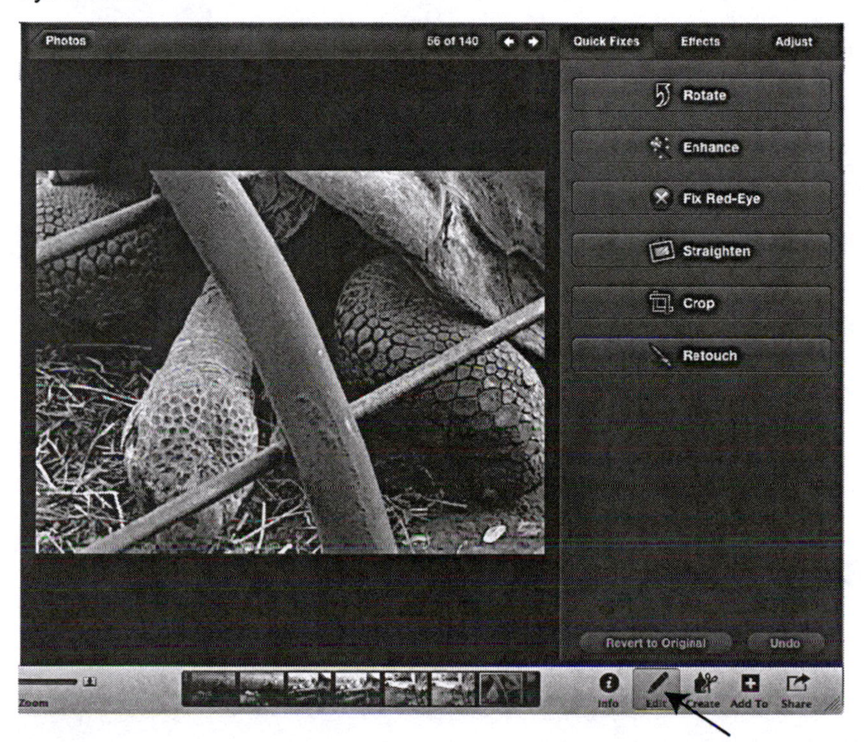

Figure 6–23. *iPhoto's editing options*

You can also use **iPhoto**'s **Footer** menu to zoom, edit, create, and share photos on Facebook, Flickr, and other social networking sites (see Figure 6–24).

Figure 6–24. *iPhoto's Footer menu*

iPhoto is one of the best applications ever made for organizing, distributing, and storing photos. It includes myriad options for image editing, and it stands out from the crowd with features such as face-recognition technology and geotagging. It will be a long time before other photo applications catch up to **iPhoto**; fortunately, as a Lion user you do not have to wait to enjoy the world's most advanced photo-organizing application.

GarageBand

GarageBand is held by many to be the most inexpensive yet most powerful music-making application that exists. Like **iMovie**, this app simultaneously caters to both amateurs and professionals. Its streamlined interface and easy-to-use navigational menus make it accessible to anyone who wants to lay down a track. Many professional audio editors and musicians begin their careers by using **GarageBand**, before moving on to more concert-oriented applications such as **Logic Studio Pro** (which is also made by Apple). As a Lion user, you get to do more than make movies and capture the essence of the photos that you take. You also get to make soundtracks that complement your movies and photos.

Working with **GarageBand** requires several things from you before you will be able to use it effectively. For example, you must have the will to learn how to create music, a good deal of patience, some kind of Midi instrument (such as a keyboard or guitar), and tons of curiosity. If you meet these requirements, **GarageBand** will help you leverage these qualities to explore music-making in all its endless possibilities. Let's see what it takes to acquire the basic skills needed to create your first track.

The GarageBand Interface

GarageBand, like all **iLife** applications, requires that you have an intimate knowledge of its user interface before you can use it effectively.

Welcome Window Pane

Like **iMovie** and **iPhoto**, **GarageBand** presents you with a **Welcome** screen when you first launch it. This screen allows you to choose between several different options, and the choices you make here will determine the type of activities you can undertake when using the application.

The first of these options is the **New Project** menu item, which lets you choose one of the instrument templates, such as the **Piano**, **Electric Guitar**, or **Keyboard Collection** (see Figure 6–25).

Figure 6–25. *GarageBand's New Project menu*

GarageBand's **Learn to Play** menu offers you the chance to follow automated lesson guides that can teach you certain chords, notes, and choruses (see Figure 6–26).

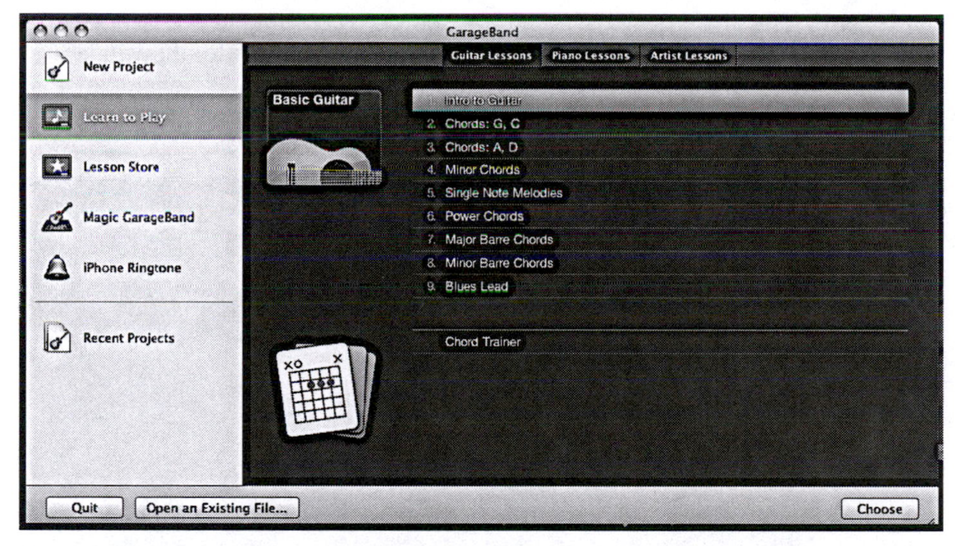

Figure 6–26. *GarageBand's Learn to Play option*

In a similar but much more advanced vein, **GarageBand**'s **Lesson Store** gives you the option to browse and download online lessons from professional musicians in three different categories: **Guitar Lessons**, **Piano Lessons**, and **Artist Lessons** (see Figure 6–27).

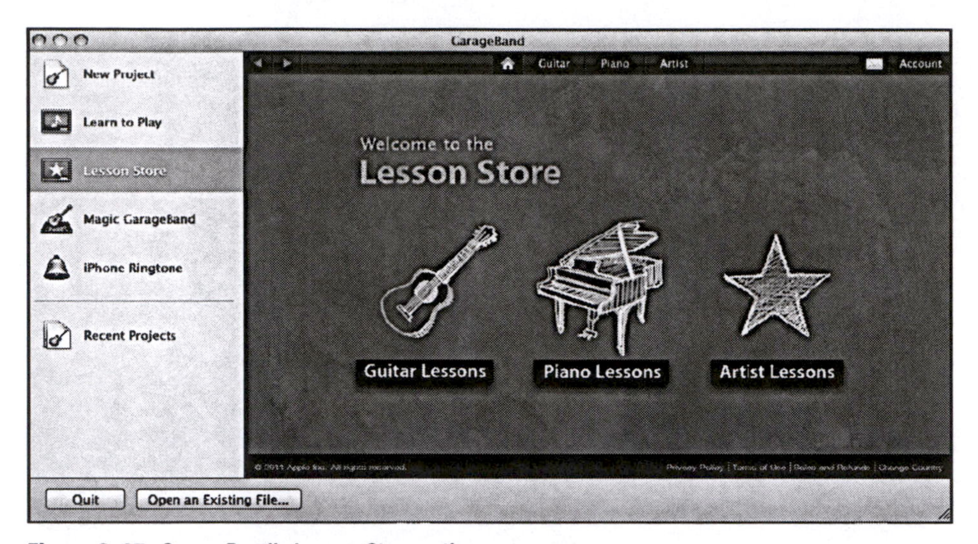

Figure 6–27. *GarageBand's Lesson Store option*

And the app's **Magic GarageBand** feature allows you to play in a virtual band of sorts, where the instruments for a given genre of music are laid out according to the template you select (see Figure 6–28). The templates in this section allow you to interact with live instruments and even to record your own playback material in real time. For example, this section's **Blues** template enables you to play in your own blues band (see Figure 6–29).

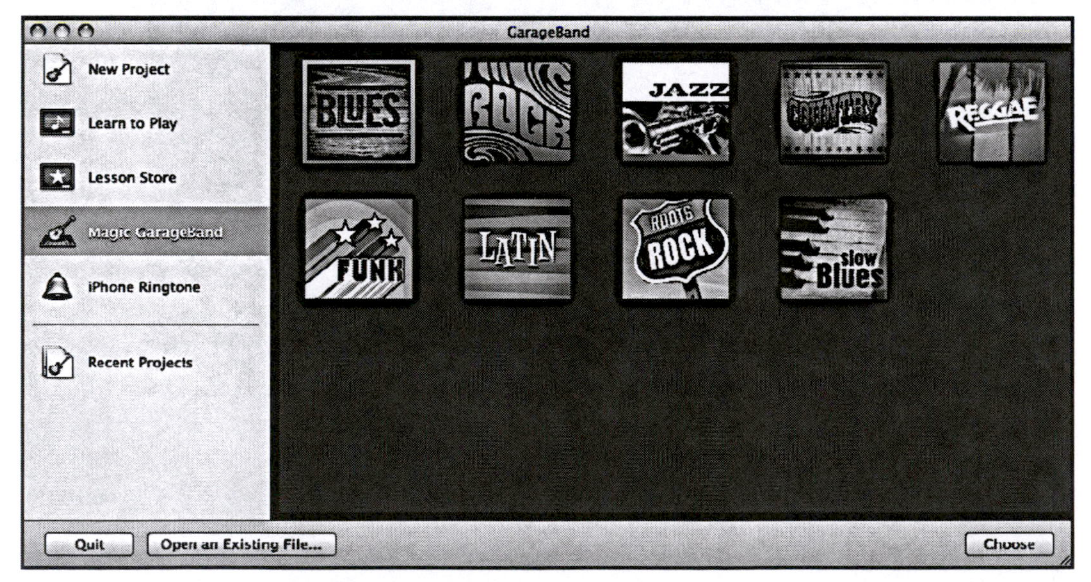

Figure 6–28. *GarageBand's Magic GarageBand templates*

Figure 6–29. *Magic GarageBand's Blues template*

Finally, **GarageBand**'s **iPhone Ringtone** option allows you to turn any audio source file into a ringtone for your phone (see Figure 6–30).

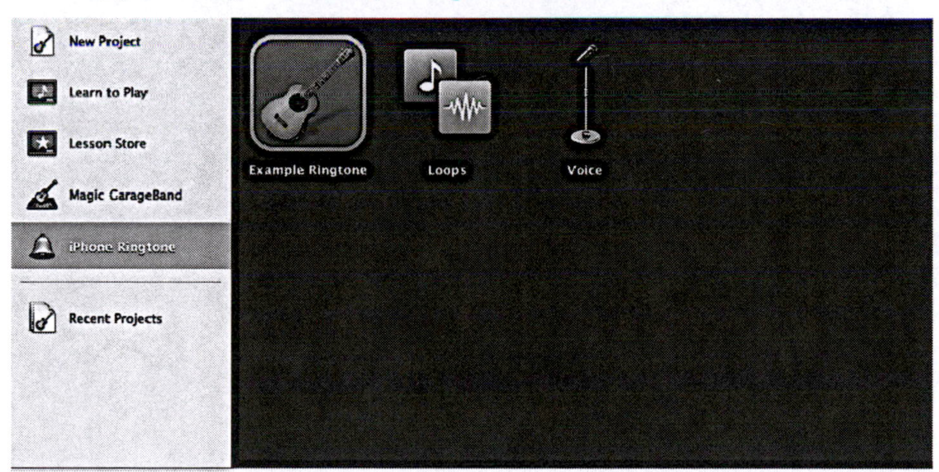

Figure 6–30. *GarageBand's iPhone Ringtone option*

GarageBand's Primary Interface

Like other **iLife** apps, **GarageBand** requires that you take the time to understand its menu options and how they work. **GarageBand**'s menus include options that help you play back, record, and edit your music. Also like other **iLife** apps, **GarageBand**'s primary menu is contained in its **Footer** menu, which allows you to play, record, and set the tempo, signature, and key. The **Footer** menu also gives you the ability to add additional tracks, to edit the tracks you're currently using, and even to access your media library directly. Hovering over any button in this menu brings up some descriptive text, so it's easy to know what any given button does (see Figure 6-31).

Figure 6–31. *GarageBand's Footer menu*

Let's break down **GarageBand**'s primary interface, which is shown in Figure 6–32.

Figure 6–32. *GarageBand's primary interface*

Tracks

GarageBand's **Tracks** submenu allows you to manipulate and add components to each individual track. This is the section where you decide what instruments and sounds to add to your tracks. This menu is quite nimble. For example, it lets you move each track up or down the list, as it suits your needs (see Figure 6–33).

Figure 6–33. *GarageBand's Tracks submenu*

Playback

GarageBand's **Playback** submenu lets you monitor and manipulate the content of the tracks that you add. You use this section to add, delete, cut, fade, and arrange the layouts of the recorded audio and loops that you have inserted in the form of track layers (see Figure 6–34).

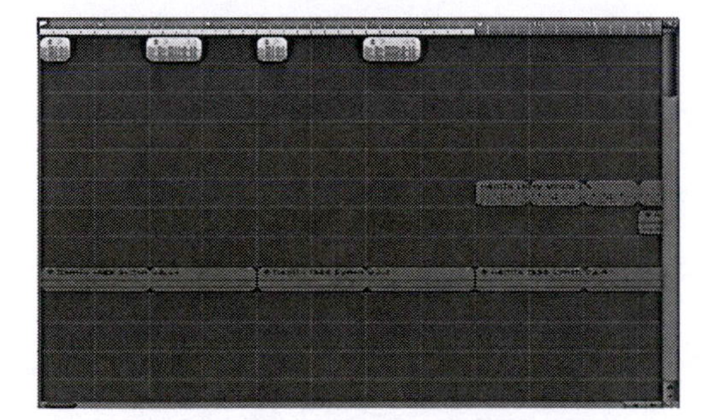

Figure 6–34. *GarageBand's Playback submenu*

Premade Content

GarageBand includes premade content in the form of loops and prerecorded audio samples that you can use and reuse in different ways with new tracks. The **Loop Sampler** and **Media Browser**

utilities make it easy to access this content (see Figures 6–35 and 6–36, respectively).

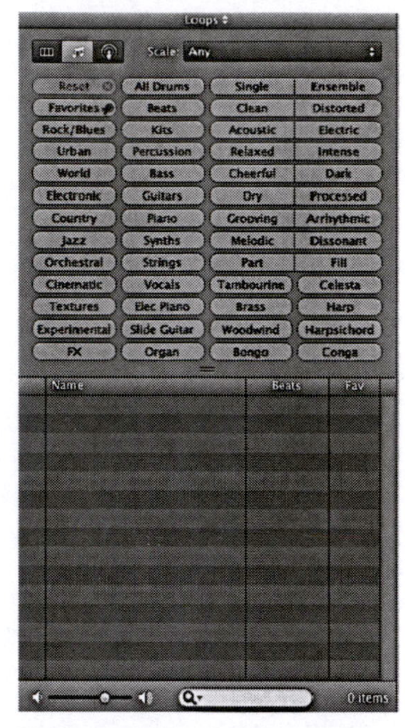

Figure 6–35. *GarageBand's Loop Sampler utility*

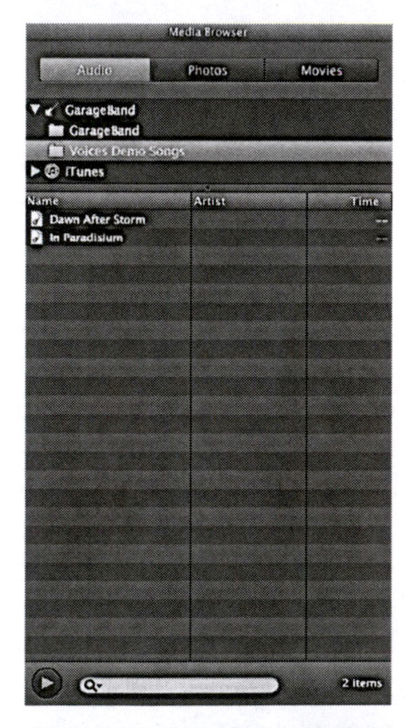

Figure 6–36. *GarageBand's Media Browser utility*

Using either of these utilities to retrieve media can dramatically decrease the time required to add content to your composition. Both utilities also let you search through either premade loops or your complete media library, including your **iPhoto** and **iMovie** libraries.

Track and Share

GarageBand also includes two very important menu items that you should you should be aware of: **Track,** which allows you to perform basic and granular track editing; and **Share**, which allows you to distribute your new composition via iTunes or a CD (see Figure 6–37).

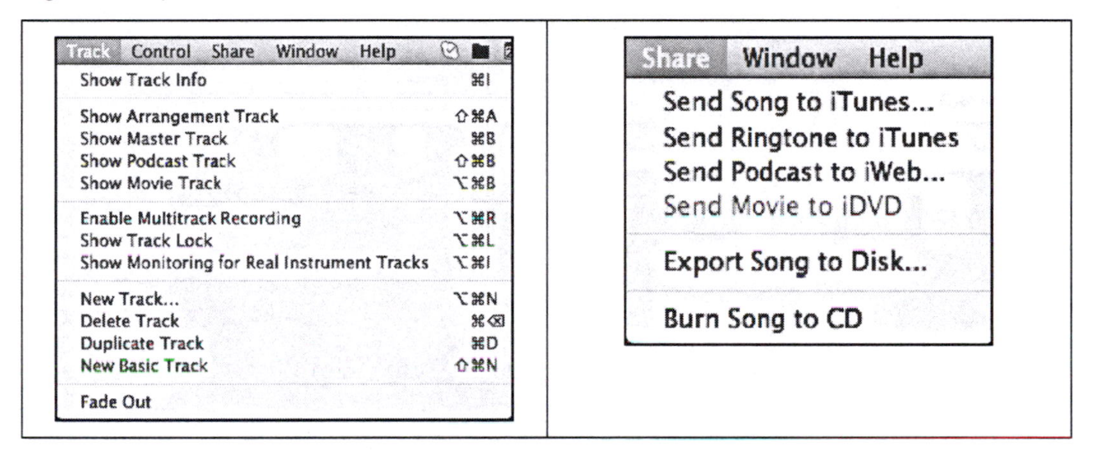

Figure 6–37. *GarageBand's Track and Share menus*

Making proficient use of **GarageBand** requires practice. But above all else, it requires a bit of talent to make music good enough for you to land a recording contract. If you have the talent and that's your goal, **GarageBand** can help you do that. However, Apple also created this app for people who do not necessarily intend to create the next number one hit. For example, **GarageBand** is also for people who simply want to create, to experiment with music and sounds, to play with instruments and loops, and/or to find their hidden musical side. **GarageBand** is the premier application in the **iLife** suite; it has taken what was once a niche only-if-you're-rich hobby and made it into a universally accessible hobby that just about anyone can afford to participate in. Now go ahead and see what *roaring* tunes your Lion is capable of creating.

Summary

Making the most out of the `iLife` suite requires that you find time to investigate your creative abilities. This suite can help you make something out of nothing or even make the something that already is into something else. Whether you want to make a movie, edit a photo to perfection, or create the next platinum album, the `iLife` suite can help create media with endless possibilities. If you've ever wanted to see what it's like to produce a movie or orchestrate a concert, then `iLife` is for you.

Chapter 7

Essential Utilities

Here's one thing that makes Lion a special operating system: it offers its users extraordinary flexibility. There are a number of ways to accomplish most tasks in Lion; and in many cases, there are small, practical apps called *utilities* that can help you make the most of Lion's innate flexibility. The real difficulty isn't so much in using these utilities, but in learning which ones might be able to address your particular issues and where you can find them. For example, you will often come across problems that require you to invest a little time learning about possible solutions. How do you find such solutions if you have no idea where to begin looking?

That is where this chapter comes in. In it, we will walk you through a handful of tools designed to help you get the most out of your Mac. Perhaps more importantly, we'll tell you where to find them. Many of these tools ship with the Lion OS; others are available from the Mac App Store; and still others are available from various web sites. This chapter will cover some of the best utilities available from all three of these sources.

You will find the Mac App Store an especially good place to turn to when you encounter problems on your Mac. This store's design makes it easy to learn about, research, and buy/download different utilities-many of which can dramatically improve the way you interact with the Lion OS. Another plus: The utilities you find at this store have been tested and approved by Apple, so they are more or less guaranteed to work with the Lion OS. At the same time, you should never, ever underestimate the power of the Internet or its ability to be a fantastic source of utilities for your Mac. Let's get started!

NOTE: Using the Mac App Store to acquire utilities gives you (a) a good receipt of purchase; (b) a way to re-download the software later; and (c) access to tested Lion–compatible applications. These are nice perks, but there are also some nice third-party apps available for your Mac that you can't get from the Mac App Store. In fact, some of the best utilities for your Mac have yet to be published to the Mac App Store. You are potentially missing out on some great applications if you limit yourself only to offerings that ship with Lion or are available from this store. If you're adventurous and willing to explore the full range of available options, you may be pleasantly surprised by what you find.

Enhancing Your Experience with Utilities

The rest of this chapter will look at a handful of both native and third-party utilities that can assist you in getting the most out of your Mac. In each application category, we'll begin by noting the native utility that ships with the Lion OS and explain what it does. Next, we'll cover one or more third-party apps in each category that build on the functionality provided by the native application that ships with Lion. As you read this chapter, you will find it helpful to keep in mind the difference between a native application and a third-party application. A *native application* is one that ships with your Lion OS. A *third-party application* is one that you must download and/or purchase, whether you do so from the Mac App Store or elsewhere over the Internet.

Third-party utilities come with a few caveats due to the fact that they are not official OS X Lion applications. Thus, they should be approached with caution because they can have unintended side effects that can affect the way Lion operates (note that all the utilities described in this chapter have been vetted and are well suited for use with the Lion OS). When evaluating third-party applications, be sure to look for reviews, which can provide strong indications of an application's quality. This is especially true when there are many reviews available for a particular app.

Monitoring Your System

The first category of utilities we'll take a look at help you to monitor your computer system's vital stats. Lion's built-in **Activity Monitor** enables you to monitor the impact various processes have on your computer system. This section will also cover a third-party utility, **iStat Menus**, which monitors a wide range of resources on your computer system.

App Name: Activity Monitor

App Type: Native Lion utility

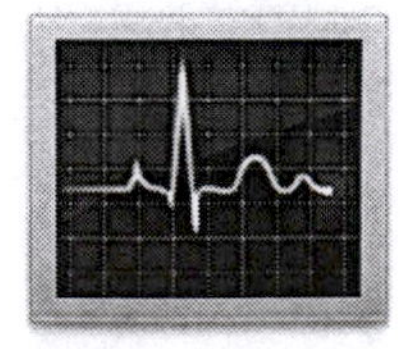

What It Does: Activity Monitor is an excellent native application that monitors the overall health of your Mac operating system. This utility allows you to view the various processes on your Mac that consume system resources. It also provides a detailed look at the kind of resources consumed. For example, this utility shows you the amount of memory, disk space, network activity, and CPU usage that each process consumes (see Figure 7-1). This information can be great for troubleshooting issues on your Mac, helping you spot those times when an application is using more than its fair share of resources. Resolving such an issue might be as simple as terminating a process or as involved as upgrading your computer system to accommodate its resource needs.

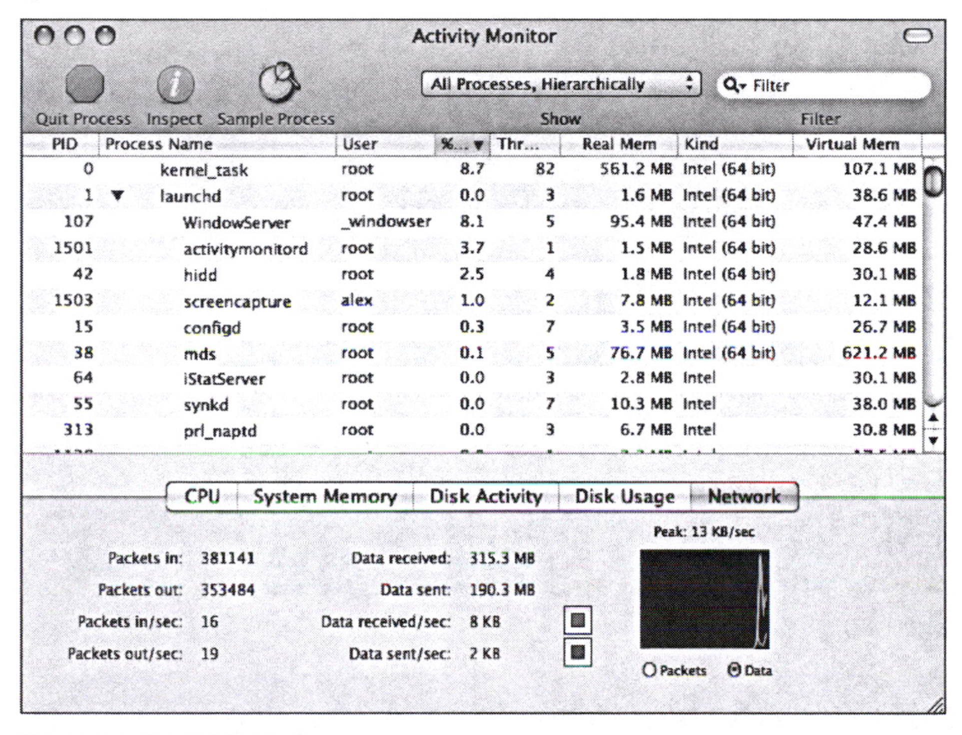

Figure 7-1. *The Activity Monitor app*

Activity Monitor also provides an effective way of measuring your computer system's ability to run certain software. You should follow these steps if you are thinking about purchasing a particular app:

1. Locate an online trial version of the app that interests you.
2. Download the app onto your system.
3. Launch the app.
4. Use **Activity Monitor** to see if your system is up to the task of running that software.

Scrutinizing System Resources

You can find many third-party utilities intended to help you monitor your system's various resources. One such utility is **iStat**, which helps you keep an eye on many aspects of your system's general performance.

App Name: iStat Menus

App Type: Third-party utility

What It Does: This system-notification utility monitors CPU, disk, battery, network, and memory activity (see Figure 7–2). You can find it at `http://bjango.com/mac/istatmenus/`.

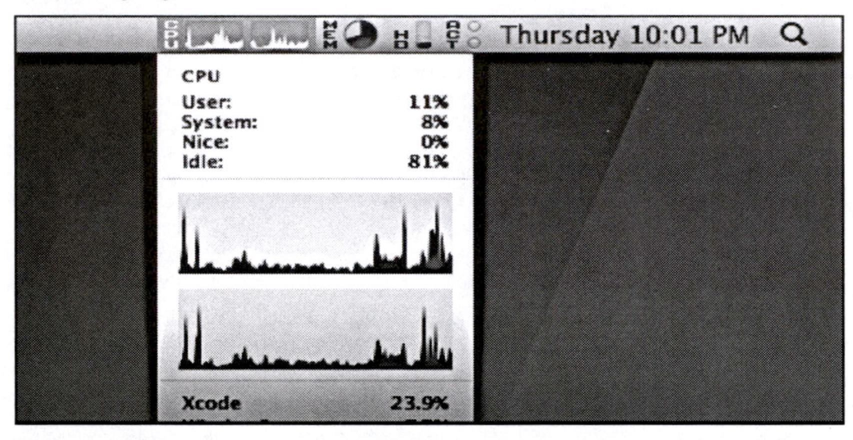

Figure 7–2. *The iStat resource-monitor utility*

Maintaining Hard Drive Health

Maintaining the integrity of your computer system's physical media (e.g., your hard drive/s) is an essential aspect of protecting your personal data. Your Lion OS ships with **Disk Utility**, a tool that simplifies the process of monitoring and maintaining your hard drives and other media; however, you can also find many third-party utilities that build on the capabilities of **Disk Utility** in significant ways.

App Name: Disk Utility

App Type: Native Lion utility

What It Does: Disk Utility can be considered the most important utility on your Mac because it is what you will use to take care of your hard drive/s, which is where all of your precious information is stored. This app lets you format new disks, repair your current disks, create new partitions, and restore data from hard drive crashes (see Figure 7–3). It also lets you create disk images, which are compressed singular disk objects that hold data.

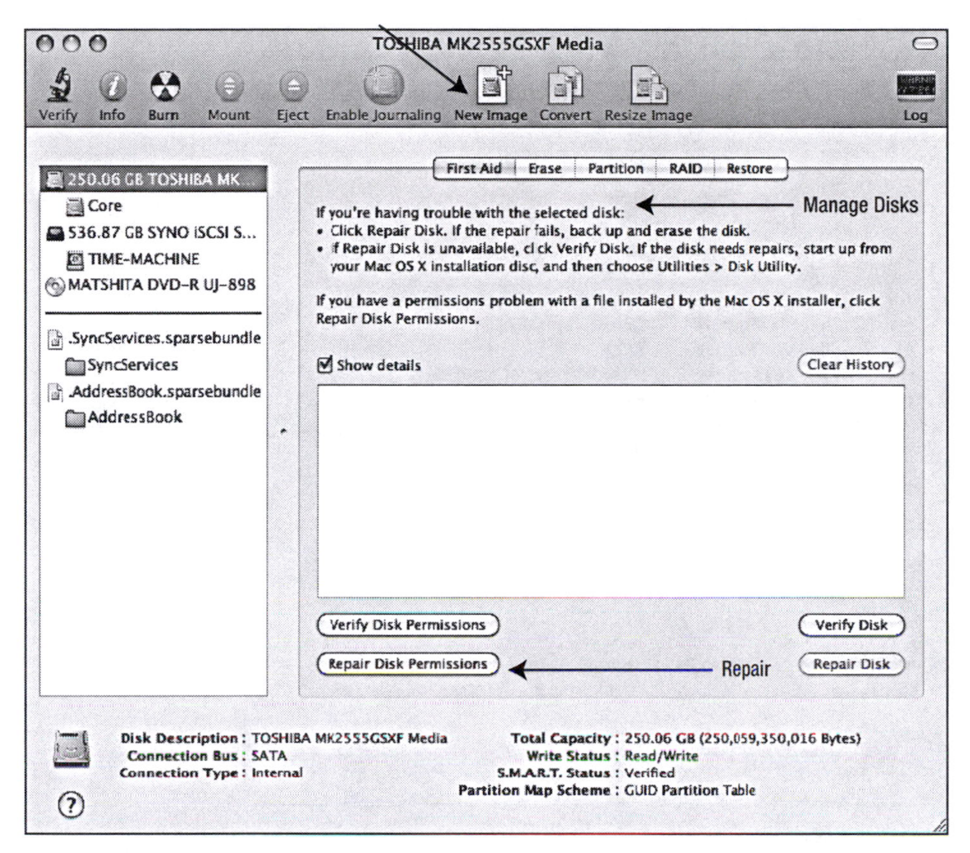

Figure 7-3. *The Disk Utility app*

Disk Utility also lets you gather information about your hard disk/s. Clicking the **Info** icon (see Figure 7-4) pulls up pertinent information about your hard drive/s (see Figure 7-5). If you have multiple drives, you can even select these drives one at a time by clicking the **Info** icon to see the details of each. This utility can help you evaluate whether it's time to upgrade a given hard drive because it tells you exactly how much storage capacity that hard drive has remaining.

Figure 7-4. *The Information button on Disk Utility's Menu bar*

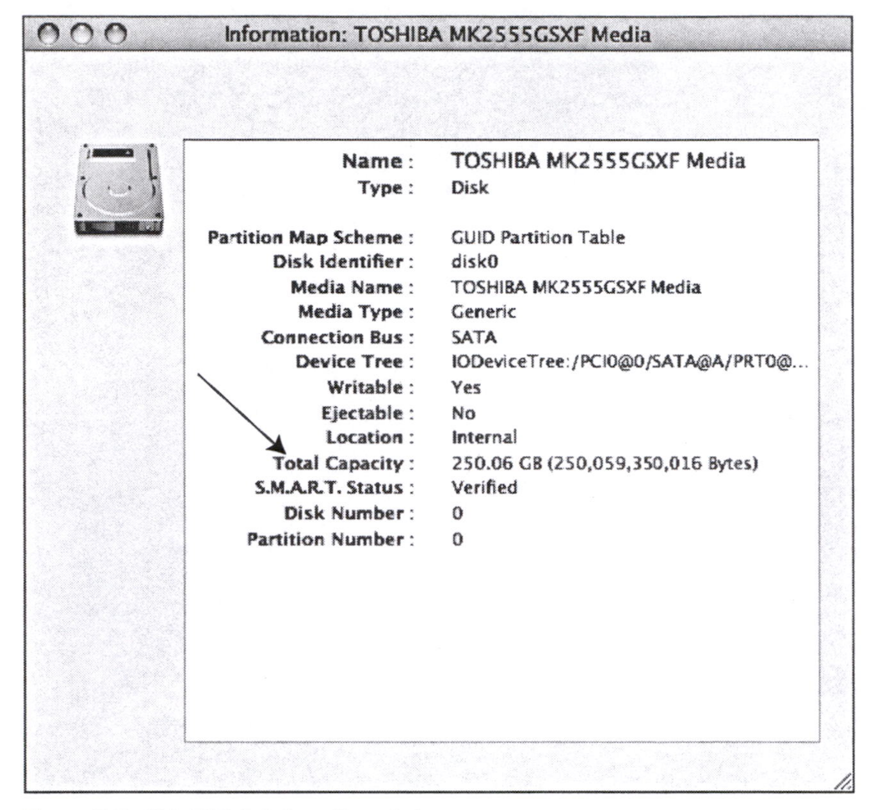

Figure 7–5. *Disk Utility's Information window*

Even if you're not interested in replacing a given hard drive, tracking how much free storage remains on that drive is important because you want to be certain that you have enough space to accommodate any applications or files you may want to install or store on it.

Beyond Disk Utility

You can find many third-party utilities that help you maintain the health of your physical media. These range from applications that simplify the process of deleting data that is no longer needed, to tools that can tap directly into the built-in diagnostics of your hard disks to warn you about an imminent drive failure.

App Name: Clean My Mac

App Type: Third-party utility

What It Does: This utility includes everything you need to keep your Mac clean and healthy. This is my favorite utility for keeping my Mac hard drives in tip-top shape. Features include the ability to delete outdated cache, log, and other files. This utility also lets you monitor your **Trash Bin** app, manage extensions, and customize your user interface. You can find it at http://macpaw.com/cleanmymac/features.

App Name: Cocktail

App Type: Third-party utility

What It Does: This is an extremely good file and cache maintenance tool for your Mac. You can find it at www.maintain.se/cocktail/.

App Name: DaisyDisk

App Type: Third-party utility

What It Does: This utility analyzes disk usage and helps you free up disk space on your Mac—effectively enabling you to store more information on your hard drives. You can find it at www.daisydiskapp.com/.

App Name: IceClean

App Type: Third-party utility

What It Does: This is a very good tool for optimizing your hard drive's speed. You can find it at www.macdentro.com/MacDentro/Home.html.

App Name: Smart Utility

App Type: Third-party utility

What It Does: SMART (Self-Monitoring, Analysis, and Reporting Technology) is a system built into hard drives by their manufacturers to report on various measurements (called *attributes*) of a hard drive's operation. These attributes can be used to detect when a hard drive is having mechanical or electrical problems; they can also indicate when the hard drive is failing. This app scans the SMART system of your hard drive/s, alerting you if it finds any issues. You can find this utility *at* www.volitans-software.com/smart_utility.php.

App Name: Drive Genius

App Type: Third-party utility

What It Does: This utility adds enhanced partitioning capabilities to the already powerful **Disk Utility** app. You can find it at www.prosofteng.com/products/drive_genius.php.

Data Security

Protecting the all-important data on your computer is essential, so much so that we will return to this topic many times in upcoming chapters. In this section, we'll explore some of the utilities that can help you simplify the process of protecting the information on your computer. Backing up your data is an important aspect of protecting your data, but that is only the start. In today's computing world, you must also consider taking steps to ensure your data remains secure, even if your computing device fall into someone else's hands. The utilities described in this section will help you do that and much, much more.

App Name: File Vault

App Type: Native Lion utility

What It Does: File Vault provides Lion users with the ability to encrypt their **Home** folder using 128-bit AES encryption. This utility uses government-approved encryption algorithms to protect your data should you lose your Mac due to theft or some other disaster whereby another party winds up with physical possession of your Mac. **File Vault** is an excellent—and easy—way to secure your files and prevent your data from leaking out.

Most Mac owners are unaware that all OSX operating systems (including Lion) come with the ability to locally encrypt files. Encryption can dramatically lessen the probability of your data being compromised should your physical computer get stolen. It also adds an extremely effective layer of security on top of an already very secure operating system.

Enabling local encryption is easy. Simply open up your System Preferences and select the **Security** icon (see Figure 7–6).

Figure 7–6. *The Security icon in the Preferences panel*

Next, choose the **FileVault** tab, set your master password (be sure you do not forget this!), and click the **Turn on FileVault** button (see Figure 7–7). That's it!

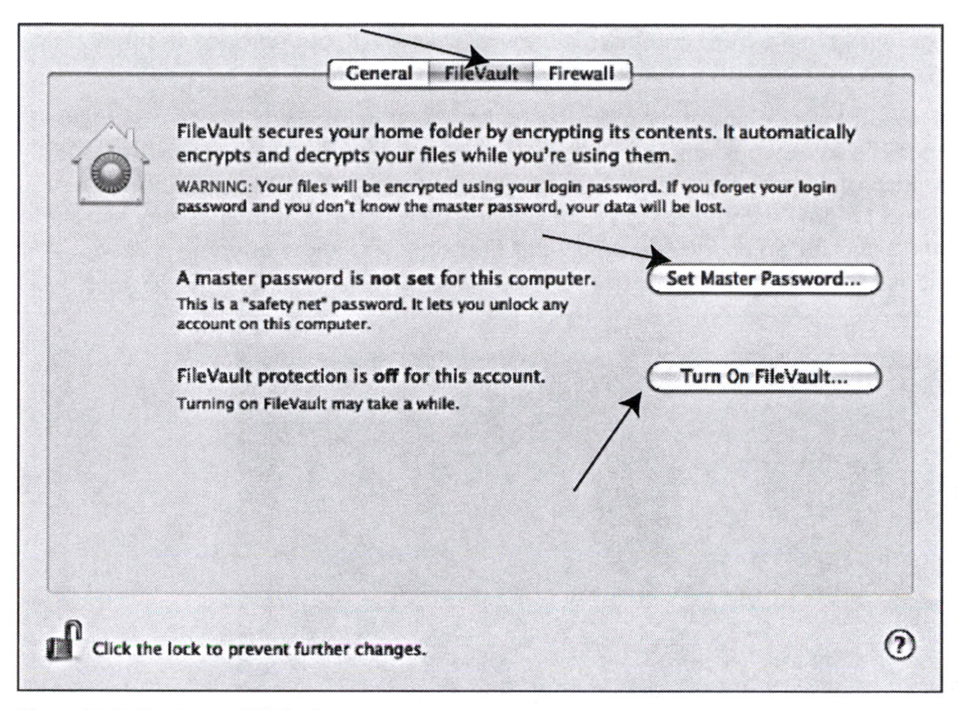

Figure 7–7. *Turning on FileVault*

Once you have enabled **FileVault**, Lion will begin to encrypt your **Home** folder and all of its contents. Moreover, all future content will be encrypted upon creation. This encryption secures all of your personal files, ensuring that no one without the master password is able to compromise your system.

Augmenting Lion's Built-in Data Security

Lion delivers a lot of useful functionality out-of-the-box with its **FileVault** utility. But as is often the case, you can also find several third-party utilities that build on the functionality provided by Lion in significant ways. This section will take a quick look at several utilities that build on the features provided by **FileVault**.

App Name: Espionage

App Type: Third-party utility

What It Does: Espionage is a file-security program from a third-party publisher that allows you to secure the information on your computer with encryption. You might wonder why you would want such a feature. Well, think about this: if someone steals your computer, she has all of your information readily available to her. This information can be used in a number of ways: to blackmail you; to expose things like company trade secrets; or to steal your grandmother's top secret recipe for her one-of-a-kind apple pie. In any case, backing up data does not preclude it from being misused. If you rely solely on backups to protect your information, you should be aware that your data is still at risk if your computer is stolen. Yes, you have a copy of your data, but so does the thief. File encryption is how you prevent a thief from accessing your data.

Espionage encrypts your information on-the-fly (i.e., as it is created), which can make it almost impossible for a would-be thief to break into your Mac and steal your precious information. **Espionage** protects both files and applications with 128- and 256-bit encryption, and I highly recommended it for anyone using a Mac. It is also very simple to use, prompting you for an encrypted password that only you know anytime a user requests access to an encrypted file or application (see Figure 7–8).

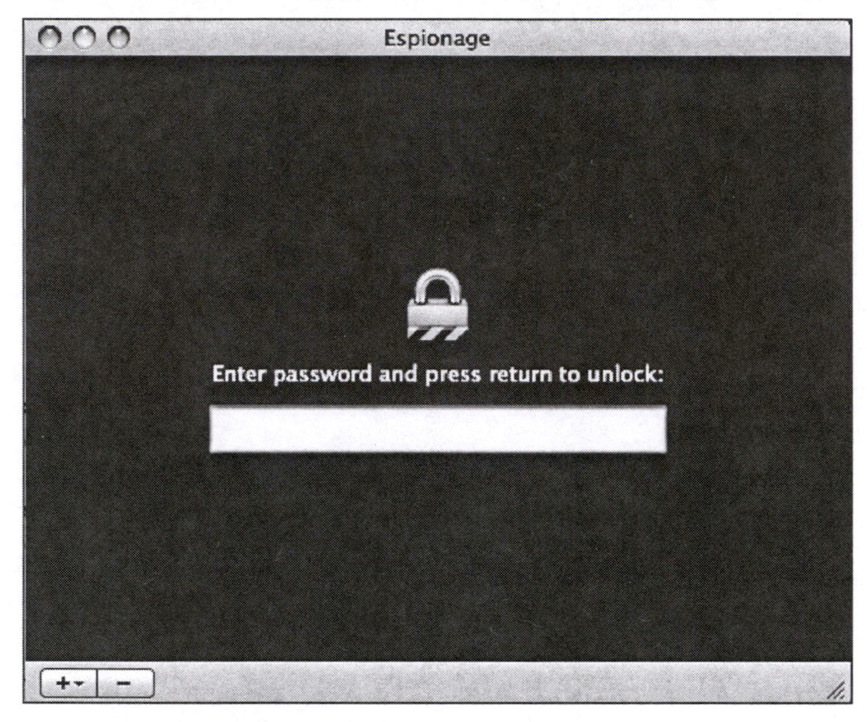

Figure 7–8. *The Espionage app's Password screen*

Espionage uses *application templates* to guide you in selecting the apps that most likely need to be secured (see Figure 7–9).

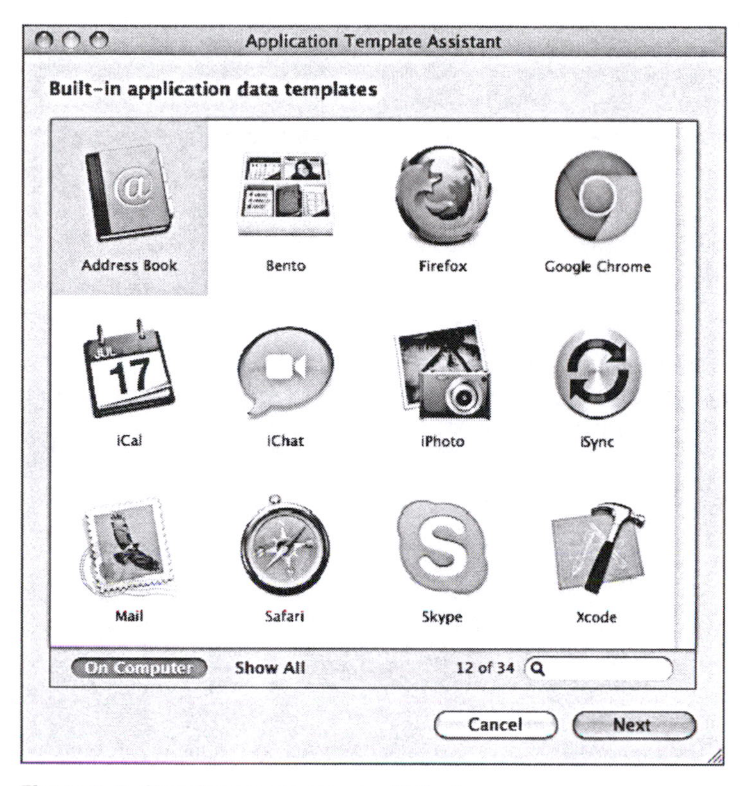

Figure 7–9. *Choosing apps to secure with Espionage*

After you select an app you would like to secure, you are prompted to select other options, including the encryption level you would like to use to secure the application (see Figure 7–10).

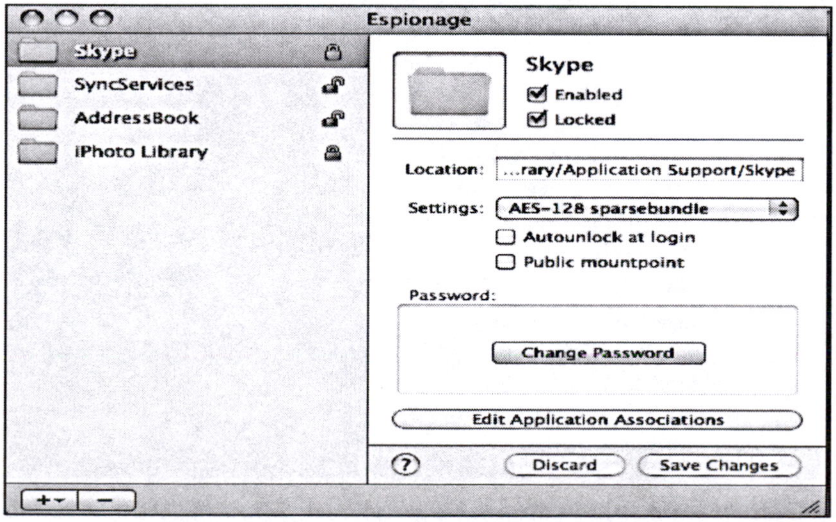

Figure 7–10. *Setting your encryption options with Espionage*

App Name: Prey

App Type: Third-party utility

What It Does: This application creates an identity trail for your Mac, which can be used to track it down if it's lost or stolen. You can find this app at `http://preyproject.com/`.

App Name: Tiptoe

App Type: Third-party utility

What It Does: TipToe is a private browser security application that can make sure your web browsing habits remain private and irretrievable by anyone else but you. You can find it at `www.zenopolis.com/software/tiptoe/`.

App Name: VigiMac

App Type: Third-party utility

What It Does: This utility is used to track your Mac in case of physical theft, and it can make it really hard for would-be thieves to take your Mac and sell it to others. It uses unique GPS tracking software to keep track of your Mac at all times. You can find it at `www.vigimac.com/`.

App Name: Watchmac

App Type: Third-party utility

What It Does: This unique program literally watches for break-ins by monitoring failed access to things like your screensaver and other password protected items on your Mac. You can find it at `http://bloo7.com/watchmac/`.

Making Input Adjustments

The utilities described in this section let you make adjustments to your mouse and trackpad settings. Making these adjustments can increase the ergonomic control you have over your Mac's input devices, enabling you to enhance the speed, proficiency, and level of interaction you have with your Mac. The end result: Such utilities can help you increase the overall usability of the Lion operating system considerably.

App Names: Mouse and **Trackpad** (in the Preferences folder)

App Types: Native Lion utilities

What They Do: Your mouse or trackpad device provides one of the primary ways of interacting with your Mac. Configuring your trackpad or mouse properly can help you be more productive. The Lion OS includes several options for altering the speed and sensitivity settings of your mouse or trackpad (see Figure 7–11).

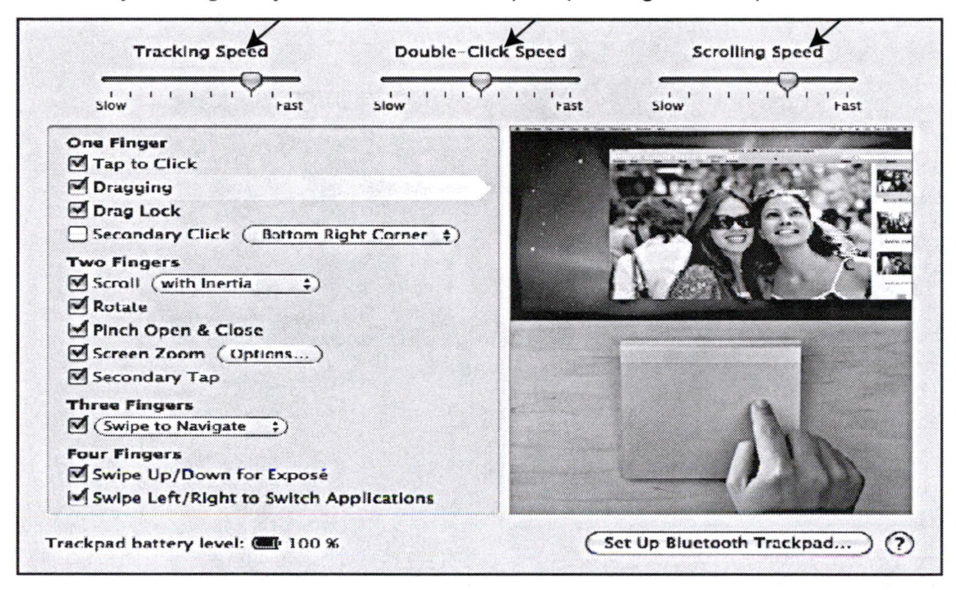

Figure 7–11. *Lion's Trackpad utility*

The **Mouse** and **Trackpad** utilities also let you make other fine adjustments, such as fine-tuning the finger motions associated with your trackpad or track-motion capable mouse (see Figure 7–12).

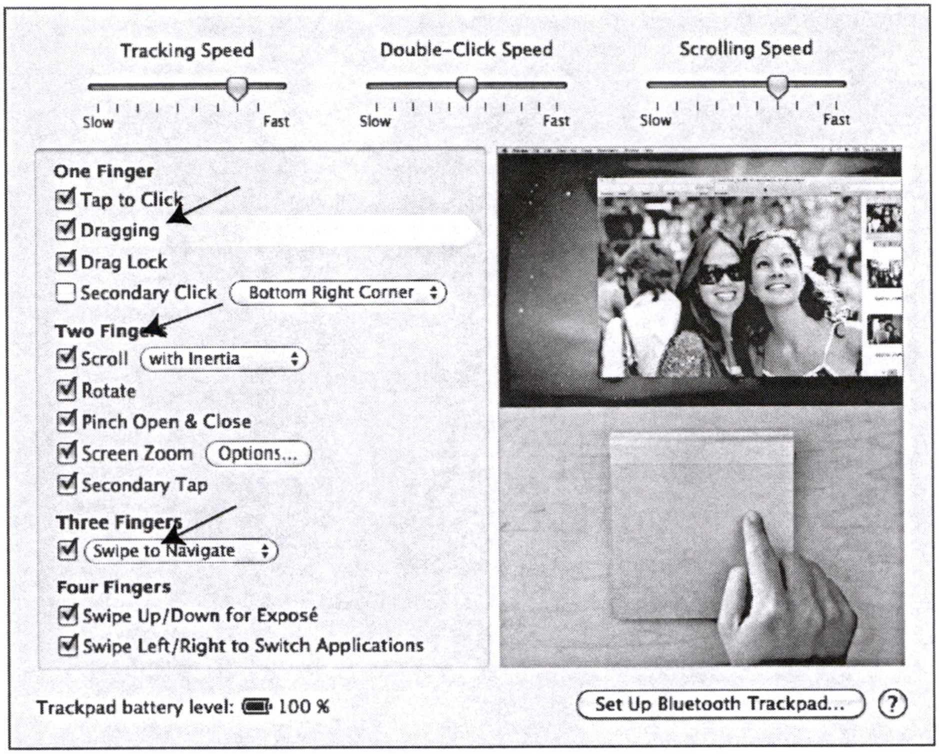

Figure 7–12. Your ***trackpad swipe options***

Customizing Your Input Devices Further

You can find several third-party utilities that enable you to augment or otherwise replace the input capabilities provided by Lion by default.

App Name: MagicPrefs

App Type: Third-party utility

What It Does: This app gives you very granular control of your Mac's preferences, such as your mouse and trackpad options (see Figure 7–13). This utility gives you significantly more flexibility in making your Mac work the way you want it to. You can see the enhanced preferences **MagicPrefs** enables for the trackpad by comparing the images shown in Figure 7–12 and 7–13. You can find this utility at `http://magicprefs.com/`.

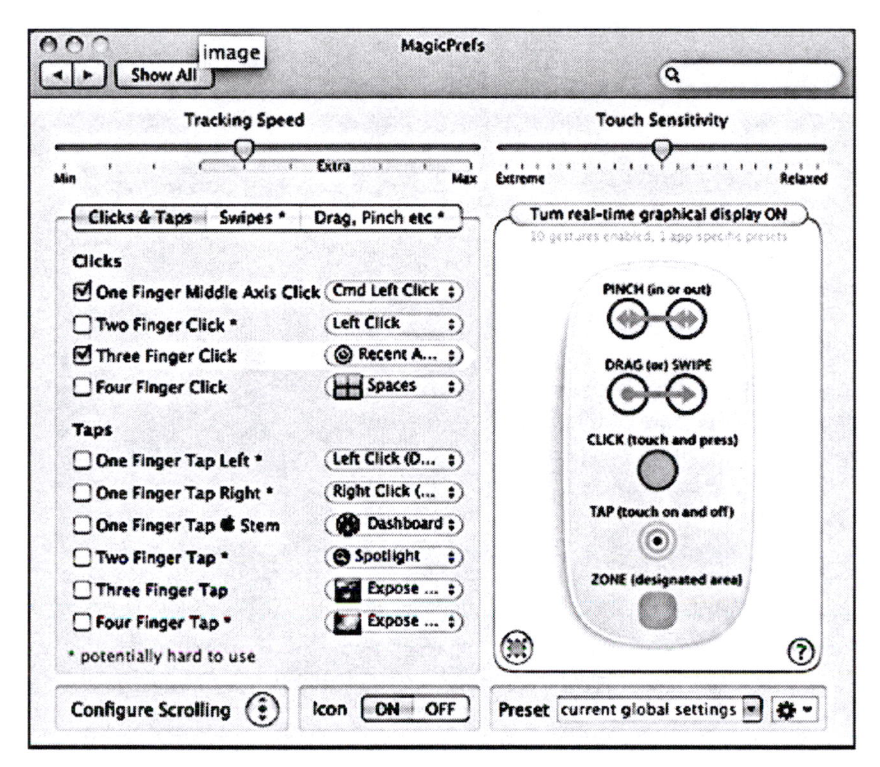

Figure 7–13. *The swipe options for MagicPrefs*

App Name: Mouseposé

App Type: Third-party utility

What It Does: This utility gives your mouse extra functionality during **PowerPoint** presentations. You can find it at `www.boinx.com/mousepose/overview/`.

App Name: MouseWizard

App Type: Third-party utility

What It Does: This utility enhances the functionality of Apple's Magic Mouse, which supports swiping gestures similar to the ones used on the trackpads on Macbooks. You can find it at `www.samuco.net/web/node/23`.

App Name: Sesamouse

App Type: Third-party utility

What It Does: This utility lets you program additional motions for your Magic Mouse that augment those provided by default. You can find this utility at `http://calftrail.com/sesamouse/`.

Staying Organized

One of the most important things your computer can do is help you create and manage your schedule. To this end, the Lion OS ships with **iCal**, a robust calendaring app. But you can also find many third-party utilities that augment the Mac's built-in schedule-management capabilities, including one called **Bento** that every Mac user should have.

App Name: iCal

App Type: Native Lion utility

What It Does: Keeping track of time, organizing events, and being on time for meetings is a normal part of everyday life for your average working adult; unfortunately, the process of managing your time can itself become a very time-consuming process. **iCal** was built from the ground up to help you manage your time better. As such, it is a great utility for managing the mundane aspects of your daily schedule, as well for tracking more irregular but significant events such as birthdays, holidays, and so on. Like most Mac apps, **iCal**'s interface is clean and very easy to use (see Figure 7–14).

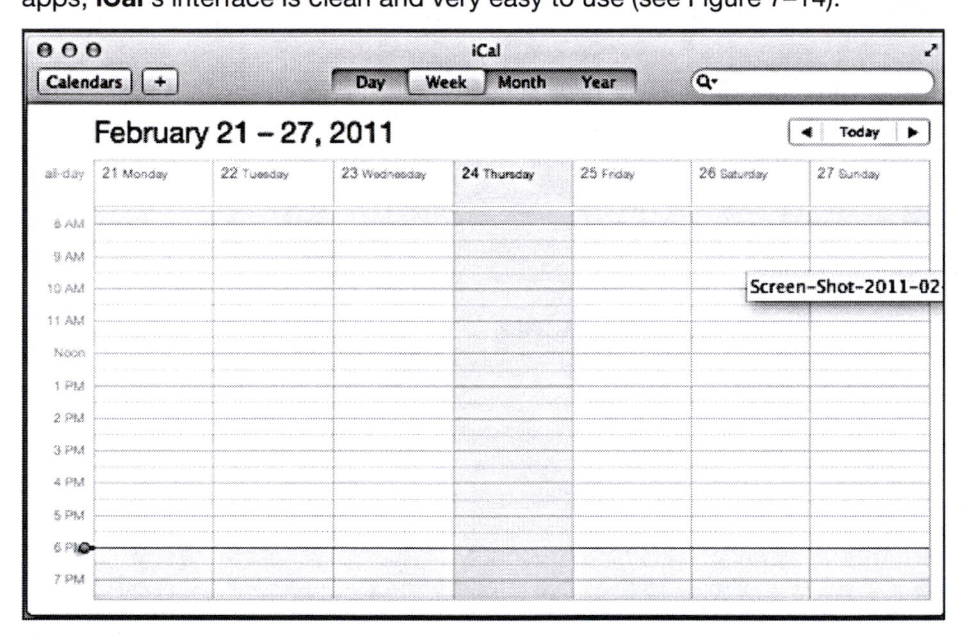

Figure 7–14. *iCal, Lion's built-in calendar app*

iCal also integrates seamlessly with your Lion **Address Book** application, enabling you to create and accept appointments from people that you already have in your contact list without firing up your email client. Furthermore, **iCal** allows you to send meeting invitations directly, without firing up another application. This speeds up the process of making calendar events. Finally, **iCal** is part of the new **iCal Server 3**, which allows groups and organizations to share and use the same calendar database for organizing meetings and other events based on the free time open to each participating member (see Figure 7–15).

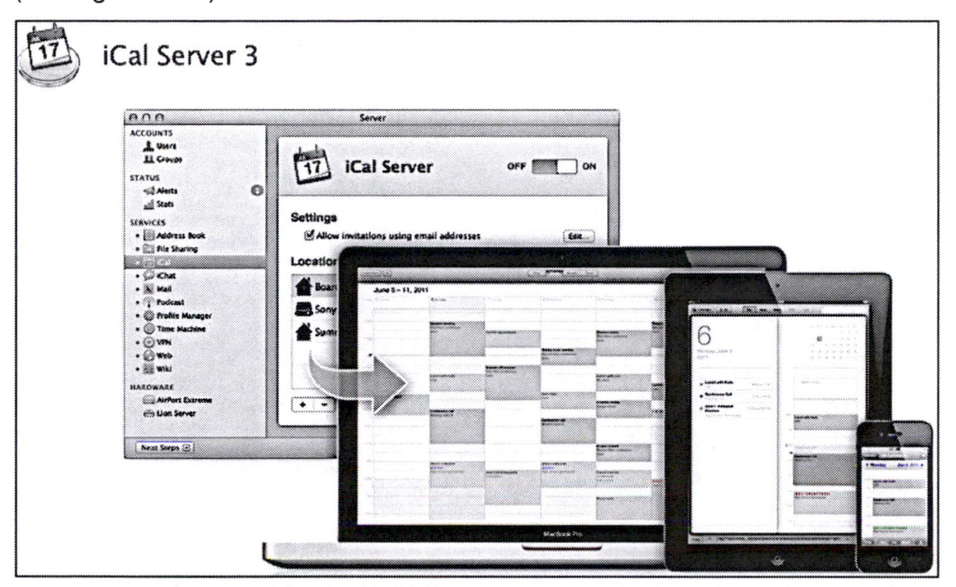

Figure 7–15. *iCal Server 3, which includes iCal integration*

Leveraging iCal's Features with Other Utilities

You can find a handful of interesting utilities that augment the functionality provided by **iCal**. We'll cover the first of these, **Bento**, in some depth. An absolute must-have utility for any Lion user, **Bento** complements **iCal**, **Address Book**, **Numbers**, and **iPhoto** by integrating all of them into one easy-to-use application.

This section will also cover a couple smaller scale (but still very useful) utilities that augment **iCal**'s functionality: **iCalViewer** and **iDeskCal**.

App Name: Bento

App Type: Third-party utility

What It Does: This database utility is one of the most well-rounded productivity applications made for the Mac. It can be used on mobile devices such as iPhones and iPads, and it can also share data between users on the same network. **Bento**'s myriad features include (but aren't limited to) project management, label printing, form creation, and a built-in customer management system (CMS) for managing your customers and clients. As mentioned previously, it also integrates seamlessly with several built-in Lion apps, including **iCal**, **Address Book**, **Mail**, and **iPhoto**. **Bento** comes with 35 pre-built templates to help you get started, as well as built-in scripting functionality. Together, the templates and scripting features enable you to embed spreadsheet-like formulas into the forms you create.

These features help you manage your projects and track the progress of your team, helping all of you to reach your goals (see Figure 7–16).

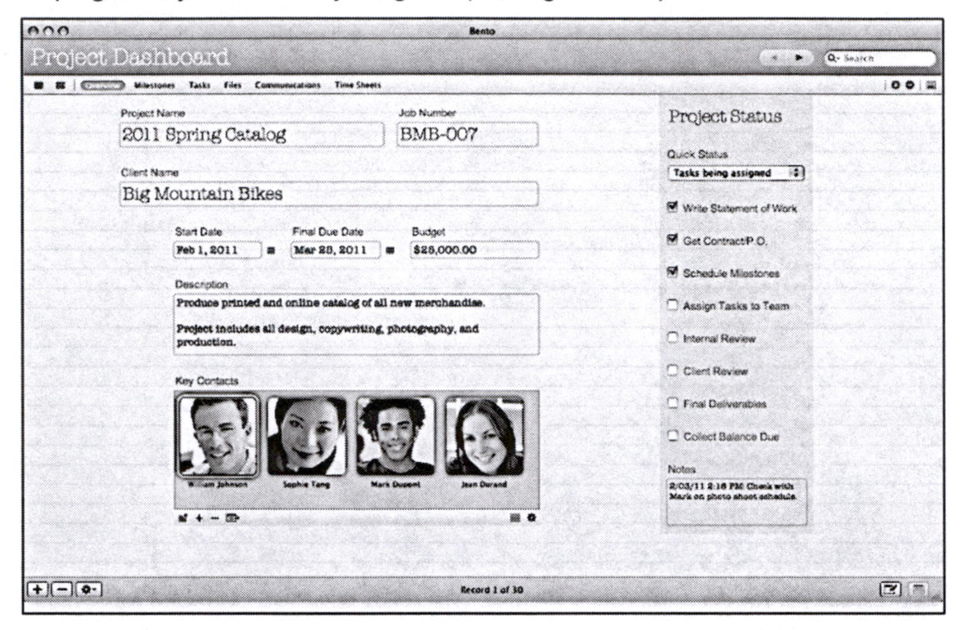

Figure 7–16. *A project management example in Bento*

Bento also lets you manage the contacts in your Mac's **Address Book** app directly, without requiring that you open up another application (see Figure 7–17).

Figure 7–17. *A contact management example in Bento*

Similarly, you can manage events in your **iCal** app without ever leaving the **Bento** application. This type of integration can significantly reduce the amount of time that it takes to look for a contact or to schedule a contact for an event or meeting (see Figure 7–18).

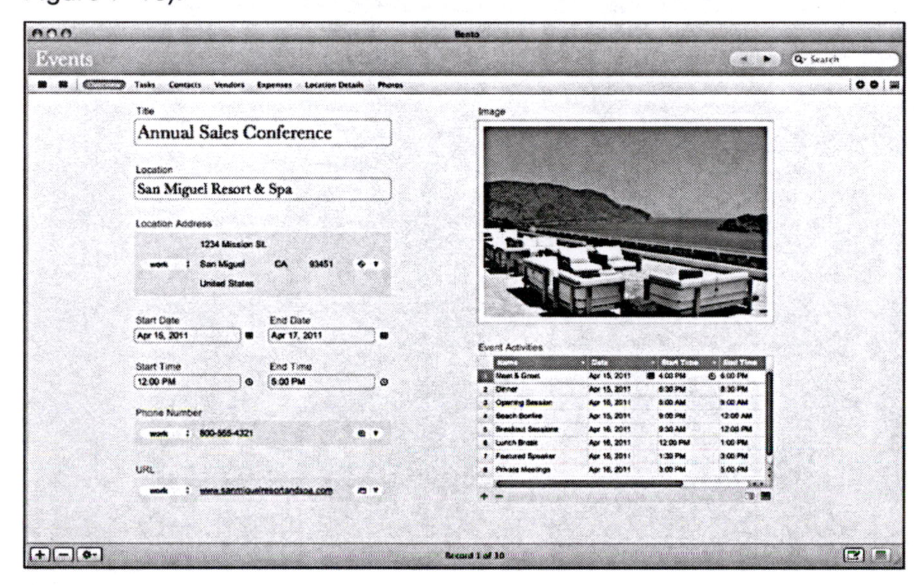

Figure 7–18. *Integration with iCal in Bento*

Another interesting feature: **Bento** enables you to build your own database applications that incorporate spreadsheet functionality such as inventory processing and record keeping (see Figure 7–19).

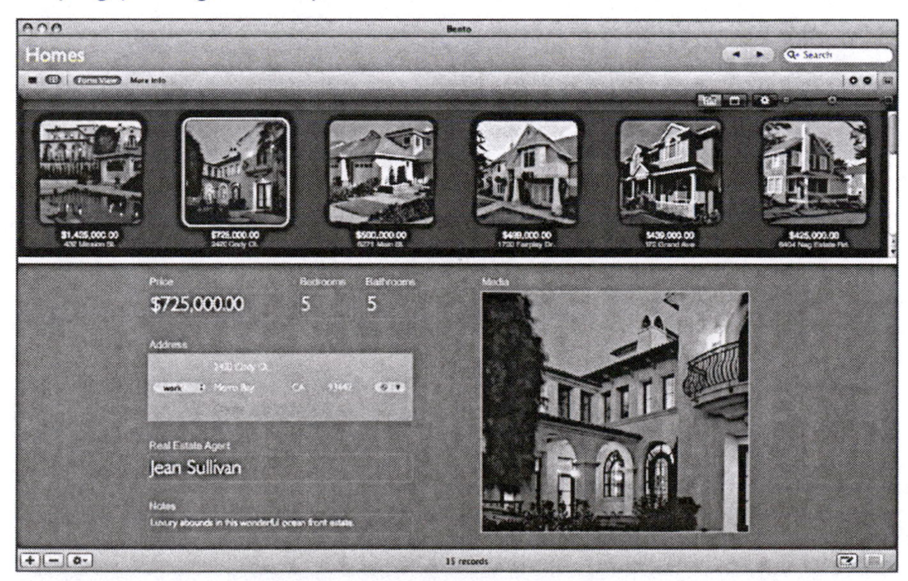

Figure 7–19. *Bento's integration of spreadsheet–like functionality*

Bento's database functionality even lets you track your products using images, so that you can get a visual view of what is going on with your merchandise (see Figure 7–20).

Figure 7–20. *An inventory example in Bento*

On the security front, **Bento** includes password protection that you can enable to control access to databases you create with it. **Bento** also allows you to export the information you store in it to a number of commonly used and widely supported formats (see Figure 7–21)

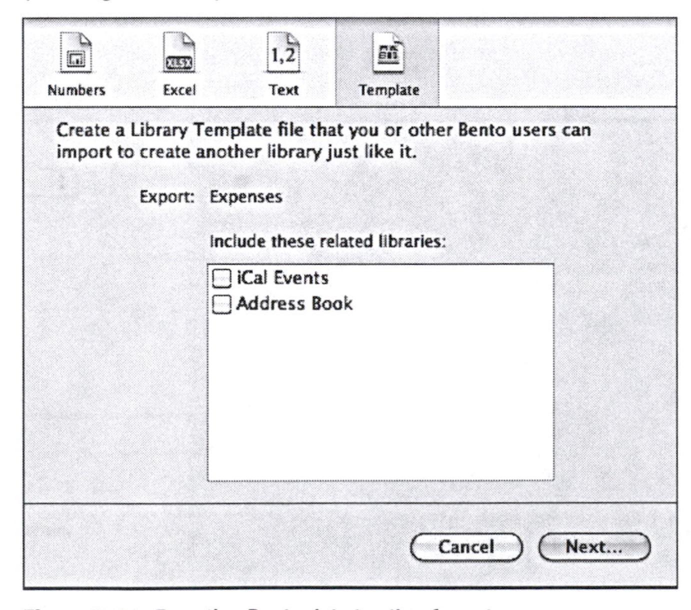

Figure 7–21. *Exporting Bento data to other formats*

Bento is the rare utility that incorporates a book's worth of functionality. You would be wise to make this one of the very first applications that you purchase from the Mac App Store. To find **Bento** on the Mac App Store, simply type "Bento" in the store's **Search** box (see Figure 7–22).

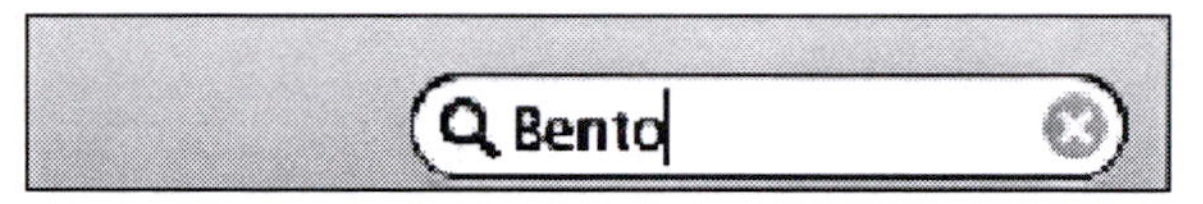

Figure 7–22. *Finding Bento with the Mac App Store's Search box*

App Name: iCalViewer

App Type: Third-party utility

What It Does: iCalViewer shows **iCal** events in a project-like view. This can help you see more clearly how soon an event will occur. You can find this utility at `www.icalviewer.com/`.

App Name: iDeskCal

App Type: Third-party utility

What It Does: iDeskCal embeds the **iCal** application directly into your desktop, so that you always have a clear view of the events in both your personal and shared calendars. You can find this utility at `www.hashbangind.com/ideskcal.php`.

Summary

Utilities help you solve many of the problems associated with computing. For example, they can help you organize information; secure your computer from would-be criminals; and ensure that the hardware your system relies on remains healthy and stable, so that you do not lose your valuable information. Thousands of utilities exist for Lion, and this chapter touched on some of the more popular ones used by Mac users today.

Of course, many more utilities are being created every day—and all of these have the potential to make your computing life easier. I highly recommend that you take the time to determine what could make your day-to-day computing experience more satisfying. When you find holes in that experience, try conducting a little research to determine whether a utility already exists that can help you fill it. Doing so is sure to make your life easier and keep your Lion OS purring.

Chapter 8

It's a Jungle Out There: Safari and the Internet

Lion, like most modern day operating systems, comes equipped with software that enables users to get online and surf the Web. There are many different web browsers available, and most behave in a very similar manner. What typically separates them is performance and usability, which can usually be reduced to two things: the speed at which a browser can render web content and the ease with which you can leverage the browser's functionality. You might think that every modern browser could accomplish these things well; however, that is definitely not the case. Fortunately, Lion ships with a web browser that is unmatched in both performance and usability.

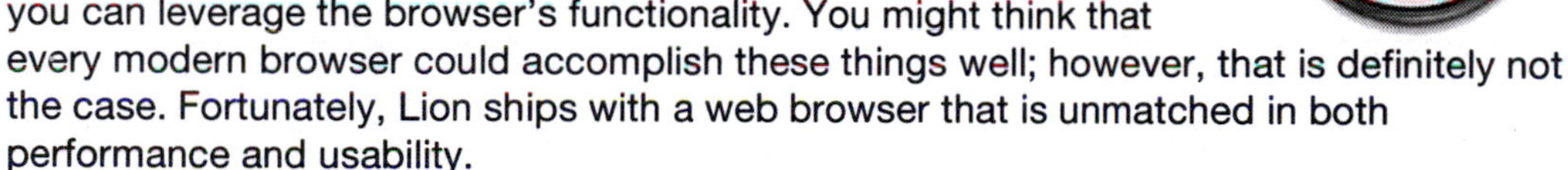

Safari is a modern day web browser built from the ground up for Mac users. It incorporates all of the functionality you would expect from a high quality Mac application—and it does so while rendering web pages extremely quickly.

Of course, there is one more feature that you cannot overlook in a web browser: security. Fortunately, Safari is all about keeping your personal information... personal. This chapter will touch on the features, benefits, and security characteristics of **Safari**. Along the way, it will explore the interface, menu system, and some of the utilities that you can use with this browser to enhance your overall Web experience.

> **NOTE:** There exist other web browsers that you can use on the Lion operating system. However, **Safari** cannot be outdone when it comes to privacy. This web browser takes strong steps to protect your personal privacy; it does not send any end-user information back to Apple; and it is also free of any malware or spyware. In contrast to **Safari**'s approach, some competing web browsers track user habits and send reports back to the parent company for statistical purposes.

The Safari Interface

Apple created Safari's user interface with the goal of making it easy to use. It achieves this goal in two ways: by stripping away unnecessary fluff that most web browsers have and by streamlining the process of information search and discovery. The Web is all about information, and web browsers are all about information retrieval. **Safari** reduces the inherent complexity of navigating the Web by keeping the user focused on browsing, gathering, and saving the information he wants. It accomplishes this primarily by discarding interruptive objects like unwanted advertisements and unnecessary buttons, so that the user has a clean, unobtrusive interface to work with. Let's look closer at how this works.

Understanding the Address Entry Bar

Safari's **Address** bar is located at the very top of its interface. It is here that you enter web site addresses that you know the correct spelling for. In Figure 8–1, you can see that I entered "http://www.msn.com" into the **Address** bar to get to the MSN web site.

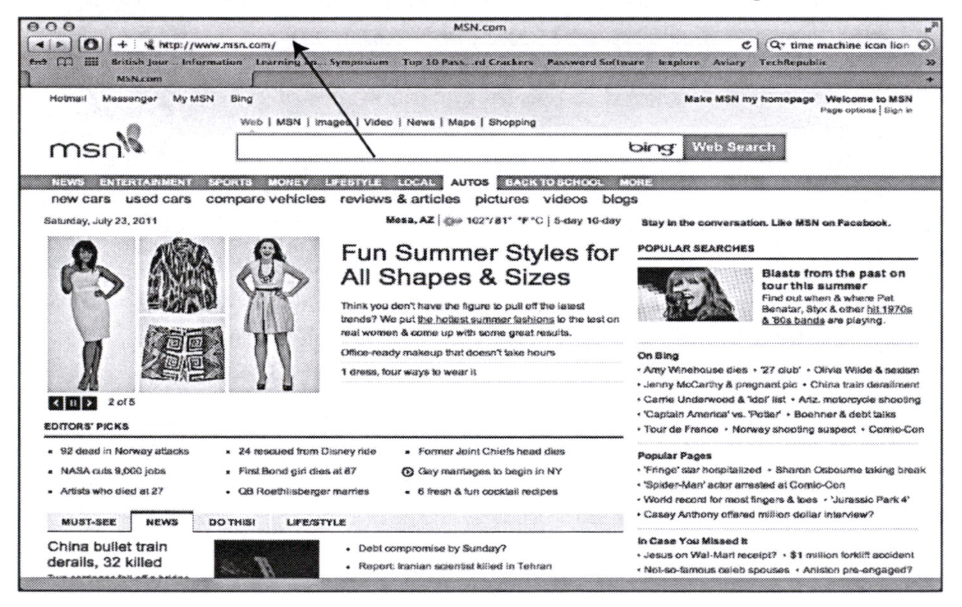

Figure 8–1. *Safari's Address bar*

Now let's suppose I did not know the exact web address for MSN. In that case, I could have easily moved to the **Search** bar, which is directly to the right of the **Address** bar, and just typed in what I was looking for (see Figure 8–2).

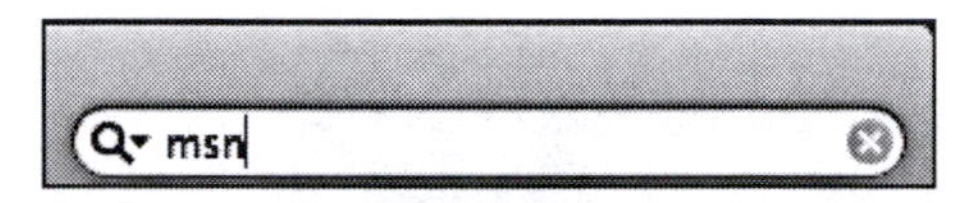

Figure 8–2. *Safari's Search bar*

The arrow in Figure 8–3 shows you exactly where you can find the **Search** bar in the **Safari** browser's main menu.

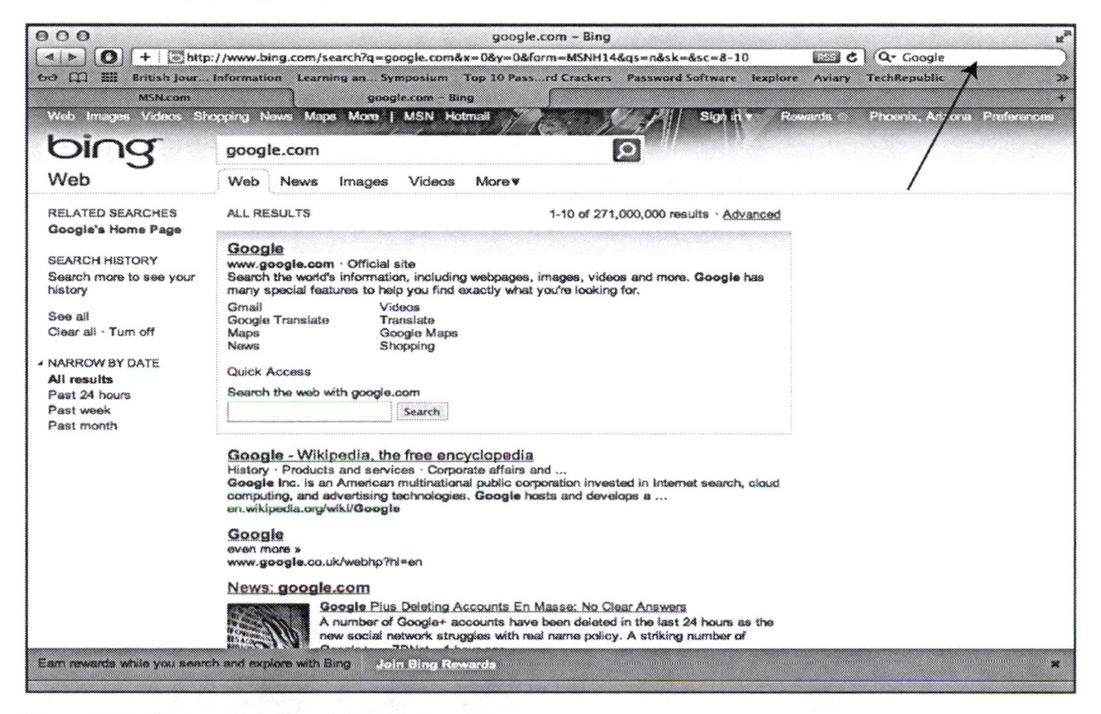

Figure 8–3. *The exact location of Safari's Search bar*

Searching with Google

As the time of writing, the default search engine for **Safari** is Google. Google's search engine basically allows users to type in whatever they are looking for and get extremely accurate results related to that search. Figure 8–4 shows the results returned by searching for the word, "MSN."

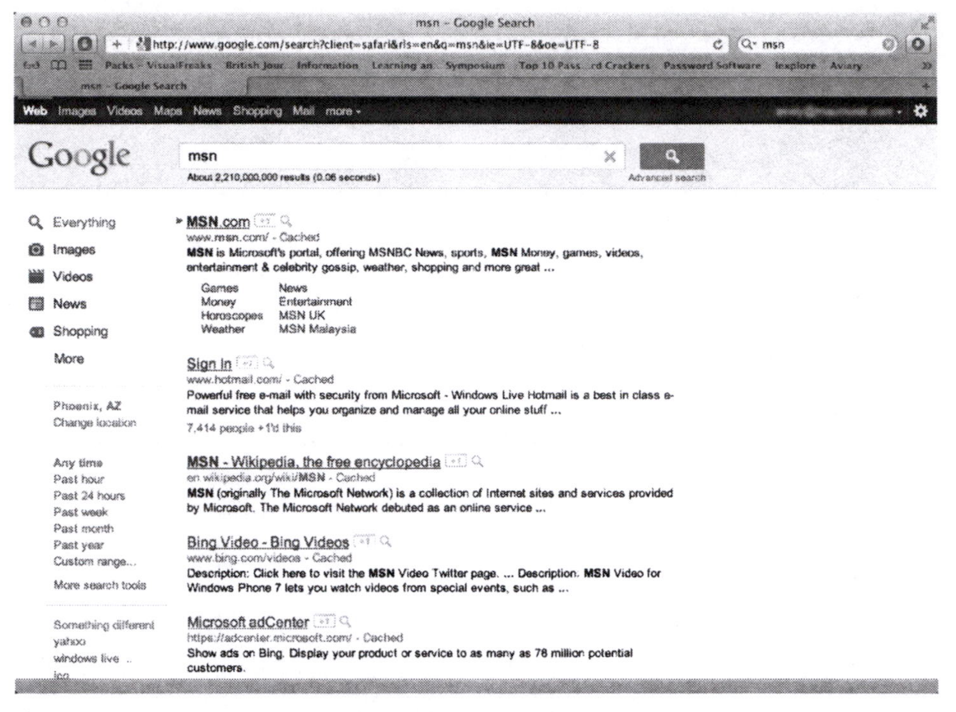

Figure 8–4. *The results of Safari's Google search for "MSN"*

As you can see, the results returned include a number of MSN–related web sites, including its gaming, entertainment, and e-mail sites. This chapter is not about Google; however, it is important to understand how Google and **Safari** work together to create a single, powerful tool for retrieving information over the Web.

When you enter information into **Safari**'s **Search** bar, it uses Google to initiate an indexed search on the information you have entered. Simply put, Google compares your search expression against its database of web sites using its special search algorithms. It then retrieves the most computationally relevant information it can find and displays it for you in your browser. Google will display the sites it finds in order of decreasing relevance (as determined by Google's search algorithms), from most relevant to least relevant. If a search does not yield the results you want, try a different combination of words and phrases that are related to the content you are looking for. Google accepts quotes for phrases such as "man in a wheel chair." Entering the preceding phrase in quotes will return much different results than searching for *man in a wheel chair* without quotes. The latter search is comprised of five separate words, rather than one complete sentence. The golden rule behind searching the Web is to experiment with different combinations of words, phrases, and numbers until you find what you are looking for.

Search Alternatives and Bookmarking

Safari ships with other search engines besides Google. The two most popular alternative search engines are Yahoo! and Bing; you can access either of these in **Safari** by clicking the **Search** box's dropdown menu selector (see Figure 8–5).

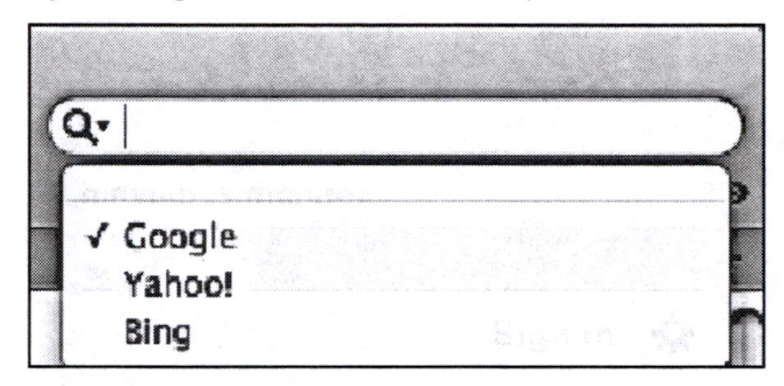

Figure 8–5. *Bringing up Safari's built-in search options*

Once you perform your search and find the web site you want, you may want to add that site to your bookmarks. Follow these simple steps to do so:

1. Click the + (**Plus**) button located directly to the left of the **Address** bar's input field to add a web site as a bookmark (see Figure 8-6).

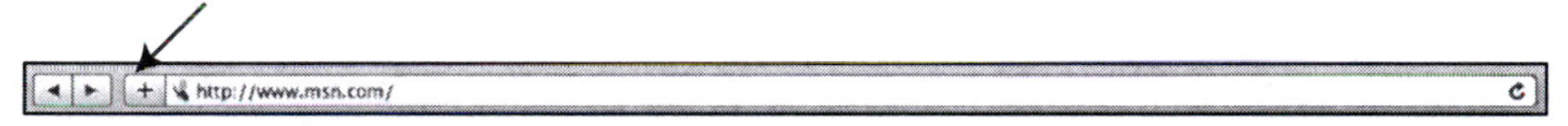

Figure 8–6. *Safari Add Bookmark*

2. This will allow you to save your site for later retrieval, adding it to your list of favorites in **Safari**'s **Bookmarks** section. To access your stored bookmarks, simply press the **Bookmarks** button on the **Safari** menu bar (see Figure 8-7).

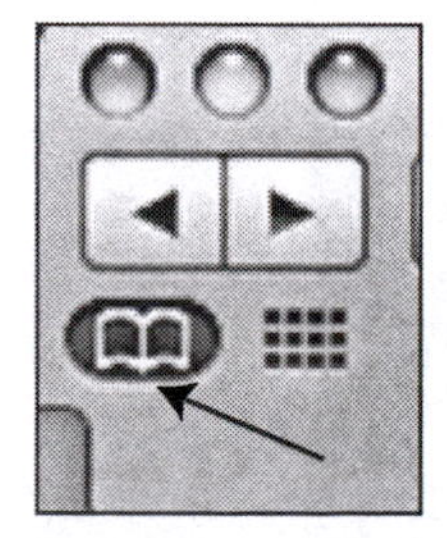

Figure 8–7. *Safari's Bookmarks button*

3. This will take you to the **Collections** section, which will automatically push you to the **Bookmarks** bar section (see Figure 8-8).

Figure 8–8. *Safari's **Bookmark** section bar*

4. If you look to the right of your screen upon entry, you will see a list of your bookmarks (see Figure 8–9).

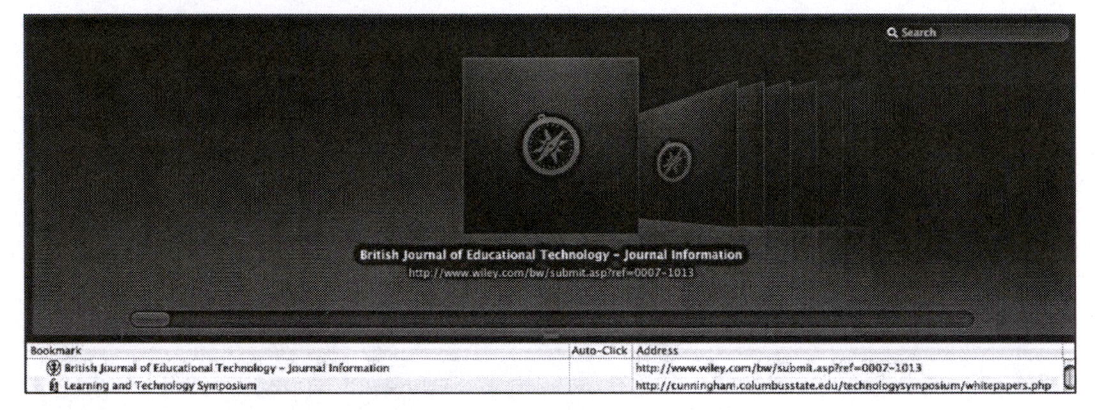

Figure 8–9. *The main windows for Safari's Bookmarks section*

5. This section lets you navigate your bookmarks, enabling you to find your favorite sites quickly and easily.

Using Top Sites

Another way to find your favorite and most visited sites is to visit **Safari**'s **Top Sites** section. This section displays the sites that you visit most often in a panel format (see Figure 8–10).

Figure 8–10. *Safari's Top Sites section*

To access the **Top Sites** section, simply click the **Top Sites** menu option on **Safari**'s main menu bar (see Figure 8–11).

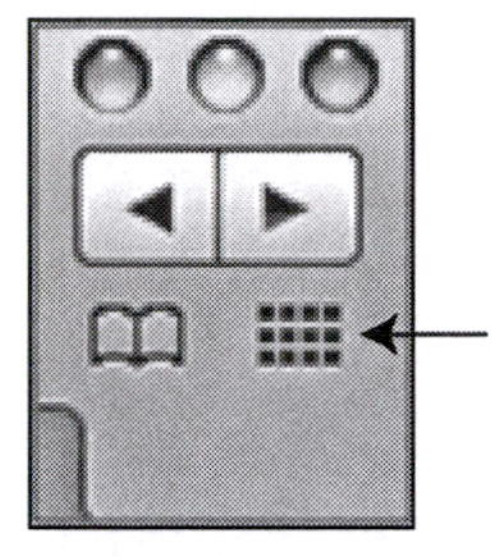

Figure 8–11. *Safari's Top Sites button*

Using a combination of top sites and bookmarks will let you find your favorite sites much more quickly than searching the Web each time you would like to visit them. If you do find yourself in the predicament where you need to look back on things you have done previously, it may be necessary to access your browsing history. You can do this simply by accessing the **Top Sites** menu option and clicking the **History** button. This option enables you to both browse and search web sites you have already visited (see Figure 8–12).

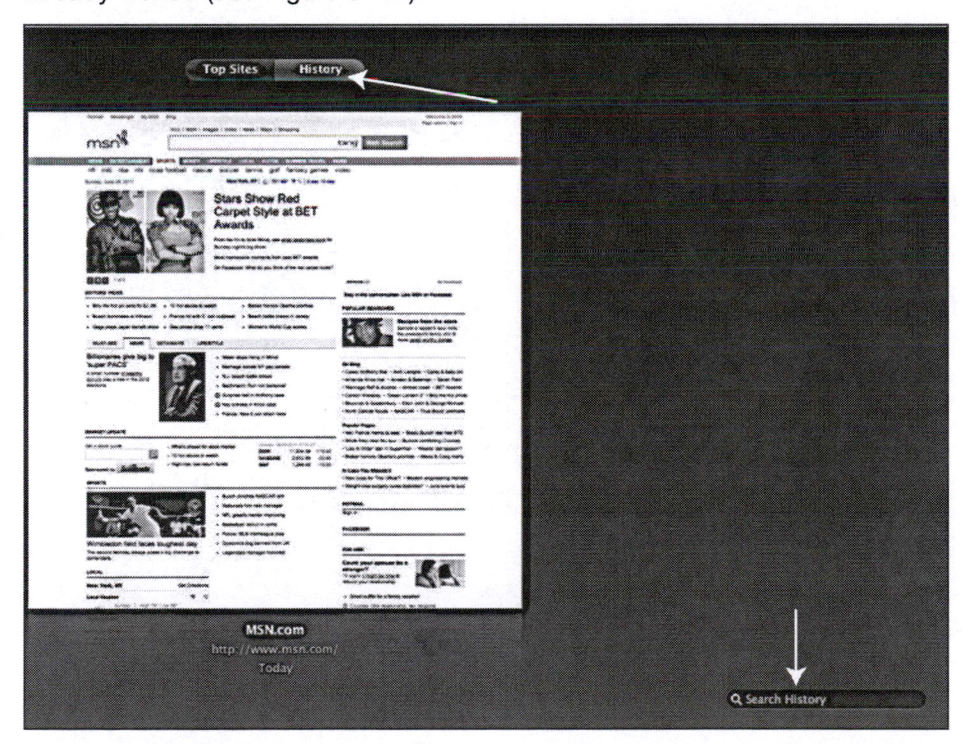

Figure 8–12. *Safari's History window*

Tabbed Browsing

Safari also supports what is referred to as *tabbed browsing*. This feature lets you use many tabs within the same window. To open a new tab, simply right-click the tab you are on, and then select the **Open New Tab** option (see Figure 8–13).

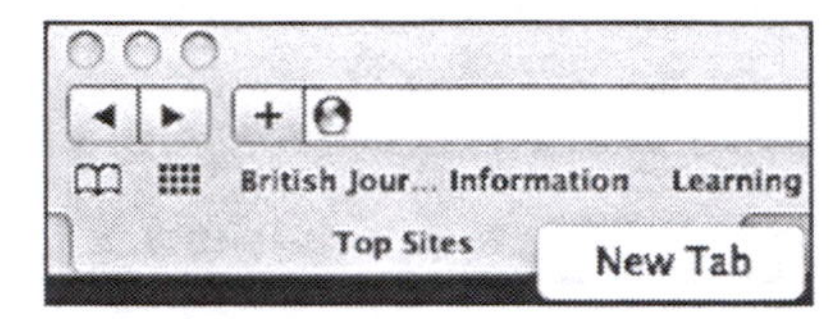

Figure 8–13. *Safari's New Tab option*

Opening many web sites in one window makes it much easier to manage your open applications because you no longer need to have one window open per web site. In Figure 8–13, I have decided to open several sites in one window. This spares me the headache of having to move between windows; instead, I simply switch between tabs to view different web sites (see Figure 8–14).

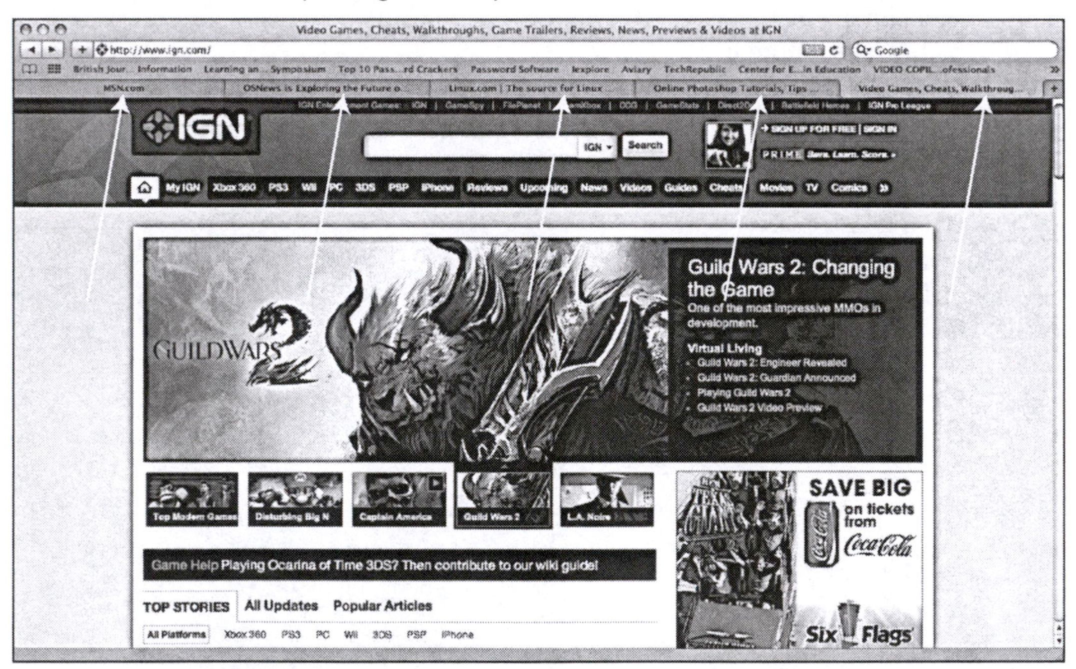

Figure 8–14. *Safari's tabbed browsing feature*

Safari is almost guaranteed to be the most-used application on your Mac, especially given the current trend to deliver an increasing number of computing services over the Web. Fortunately, **Safari**'s easy-to-use interface has a welcoming simplicity that invites you to explore its functionality. As with anything, the more you use it, the more comfortable you will become with how it works.

Safari Preferences

Safari includes a lot of preferences that let you tailor the way the web browser works. Everyone browses the Web a little differently because everyone has a different reason for using the Web. In this section, we will look at how you can adjust these preferences to make your web surfing more pleasurable.

To access **Safari**'s various options, open your **Safari** browser and then select **Preferences...** from the **Safari** menu (see Figure 8–15).

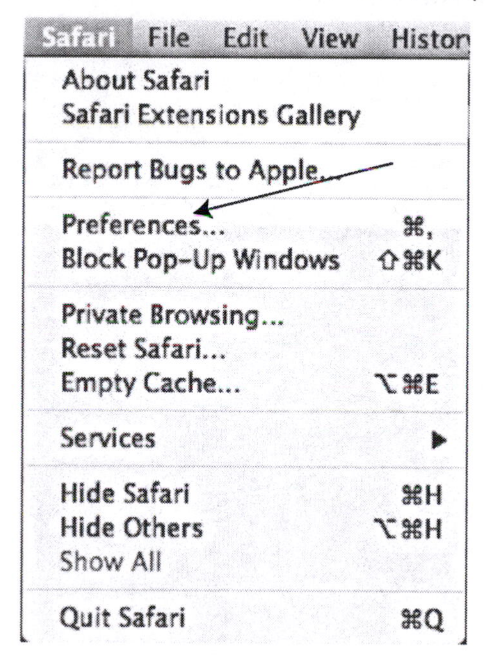

Figure 8–15. *Safari's Preferences... menu option*

Selecting this option will bring up **Safari**'s **General** options section (see Figure 8–16). You can also access a series of other tabs along the top of this window's toolbar. Let's review these options now, beginning with the **General** preferences tab.

General

The **General** preferences tab allows you to do the following:

- Change your default web browser (if you have more than one installed).
- Change your default search engine (in case you want to use Bing or Yahoo! by default).
- Set your **Home** page.
- Change your **Remove history items** settings (i.e., set how far back you would like retain a history of your web browsing).
- Set the **Open "safe" files after downloading** option. Clicking the checkbox for this option indicates that you want to open the files you download in their associated application immediately after they download. It is recommended that you keep this option turned off.

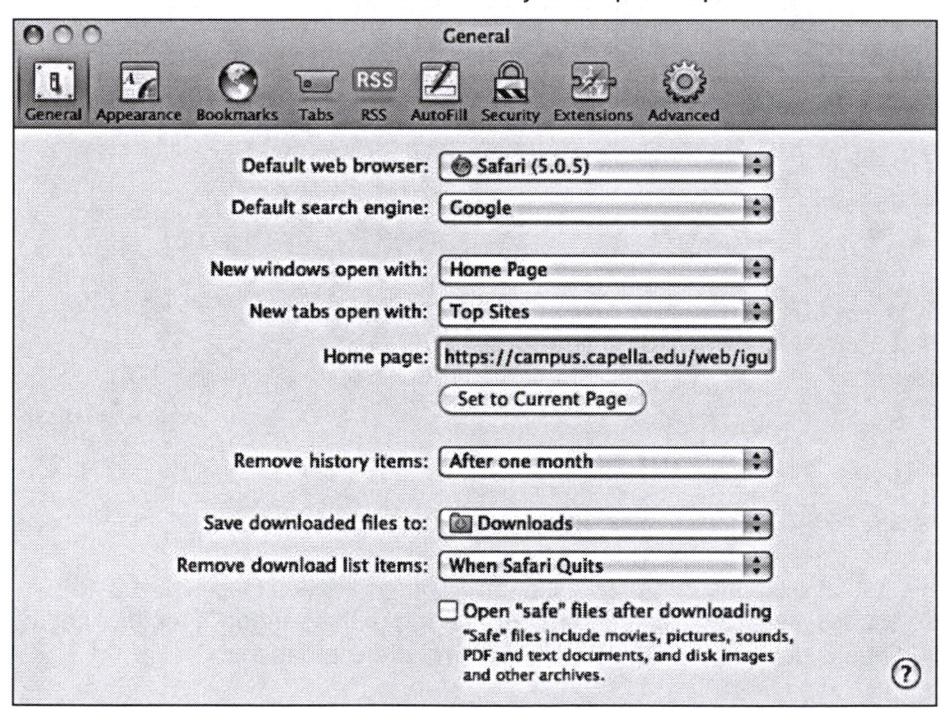

Figure 8–16. *Safari's General preferences tab*

Appearance

The **Appearance** preferences tab allows you to set the specific font sizes and types you would like to use (see Figure 8–17). This option is especially useful if you have issues with your vision that are not accommodated by the default installation of **Safari**.

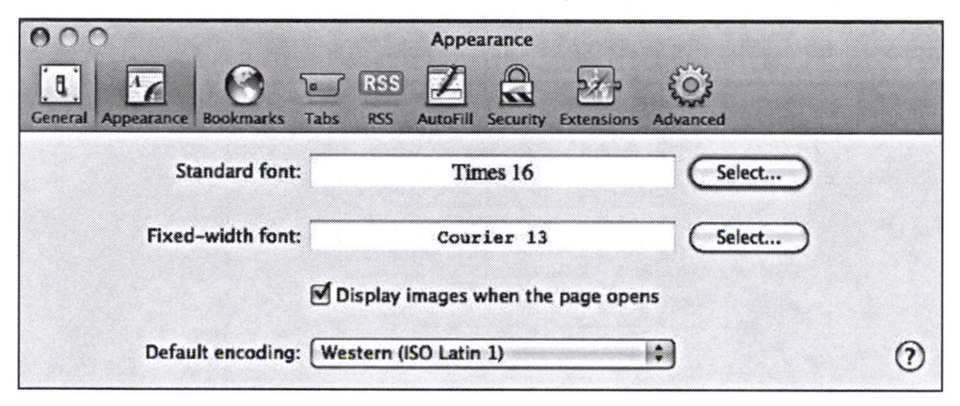

Figure 8–17. *Safari's Appearance preferences tab*

Bookmarks

The **Bookmarks** preferences tab allows you to select what you want your **Bookmarks** window to display. It also lets you dictate whether you would like your bookmarks synced with your MobileMe account (if you have one). This tab provides a great way to limit what you see when browsing your bookmarks, which in turn can help you keep clutter to a minimum (see Figure 8–18).

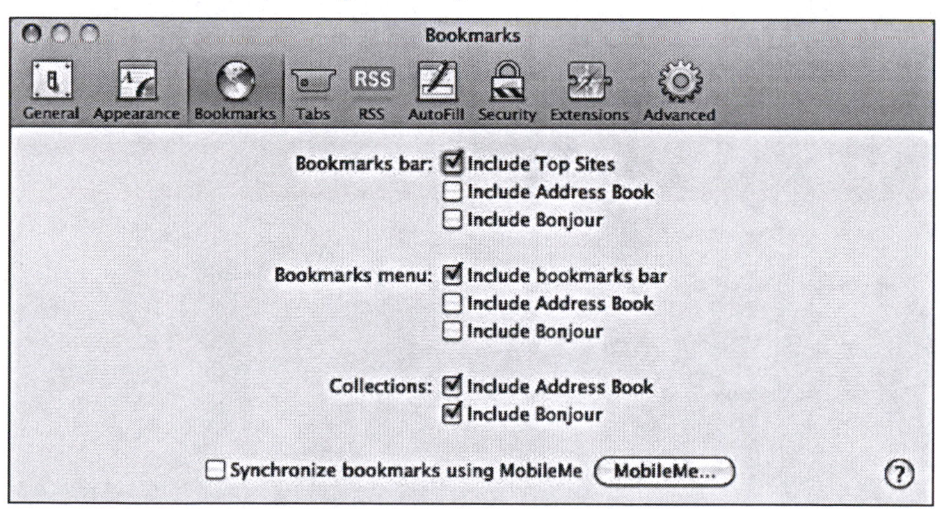

Figure 8–18. *Safari's Bookmarks preferences tab*

Tabs

The **Tabs** preferences tab allows you to determine how your tabs are integrated into your web browsing experience. For example, it allows you to choose how new windows and web sites will display when you first visit them. This is a great way to make your tabs support your browsing habits if you surf multiple web sites at once—a quite common approach for surfing the Web (see Figure 8–19).

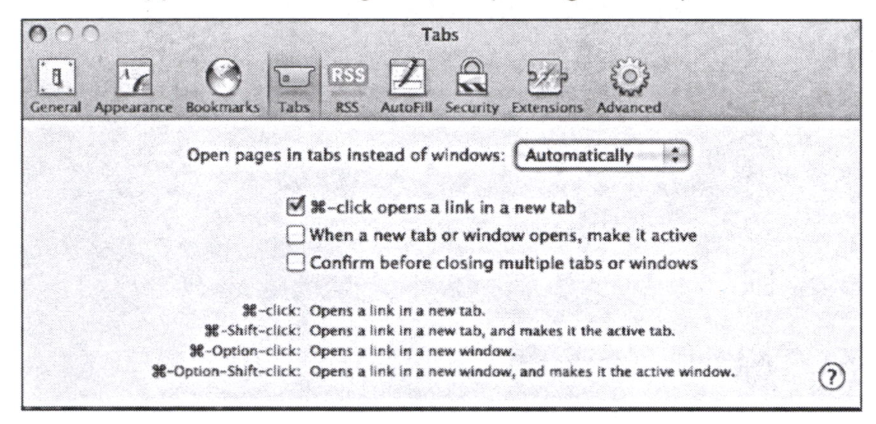

Figure 8–19. *Safari's Tabs preferences tab*

RSS

The **RSS** preferences tab allows you to integrate RSS feeds from other sites directly into your web browser. RSS feeds enable you to keep up with news contextually by giving you a streaming feed of information. RSS stands for *really simple syndication*, and it gives you a great way to minimize your web footprint, while simultaneously maximizing your ability to retrieve information over the Web (see Figure 8–20).

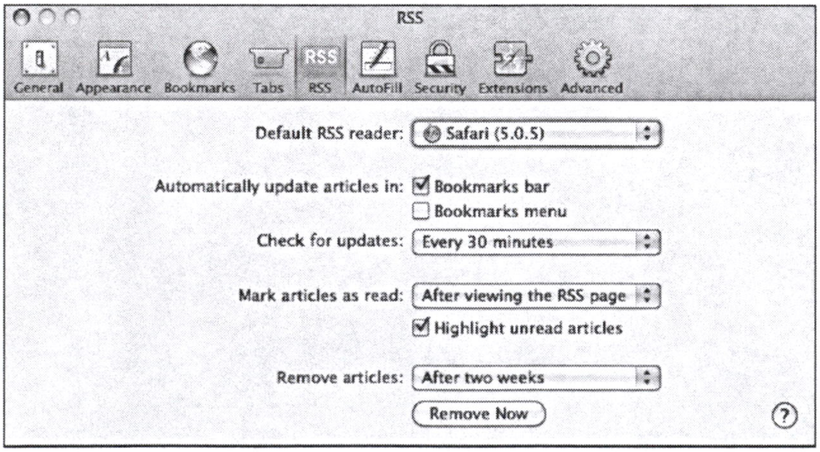

Figure 8–20. *Safari's RSS tab preferences*

Autofill

The **Autofill** preferences tab helps you fill out forms on the Internet automatically. This feature can allow **Safari** to take information from your address book, password list, and other forms you have filled out, and then automatically insert that information into new forms that you need to fill out. Enabling this feature means that you do not have to fill in redundant information such as your name, address, and telephone number. This is a very handy tool when doing registration-related activities on the Internet (see Figure 8–21).

Figure 8–21. *Safari's Autofill preferences tab*

> **NOTE:** We will cover the security and extension preferences in this chapter's upcoming "Safari Privacy and Security" and "Safari Extras" sections, respectively.

Advanced

The **Advanced** preferences tab lets you set your preferred font size when surfing the Web (see Figure 8–22). It also lets you change the style sheets associated with each page. Moreover, this section is where you must adjust your network and proxy settings to ensure that you have web connectivity—only if necessary, of course. Unless you know what you are doing, however, it is advised that you leave this tab's settings at their default values.

Figure 8–22. *Safari's Advanced preferences tab*

For a lesson on style sheets, I recommend that you visit `www.w3.org/Style/CSS/`, which has a wealth of information about how style sheets and web pages work together.

All of the options in **Safari**'s **Preferences...** menu can significantly impact the way you choose to browse the web. With **Safari**, Apple has done away with those options intended solely for developers and programmers; instead, it has put all the power of its browser into the hands of your basic, everyday user. Therefore, I recommend that you take the time to explore all of these options. I further recommend that you try changing some of **Safari**'s default settings—you may be pleasantly surprised by the degree to which this browser can be manipulated to meet your web browsing needs.

Safari Privacy and Security

When surfing the Web, it is important that you put privacy and security before all of other aspects of web browsing. Fortunately, **Safari** has a few built-in features that can make browsing the Web a safe experience, helping you to keep your information from reaching the hands of would-be Internet criminals.

The **Security** tab under the **Safari** menu's **Preferences...** submenu allows you to set several options that can significantly impact the security level of your web browsing. By default, **Safari** comes with most of the security features you need enabled by default; however, it is always good to make a few adjustments. In this section, I will recommend a handful of adjustments you can make to ensure you are surfing the web in the safest manner possible (use Figure 8–23 as a reference for making these adjustments).

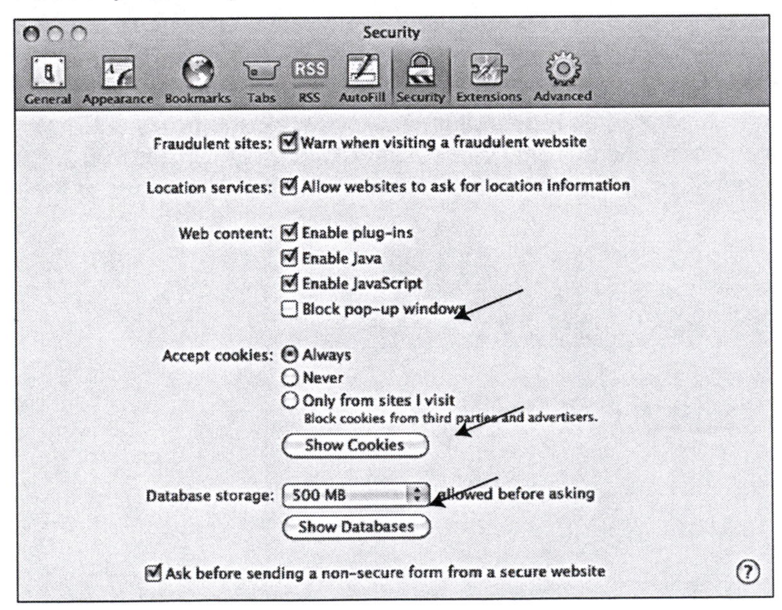

Figure 8–23. *Safari's Security preferences tab*

Security Recommendations

By default, **Safari** does not block pop-up windows. It is a good idea to enable this option by placing a check in the appropriate box (see Figure 8–23). This will ensure that you are not bombarded by unwanted advertisements or intrusive—and potentially dangerous—web scripts. Furthermore, it is a good idea to change the **Accept cookies:** option from **Always** to **Only from sites I visit**. The reason for this change: Many web sites today contain malicious code that attempts to grab your information on the fly. Making this change helps you ensure that you do not acquire any unwanted cookies in your web browser's database cache. Cookies are used by **Safari** to sync information with web sites that require certain information. Cookies were originally a programming tool intended to enhance the security of web sites; however, today many web sites use these cookies to track and harvest your personal information. For this reason, it is advisable that you only accept cookies from sites that you trust. For more information about cookies, I recommend that you visit `http://en.wikipedia.org/wiki/HTTP_cookie`. This site provides a thorough explanation of what a cookie is and what it does (see Figure 8–24).

I also recommend that you decrease the database storage for web sites that require local information storage. This keeps foreign information on your computer to a minimum, thereby reducing the possibility that you will store unwanted information on your Mac (see Figure 8–23).

Surfing Privately

When you surf the web, you leave a trail of evidence that indicates where you have been and how long you were there. This type of information could put you in an awkward position if you do not want others to see what you are using the Internet for. For example, if you run or are part of a business of any kind, it is important to keep your Internet surfing tracks clean. This will ensure that, if your Mac is somehow compromised, the would-be criminals would not immediately have access to your company's most important—and potentially damaging—information. Fortunately for **Safari** users, covering your tracks is a simple as enabling the **Private Browsing...** option from the **Safari** menu (see figure 8–24).

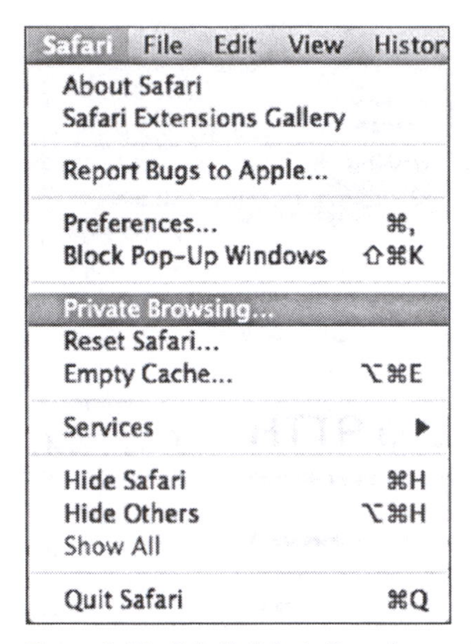

Figure 8–24. *Safari's Private Browsing... option*

After you select the **Private Browsing...** option, you will see a window that explains what this feature does. Simply click the **OK** button and proceed to browse the Web privately (see Figure 8–25).

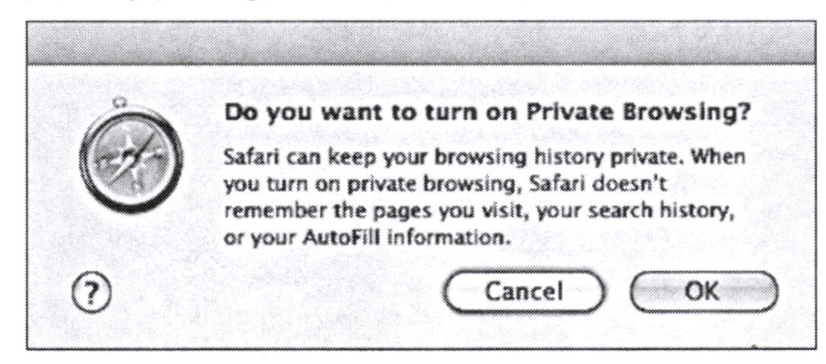

Figure 8–25. *Safari's Private Browsing... prompt*

Browsing the Web can be fun and entertaining; however, a big part of browsing the Web means acting responsibly. Taking the right precautions will help you browse the Web with maximum safety, keep your information safe—*and* let the Web continue to be an interesting place to visit.

Safari's Extras

Safari adheres to web standards when it comes to browsing. This helps to ensure maximum compatibility with today's dynamic range of modern web sites, which use hundreds of differentiating pieces of technology to create rich user experiences. At the same time, you can use extensions to take **Safari** far beyond its original, default functionality. To access the menu for enabling and acquiring more extensions, simply click the **Preferences...** option under the **Safari** menu, and then click the **Extensions** preferences tab (see Figure 8–26).

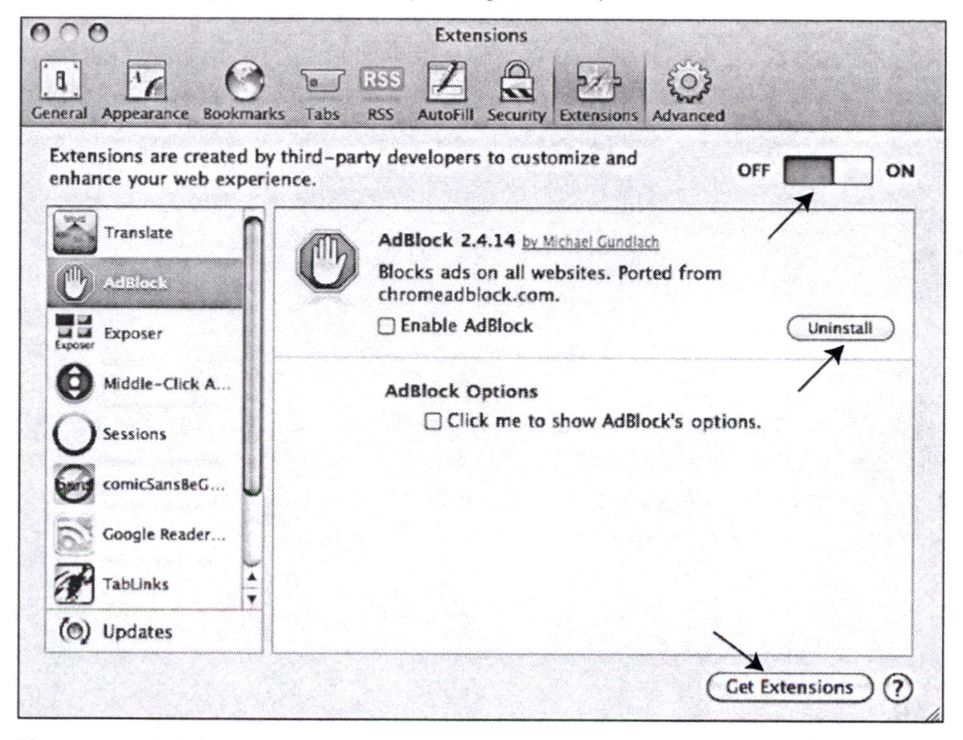

Figure 8–26. *Safari's Extensions preferences tab*

As you can see, I have enabled several extensions; these are listed in the order they were installed. To add extensions, simply click the **Get Extensions** button. This will take you to `https://extensions.apple.com/`, from which you can download and install extensions. The process for downloading and installing extensions is very similar to the process for downloading and installing an app from the Mac App Store. You can enable or disable extensions simply by turning them on or off. You can even uninstall an extension you no longer want by clicking the **Uninstall** button (see Figure 8–26.

Another nice feature: You can install and use extensions without restarting **Safari**. This adds a great deal of flexibility to an already outstanding browser. One extension I highly recommend is the **Add Blocker** extension, which blocks unwanted advertisements from showing up on web pages (see Figure 8–27).

Figure 8–27. *Enabling Adblock*

Once this extension is installed and enabled, it shows up in **Safari**'s main menu bar (see Figure 8–28).

Figure 8–28. The *Ad Blocker extension on Safari's main menu bar*

NOTE: Not all extensions work perfectly or as advertised. However, most are relatively harmless and will indeed enhance your browsing experience. Be aware that sometimes extensions can have side effects that detract from your browsing experience, so it is best to test them immediately after installing them. When an issue does occur, it is best to resolve the problem by disabling or uninstalling the problem extension.

Summary

Safari is a very flexible and powerful browser application for the Lion operating system. It takes the best web browsing technologies and wraps them into one easy-to-use application that can be significantly enhanced in functionality through the use of extensions. **Safari**'s **Private Browsing...** option also gives you the means to secure your personal information and cover your browsing tracks. Other options in the **Preferences...** menu can help you keep things organized and uncluttered. **Safari**'s possibilities are practically endless; indeed, this app is where the smart Lions go to interact, socialize, and retrieve information over the Web.

Chapter 9

Mail and Other Ways to Say Hello

The main reason most people use computers is to communicate with others. Computers allow us to connect with our family, friends, and business associates, as well as to meet new people. They also give us several different ways to communicate—through e-mail, video, voice, SMS (texting), and so on.

To truly appreciate just how powerful computers have become as communication tools, it's helpful to reflect on where they started. In the early days of home computing, using a computer to communicate was a rather complicated task, so much so that computer users often avoided using their computers as communication devices. Things have changed tremendously since then: communicating on modern-day computers is a relatively easy and straightforward affair.

The Internet has played a particularly important role in making computers the powerful communications devices they are today. The Internet provides an always-on, universally connectable medium for our computing devices to connect to. This in turn enables us to participate in far-reaching digital dialogs that span the globe.

Macs are the most communication friendly devices made, not least because Apple has engineered its hardware (your Mac) and software (the Lion OS) to make computer communication easy and intuitive. Whatever medium you use to communicate electronically—e-mail, video, audio, or SMS—Macs make it easy to communicate with others, especially other Mac users. And you can do so without having to acquire any third-party software, which enables you to keep your social life thriving as you communicate in a safe, innovative way. In this chapter, you will learn how to make Lion roar using the wide array of communication tools and utilities available for Lion. Let's get started!

NOTE: You must exercise caution when using some of the applications we will be exploring in this chapter. Communicating openly on the Internet is fun, but it also requires that you do so in responsible way. Just as in face-to-face communication, communicating over the Internet requires that you adhere to common, widely accepted standards of behavior. Be safe, be kind, and be sensible.

Using Mail

Most communication today is done asynchronously; that is, communication happens in one direction at a time. This is true even if you are on a cell phone. After all, if two people are talking to one another at the same time, neither can be heard. Computers do make synchronous communication possible; however, humans still prefer the get-and-send approach to communicating because we are not very good at talking and listening at the same time. For this reason, many of the communication applications we use today have been designed around our natural tendency to communicate asynchronously.

E-mail applications have always been at the forefront of communication applications for computers. E-mail applications provide us with a way to communicate somewhat naturally with anyone, anywhere in the world. Lion ships with an e-mail application simply called **Mail**. Fortunately, using it is as simple as saying its name. Let's explore some this app's functionality, with an eye toward what it takes to use it effectively.

Mail's Interface

The **Mail** app's interface is sleek and simple. It does away with any extra images, buttons, colors, and annotations that would distract you from reading your e-mail. Its main menu is very easy to use and consists of what you need to create, delete, reply to, and organize various pieces of information in your e-mail accounts (see Figure 9–1).

Figure 9–1. *Mail's main menu bar*

Mail includes a handful of functions in addition to its ability to create and send messages. In the next section, we'll take a look at what each of the functions on its main menu bar does, covering the buttons from left to right.

Reviewing Mail's Main Menu Functions

The **Get Mail** button at the far left of **Mail**'s main menu bar does exactly what it name purports.

If you are impatiently waiting for an e-mail to arrive, pressing this button will override the built-in timer used to check your e-mail periodically and perform what is known as a *force check* of your e-mail.

Next, you see the **Delete** and **Junk** buttons.

The **Delete** button moves your e-mail to **Mail**'s trash bin. After a certain period of time, you can request that **Mail** permanently delete this e-mail to save disk space on your hard drive. The **Junk** button is a great way to ensure that the mail you are receiving is the mail you want to receive. This feature enables you to let **Mail** know that you do not want to receive a particular type of e-mail. To use this feature, select an e-mail and click the **Junk** button.

Next, you can see the message redirection options. These allow you to reply to a single person or reply to a group of people if you have received an e-mail that contains multiple contacts. You can also see a **Forward** button, which allows you to send an e-mail you've received to people who weren't among that e-mail's original recipients.

Moving further to the right along the main menu, the **Compose New Mail** button allows you to create a new e-mail message for your intended recipients.

Next, you see the **Note** and **To Do** buttons. The **Note** button allows you to jot down notes about anything, not just e-mail.

You can keep the notes on your e-mail server for safe retrieval later. In a similar vein, the **To Do** button lets you create **iCal**-like reminders to perform certain tasks in response to receiving e-mails that contain activity requests.

Sitting immediately to the right of the **To Do** button is the **Related Messages** button, which allows you to group messages that correspond to the same e-mail dialog.

This feature will organize and sequence the messages you have sent and received in a particular e-mail discussion. This feature will display these messages all at once, so you can see the flow of dialog between yourself and the other respondent/s.

The **Mail Flag** button enables you to highlight and prioritize the messages in your inbox based on their importance and significance.

This a great feature to use when you need to filter and organize the messages you deem more important than others.

Finally, you can see a **Search** box at the far right of **Mail**'s main menu bar. This box lets you search your e-mail by content, subject, title, recipient, and date.

Other Noteworthy Mail Items

The **Mail** app includes a few other features worth highlighting. The first is a window pane that includes **Reminders** and **Mailboxes** sections. This pane also includes a **Notes and Folders** menu bar that allows you to drill down into your notes, as well as access the folders associated with your e-mail account (see Figure 9–2).

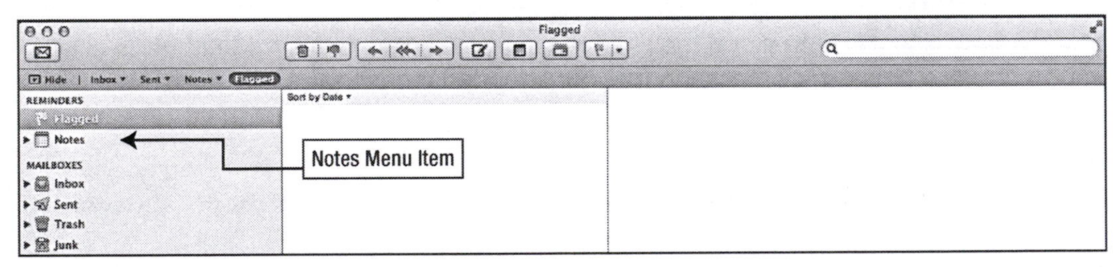

Figure 9–2. *Mail's Notes and Folders menu bar*

Activity Section

This same window pane includes an **Activity** section that allows you to view e-mail activity in real-time (see Figure 9–3). Watching this section as you send or receive e-mails can give you a better view of the e-mail activity occurring on your system. This section also includes a bar that shows time elapsed. This feature allows you to see whether a message was sent or whether a message you were trying to send reached its destination.

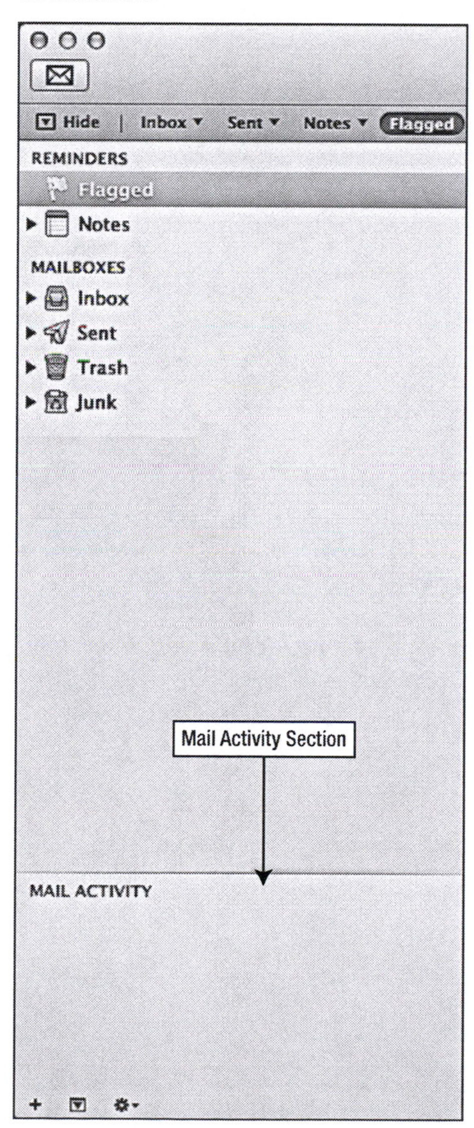

Figure 9–3. *Mail's Activity section*

Listing and Content Windows

A listing of your e-mail and its content will be shown in **Mail**'s **Listing** and **Content** windows, respectively. The **Listing** pane displays your e-mails, while the **Content** pane displays the contents of the message you have currently selected in the **Listing** window (see Figure 9–4). Panes can be rearranged, but I recommend you leave them in their default positions for the sake of clarity.

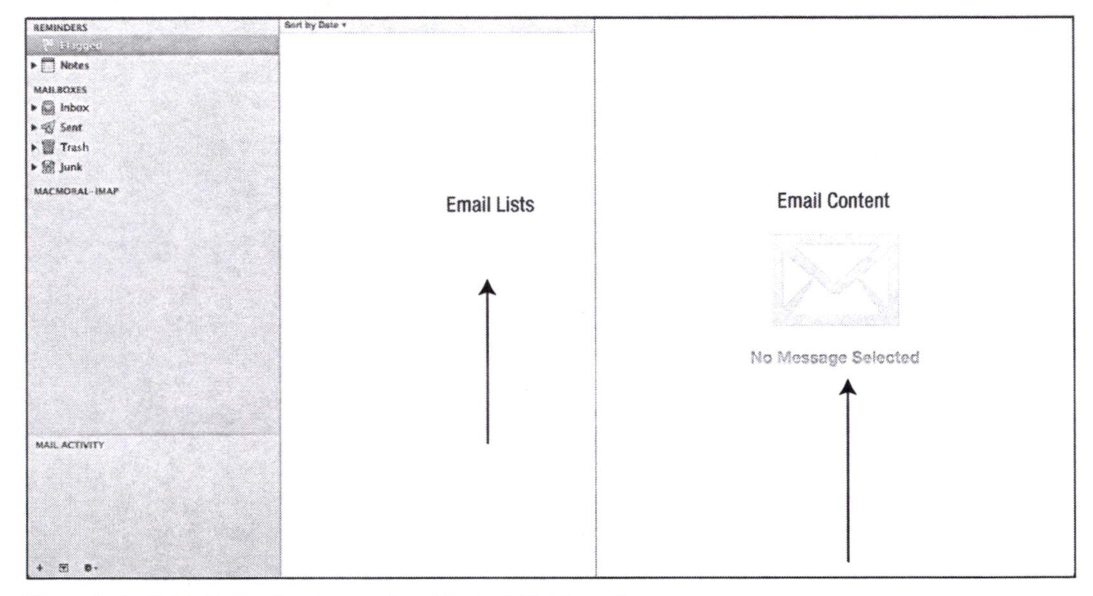

Figure 9–4. *Mail's Listing (center pane) and Content (right pane) areas*

Mail's default layout is standard for most e-mail clients, and it provides a very easy way to view many e-mails at once.

E-mail Contextual Menus

Mail also includes a **Mailbox** menu in the menu at the top of its interface. You can use this menu to interact with the program in additional ways (see Figure 9–5). For example, this menu allows you to do several things related to managing and connecting to your e-mail account, such as create what are known as *Smart Mailbox folders*.

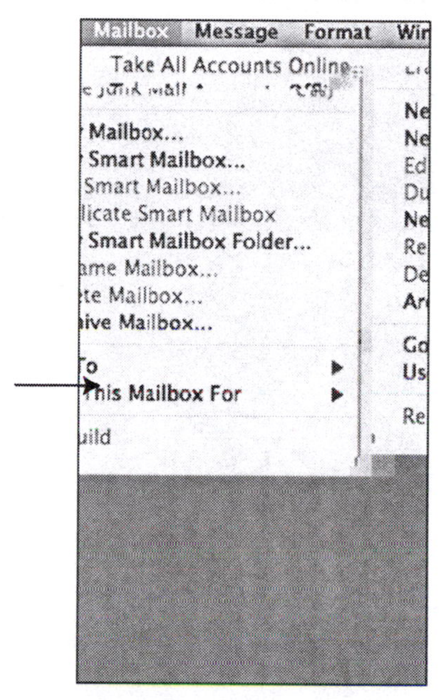

Figure 9–5. *Mail's Mailbox menu*

Smart Mailbox

Smart Mailbox folders differ from other mailbox folders in that they are not actual folders that take up physical space on your hard drive; rather, they are virtual folders that use rules to fill and sort their content. Upon creating a Smart Mailbox, you are asked to supply the filter that will be used to designate the exact content that will fill the folder (see Figure 9-6). This content is not copied to the folder; rather, it is merely displayed in the folder, giving you the illusion that you have a folder dedicated to holding information in the manner you have specified. The benefit of such folders is that they do not take up extra space on your hard drive or the e-mail server you use for your e-mail. Also, you can create as many Smart Mailbox folders as you need. This feature provides the one of the best ways to keep your e-mails organized.

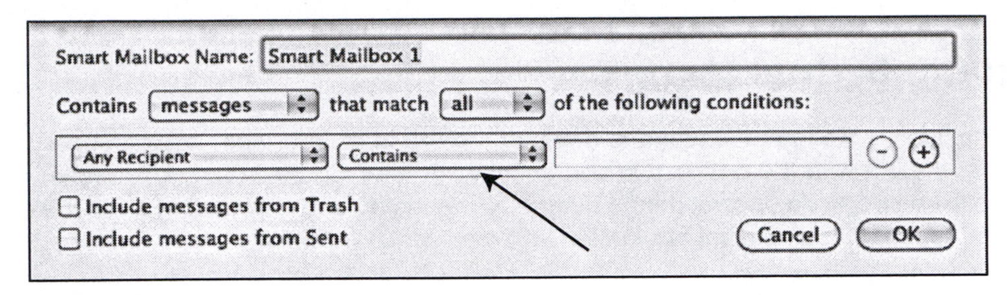

Figure 9–6. *Smart Mailbox folders*

Composing a Message

When composing a new mail message, you can use the message option buttons located in the upper right of the **New Message** window to manipulate the content of your message in several ways (see Figure 9–7).

Figure 9–7. *Mail's message option buttons*

This section contains four option buttons: **Attachments**, **Fonts**, **Photo Browser**, and **Stationery**. In the upcoming sections, we'll look at both their functionality and what they can do for you.

Attachments

Clicking the **Attachments** button allows you to insert file attachments of almost any type into your e-mail.

You can use this feature to send an accompanying file with your message to the intended recipient. You can also check an option to ensure that the attachment is formatted properly when going to someone using a Windows operating system (see Figure 9–8).

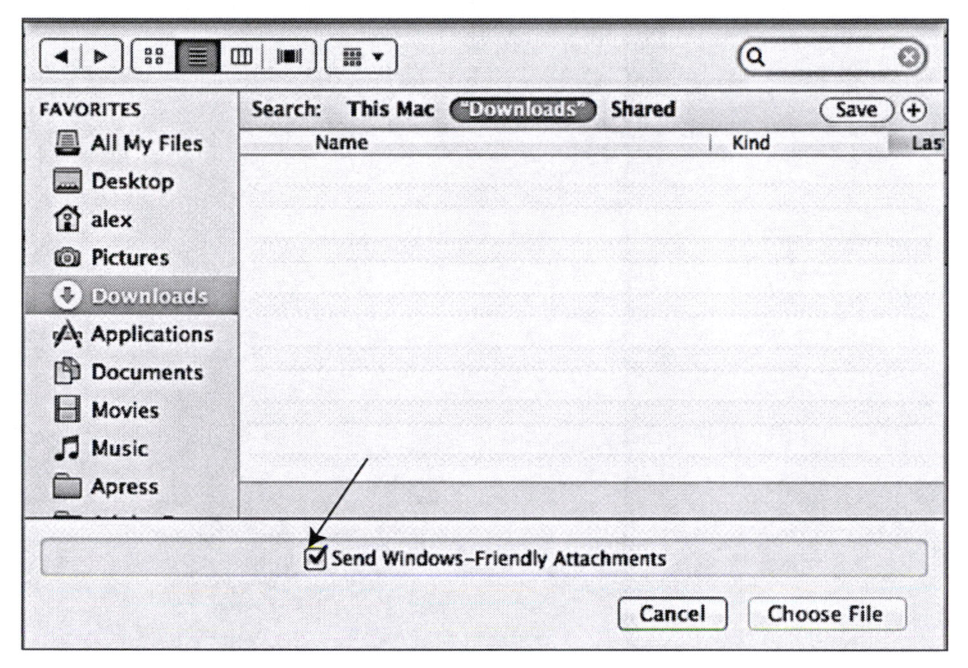

Figure 9–8. *Mail's Attachments window*

Fonts

Clicking the **Fonts** button brings up a formatting toolbar that lets you edit the font properties of your message's text.

With this feature, you can create messages that use different fonts, font sizes, and other custom font attributes, much as you would in a word processor such as **Pages** (see Figure 9–9).

Figure 9–9. *Mail's formatting toolbar for fonts*

Photo Browser

Clicking the **Photo Browser** button allows you to incorporate images from **iPhoto**.

Clicking this button takes you directly into **iPhoto**, so that you can import pictures straight into your e-mail (see Figure 9–10).

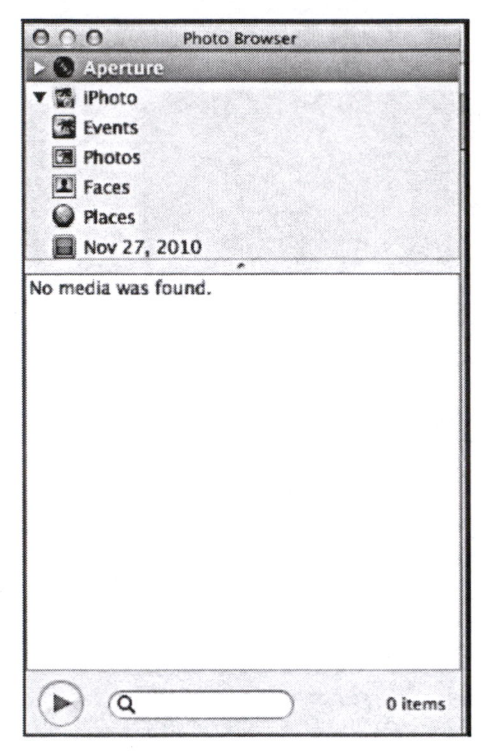

Figure 9–10. *Mail's Photo Browser feature*

Stationery

The final, right-most button at the top of all new messages is the **Stationery** button.

This button brings up interactive templates that you can use to spruce up your otherwise dull e-mails. Figure 9–11 shows a detailed view of the **Stationery** menu.

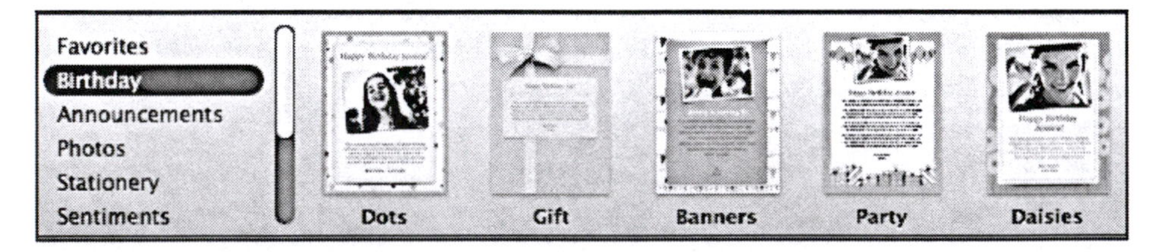

Figure 9–11. *Mail's Stationery menu*

After you select your desired Stationery template, **Mail** automatically applies that template to the body of your e-mail. At this point, you can proceed to replace the default images and text supplied by the template with images and text of your own (see Figure 9–12).

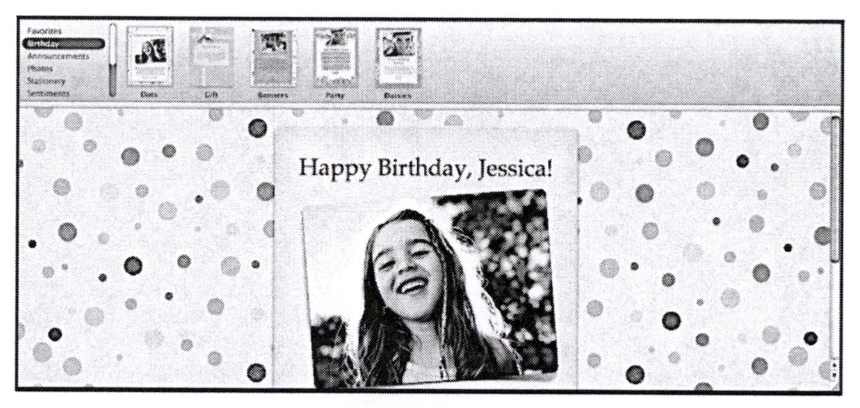

Figure 9–12. *Applying a Stationery template*

Other Communication App Alternatives

Applications, like operating systems, are about choice. And the breadth of applications available for Lion OS X—and the way they enable you to go beyond the default functionality provided by the operating system—is one of the things that make Lion so great.

Application flexibility is more than just a good thing to have—it is an absolute necessity in today's modern computing and technology environments. This is especially true where communication is concerned. Being aware of other ways to communicate on the Lion OS can save you time and grief in those cases where the application you are used to using just will not suffice. In this section, we'll take a look at some alternative communication applications, exploring how these apps can help you stay in touch with your family, friends, and co-workers.

iChat

iChat gives you yet another way to communicate with other Mac users (see Figure 9–13).

> **NOTE:** At some future point, **iChat** will likely be completely replaced by **FaceTime** (this app will be covered in some depth later in this chapter). Nevertheless, **iChat** remains a great way to communicate using your Mac at this time.

iChat has several nice features and one significant drawback. **iChat**'s drawback: Both you and the person you're chatting with must connect to a Jabber communication server. One the plus side, it supports Yahoo, AOL, and MSN Messenger buddy lists and communications. Another plus is that it's available at no cost to Mac users.

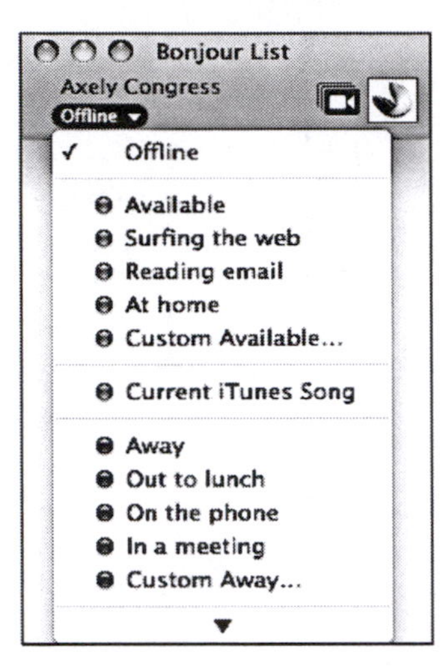

Figure 9–13. *iChat's interface*

FaceTime

FaceTime is Apple's premier native communications application. It provides a private, secure connection for communicating with anyone else who owns any other type of Apple **FaceTime**-`compatible` computing device, including the iPad, the iPhone, and (of course!) any Mac computer. Figure 9–14 shows the **FaceTime** interface running on the iPhone.

Figure 9–14. *FaceTime's iPhone interface*

FaceTime does not require you to connect to any type of server manually, and you can use it to interact with anyone already in your address book. Another plus: **FaceTime** has no learning curve, which makes it the easiest of the available communications applications to use.

Before you can use **FaceTime** to chat with someone, you need to enter that person's phone number or e-mail address, and then request that this person add you as a contact. At that point, initiating a **FaceTime** chat is extraordinarily simple. Simply select the person you wish to chat with and click the **FaceTime** button. That's all there is to it (see Figure 9–15).

FaceTime represents a revolutionary step forward in how we communicate using handheld and other computing devices. It is exclusively available to Mac users from the App Store for $0.99.

Figure 9–15. *FaceTime on your Mac*

Skype

Skype is a user-friendly video, audio, and chat program that provides another great way to communicate with others. It has a ton of features and is extremely easy to use.

Skype is also a phone utility that serves both home and business users. The program lets you make and receive phone calls through your computer. And unlike **FaceTime**, **Skype** lets you do much more than call other **Skype** users. In fact, it lets you call any phone in the world, anywhere in the world.

Skype is available on a broad range of platforms, including the Windows, Linux, and Mac OS X operating systems. It is also available on most mobile computing devices, including the iPhone (see Figure 9-16).

Figure 9–16. *Skype on your iPhone*

Skype is a very flexible application; it rivals **FaceTime** in functionality, yet exceeds it in accessibility. It is one application you should look into using if you want a way to transparently communicate with the rest of the world. Skype can be downloaded and installed from `www.skype.com`.

Summary

You Mac can serve as your communications gateway to the rest of the world. It has a wealth of applications that enable you to communicate with anyone, anywhere, and at any time. Most of these applications are very cheap or free to use. They are also very popular, which means that you will find it easy to use them to contact others.

I recommend that you give all of the applications mentioned in this chapter a try, so you can see which one fits your communication needs best. In any case, the Lion OS offers you powerful tools that give you a way to talk to—and see—just about anyone else in the world. But this power also comes with significant responsibility. Remember to stay vigilant, and be sure to keep track of others who have your contact information. You should also remember to be tactful when you communicate with others over the Internet. You never know who is watching, and it is a good idea to be on your best behavior when your actions are potentially visible to the rest of the world.

Chapter 10

Keeping Things Safe: Time Machine and Security

Backing up your precious files is something that every Lion user should take seriously. After all, there are two kinds of hard drives: those that have already failed, and those that will. The point is that all hard drives eventually fail; and while technologies like *solid state drives* (SSD) may give us the impression that our hard drives are impervious to failure, that is not the case. Happily, Apple has developed multiple solutions to the problem of making sure that you have copies of your data in a place other than your Mac.

There are thousands of technologies and software applications available that are designed to back up your data. That said, most of these applications focus on allowing you to back up and retrieve your data in a way that does not permit you to view the contents of what it is you have chosen to back up. Furthermore, these applications do not give you the amount of control necessary to search and retrieve your files as if they were still in the exact same location that you originally saved them. For example, most backup applications do not store or remember the exact file and folder structure of your hard drive. Instead, they simply duplicate your data, and store it in the best way they know how. Fortunately there is a solution to this available to all Mac users: **Time Machine**.

Time Machine Overview

Time Machine separates itself from all other backup programs by offering its users a granular backup application with unparalleled flexibility for both backing up and retrieving data. **Time Machine** works on the premise that people can best remember where a file is when they are able to go back to the exact same place that they first witnessed or stored that file. **Time Machine** allows you to literally search through your periodic backups in the exact same manner that you would look for a file on your hard drive in normal use cases.

As a consequence, **Time Machine** can dramatically reduce the amount of time it takes to search and retrieve files that you need to restore. It also offers a very flexible range of ways to store your data. In the upcoming sections, we'll take a closer look at how to use **Time Machine**, so that you can start taking advantage of secure local and remote backups for your Mac.

NOTE: Time Machine's performance is dependent on the medium and the type of storage used to save your data. You should make sure you have a strong and speedy wireless connection if you plan on using wireless technologies to back up your data using **Time Machine**. You should also be sure that you back up your data to a decently sized hard drive. The rule of thumb for choosing a hard drive is to select one that is at least quadruple the size of your computer's hard drive. This will enable you to maintain and retrieve a long history of the files you intend to back up. Finally, be sure to store your backup media in a safe place, so that it is not readily visible to just anyone. Remember: All of your files are on this backup hard drive, so you need to be extremely vigilant when allowing access to this device.

Setting up Time Machine

Using **Time Machine** is quite easy, so much so that it requires no learning curve to use it proficiently. To start using this utility, follow these steps:

1. Open the **Preferences** application for your Mac (see Figure 10–1).

Figure 10–1. *The Preferences icon*

2. Select the **Time Machine** icon (see Figure 10–2).

Figure 10–2. *The Time Machine icon in the Preferences menu*

3. You will now see a window prompting you to turn on **Time Machine** (see Figure 10–3). This window also allows you to select the media that you want to use for backups, as well as to specify certain folders and files that you do not want included in your backups.

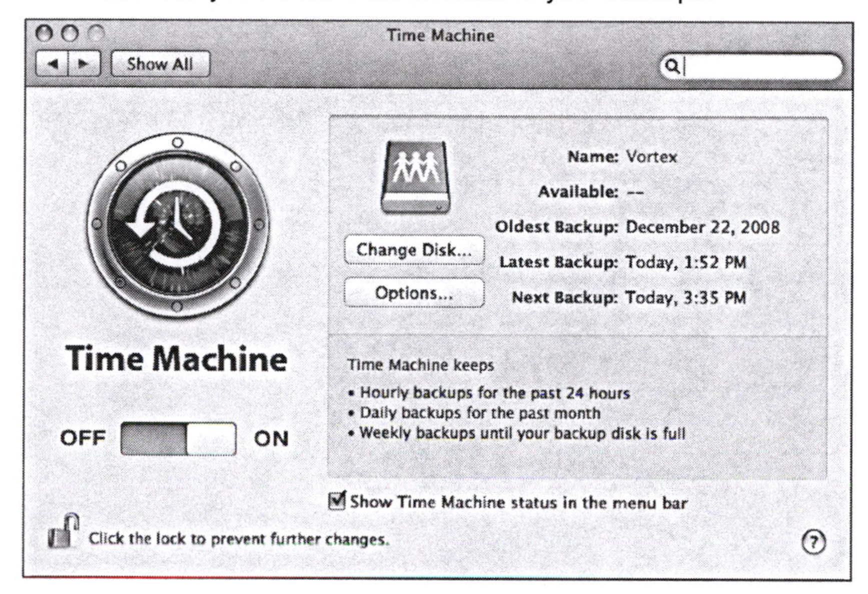

Figure 10–3. The *Time Machine window prompt*

4. After selecting your **Time Machine**-compatible device of choice (see Figure 10–4), all you need to do is make sure that your backup device is connected to your Mac thereafter, so that your future backups can take place.

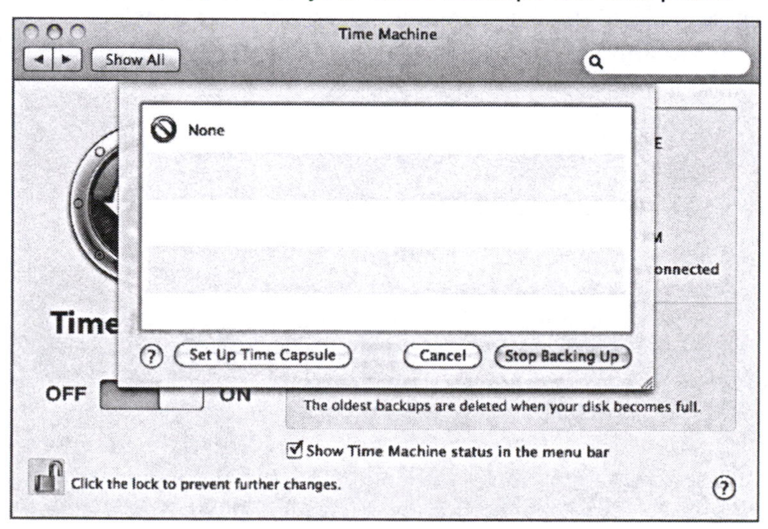

Figure 10–4. *Time Machine's backup selection dialog*

Believe it or not, that's all there is to it. Apple wanted to make it easy for even the most novice Mac users to back up their files remotely (or locally), without sacrificing performance or usability.

Using Time Machine

Time Machine will recognize compatible media, such as USB hard drives, external SATA, and FireWire hard drive enclosures. It will also recognize Mac-compatible network attached storage (NAS) devices without requiring that you do anything at all. Simply plug in a blank or newly formatted hard drive, and you will be asked whether you would like to use it as a **Time Machine** backup disk (see Figure 10–5).

Figure 10–5. *Time Machine's backup media prompt*

This prompt is how you tell your Mac that you wish to use a disk as a **Time Machine**-backup device. As noted previously, **Time Machine** is not limited to local media that you have to carry around with you and plug into your computer. **Time Machine** also works with networked media. For example, there are third-party NAS (Network Attached Storage) devices that work with **Time Machine**, enabling you to back up your computer to your wireless device. However, Apple has also created its own network device specifically intended for **Time Machine.** This device, called a *Time Capsule*, takes very little time to set up, and you can have it backing up your wireless network in mere minutes.

Using Time Capsule for Network Storage

Time Capsule devices come with hard drives built into them, so you do not have to put any effort into looking for the right type of or size of hard drive. At the time of writing, these devices come in 2 TB and 3 TB sizes, which is more than enough to keep several months of files in your backup archive. Your Mac will automatically detect your Time Capsule and ask you if you would like to use it as a backup device immediately after you give it power and attach it to your Mac via Wi-Fi. Simply say **Yes** to initiate this process. If for some reason you are not automatically prompted, you can use the **Set Up Time Capsule** option located in **Time Machine**'s **Preferences** window to initiate this process (see Figure 10–6).

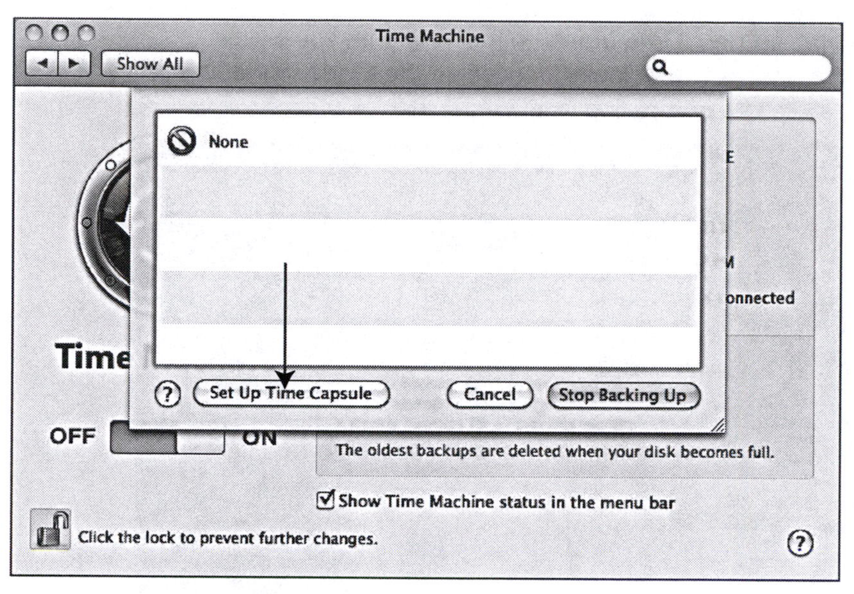

Figure 10–6. *Time Capsule's Set Up Time Capsule button*

After clicking the **Set Up Time Capsule** button, you simply select the desired Time Capsule device and proceed to back up your data.

> **NOTE:** Your first backup will take a very, very long time over wireless, so be patient. Successive backups will only take minutes or even seconds to complete.

Retrieving Data

Retrieving data with **Time Machine** is dead simple. For example, suppose you need to retrieve a file you have lost or one that has been corrupted. Simply follow these steps to do so:

1. Select the **Time Machine** icon from your Mac's main menu and choose the **Enter Time Machine** option (see Figure 10–7).

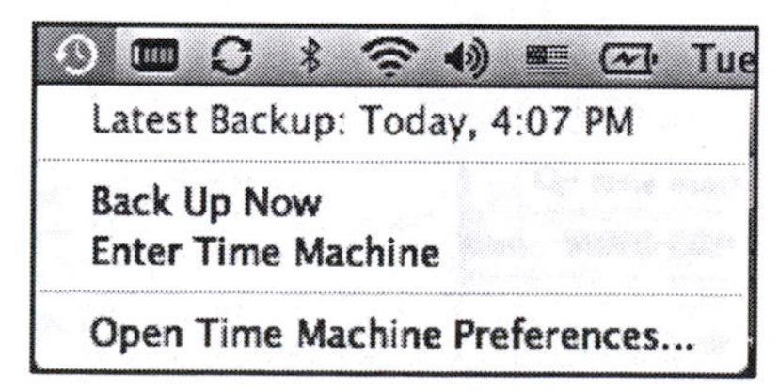

Figure 10–7. *The Enter Time Machine menu option*

2. After choosing the **Enter Time Machine** menu option, you will be presented with a window that looks identical to the **Finder** window you use in your day-to-day computing (see Figure 10–8).

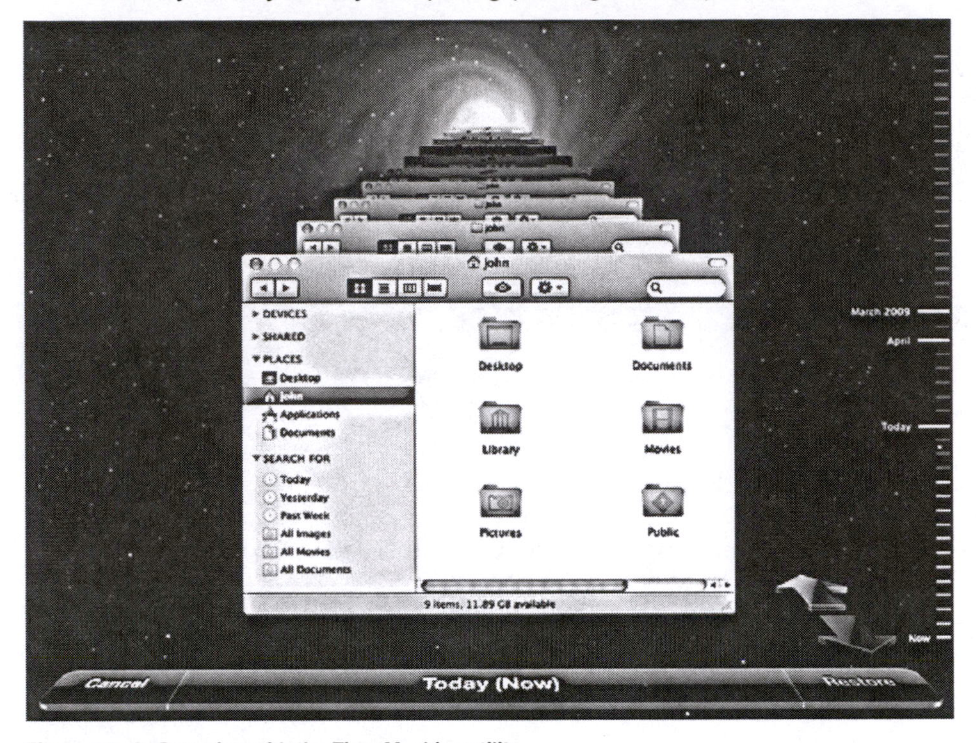

Figure 10–8. *Browsing with the Time Machine utility*

3. From here, simply select the time and date you wish to go back to by using the date slider located on the right side of the window (see Figure 10–9).

4. Next, drill down to or search for (yes, search also works here) the file you wish to retrieve, and then restore it with a simple right-click.

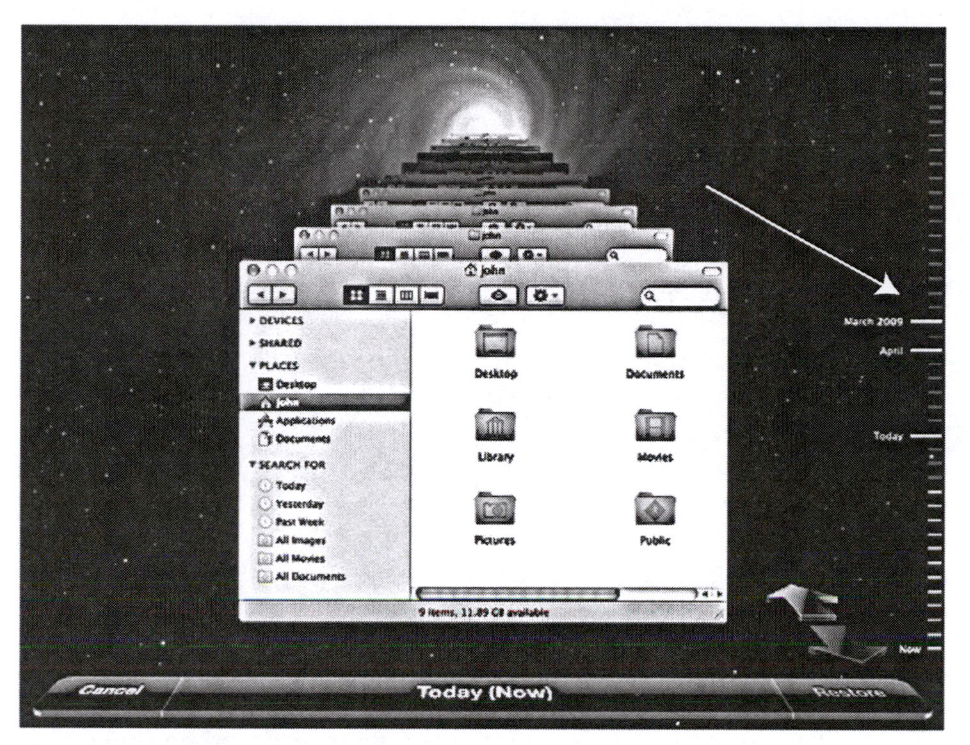

Figure 10–9. *Time Machine's Date slider*

5. After you restore the file, you're done. **Time Machine** then moves out of the way, so you can continue working. Note that this is exactly how Apple intends for this technology to work.

Time Machine should be used as your first line of backup because it provides you with an easy and fool-proof way to back up your files without being an IT expert.

> **NOTE:** Be sure to lock your **Time Machine** preferences after you configure the utility, and then select the checkbox that allows you to access **Time Machine** from your Mac's main menu (see Figure 10–10).

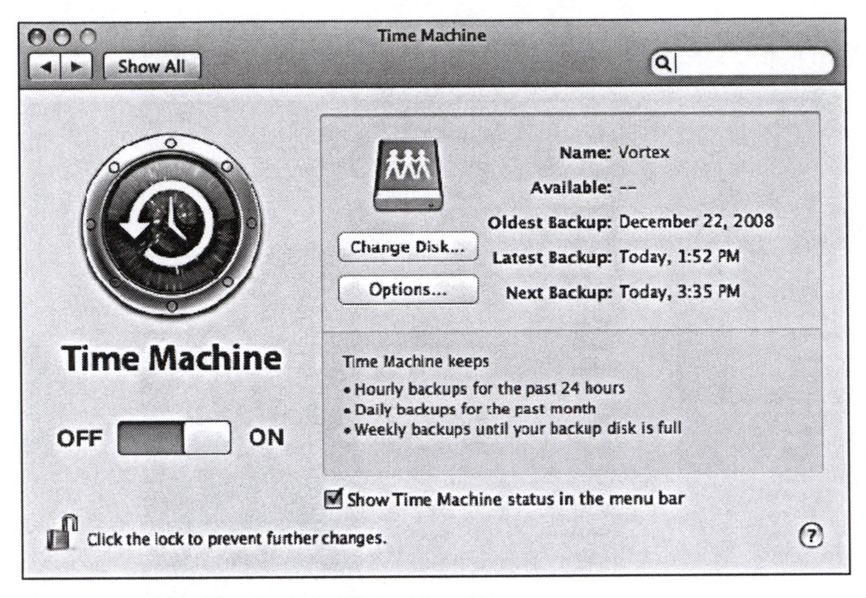

Figure 10–10. *The Time Lock and Status bar options*

Time Machine is a breeze to use and even the most non-savvy computer user can leverage this utility to its full potential. That said, there are a couple of alternatives to this software that I would also recommend: **Super Flexible Backup** and **Carbon Copy Cloner**. Both of these utilities are intended to give you an instant data recovery solution that does not require file restoration to get you up and running again. We'll review both of these backup options later in this chapter. First, however, let's look at another useful feature in Apple's Lion OS: Versions.

Versions

Time Machine is a great way to keep multiple versions of a single file (or group of files); however, it is not the only way to achieve file redundancy. Lion also ships with *Versions*, a feature that allows you to control the snapshots taken of a single file from within certain applications. This feature helps you eliminate two known issues users commonly have with **Time Machine**.

First, it eliminates the need to use alternative storage as a means of keeping multiple backups of your files. **Time Machine** requires a hard drive other than the drive that Lion is installed on to do this. This means you must acquire some extra hardware and spend a bit more money in the process.

This extra hardware requirement is also the principle cause of the second problem the Versions feature eliminates: connectivity. To use **Time Machine**, you must be within a certain proximity to your backup source. This severely limits mobility for those who are on the go, but still require access to previous versions of their files.

Versions eliminates this restriction by giving you immediate control of the snapshots taken for file backup. Versions is always aware of the changes you've made to a document, and it allows you to create a copy of the document at hand with your new changes intact. Versions also keeps up with you by taking automatic snapshots when you open, save, lock, rename, or duplicate a file. Thus, this feature provides a very good safety net for anyone who wants to go back in time to retrieve the version of a file from ten minutes ago. (Note that **Time Machine** backs up your files at hourly intervals, so restoring a file to its state ten minutes ago probably wouldn't be possible with that app.)

Using Versions is relatively easy because it is built into some of the more recent native Lion applications, such as **iWork**. Another plus: You can use Versions without buying any extra hardware. While Versions is not featured in every Lion application or in most third-party applications, it is integrated into enough native Lion applications to make it a very useful tool for backing up your information. Let's take a closer look at how this feature works.

Using Versions

Using Versions is rather simple. To access Versions, simply open an application that supports it, such as **Pages** from the **iWork** suite, and then navigate to the very top of the document screen after you have saved the file at least once. Figure 10–11 shows four different options enabled by the Versions feature: **Lock**, **Duplicate**, **Revert to Last Saved Version**, and **Browse All Versions...**

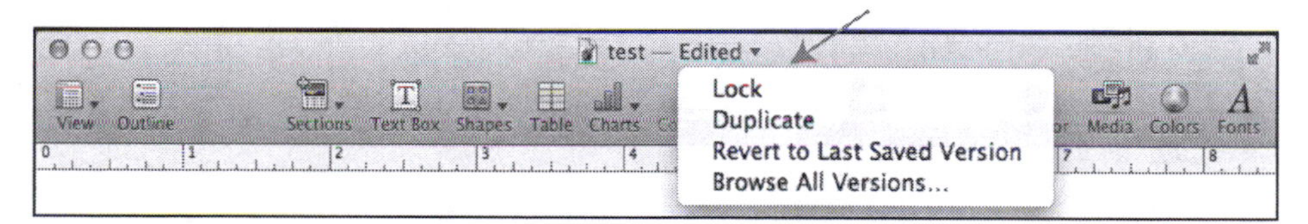

Figure 10–11. *Accessing Versions from the menu bar*

Versions can also be accessed from the Mac's main **File** menu, as shown in Figure 10–12.

Figure 10–12. *Accessing Versions from your Mac's File menu*

Locking a Document

Locking a document prevents you or anyone else from making any changes to it. This is useful if you want to make a master template document that is used as a source for feeding other documents you make. You might also use this feature to ensure that a perfectly made document stays that way! For example, you might want to use this feature on a resume you have created, guaranteeing that no accidental changes can be introduced into the document before you send it off to a potential employer.

Duplicating a Document

The **Duplicate** function creates an exact copy of the current document. It allows you to do so without having to revert to a former version of the file in the **Finder** or without having to use the contextual menu to create another saved file (albeit one with a different name). Duplicating a document is the equivalent of taking a snapshot of the file. Doing so puts a working copy of the file on your hard disk for later retrieval, should you need it. Using the **Duplicate** option gives you the choice of creating a new duplicate or reverting to a previously created duplicate (see Figure 10–13).

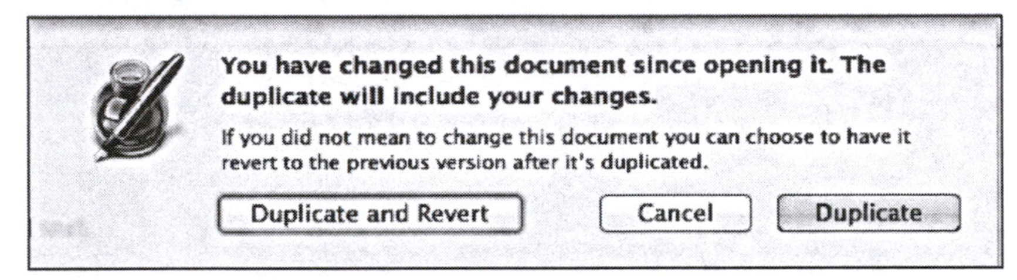

Figure 10–13. *Versions' duplication options*

For example, the **Duplicate and Revert** option allows to you to go back to a previous duplicate copy of your file. This is actually the core function of the Versions feature. It allows you to take a snapshot or make a duplicate of a file, and then restore to that snapshot or duplicate later (should that be necessary). I recommend that you use the **Duplicate** feature heavily when working with important, time-sensitive documents.

Reverting to the Last Saved Version of a Document

The **Revert** option allows you to go back and retrieve a file that has been previously worked on (see Figure 10–14). The primary difference here is that this option reverts to the last *saved* version of your file, rather than the last duplicate version you made. This option retrieves the file from your local hard disk, taking it from its at-rest state. It then replaces your current working document with the last saved version of it, making that the new active document. This is a quick way to take a single step backwards and return to an earlier version of the document you are working on. You can also use this feature to retrieve older versions of the same previously saved file.

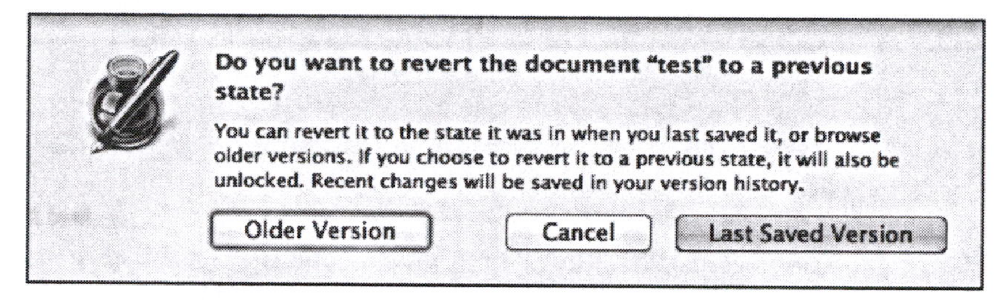

Figure 10–14. *Reverting to a prior saved version of a document*

Should you decide to revisit older versions of your document, you will be shown a **Time Machine**–like window that lets you specify specific points in time that you can return to in a given document's history (see Figure 10–15).

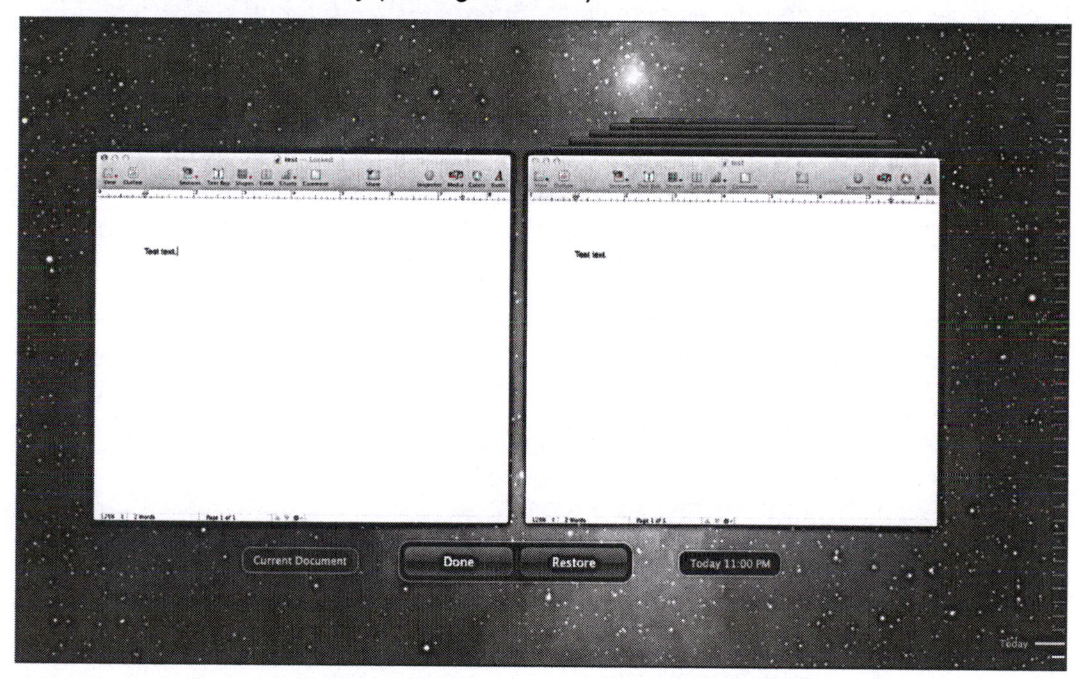

Figure 10–15. *Restoring an older version of a file*

Using Versions can save you time and money compared to **Time Machine**. Although Versions uses your local hard disk, it consumes a minimal amount of space. This is a good trade off in terms of convenience compared to the more heavy-handed approach of an alternative like **Time Machine**. Use Versions often and you may see that you can travel back in time without a **Time Machine**.

Time Machine and Versions are both useful native features provided by Apple in Lion; however, you also have a number of third-party options you can turn to if the native applications included with Lion don't meet all your needs.

Backup Alternatives

If you're considering backup alternatives to **Time Machine** and Versions, I recommend that you take a long look at **Super Flexible Backup**. In my opinion, this is the most effective and secure piece of backup software that exists today. (Later in this chapter, we'll also cover **Carbon Copy Cloner**, which is another suitable choice for backing up the files on your hard drive.)

Super Flexible Backup

Super Flexible Backup has so many options that writing about them all would require a book longer than this one! For all its features, **Super Flexible Backup** is easy and intuitive enough for novices to use—yet powerful enough for IT professionals to consider.

When you first launch **Super Flexible Backup**, the app presents you with a wizard-type interface. If you prefer, you can click the `Switch to Advanced Mode` link in the upper-right corner of this initial screen to see the program's more advanced options (see Figure 10–16).

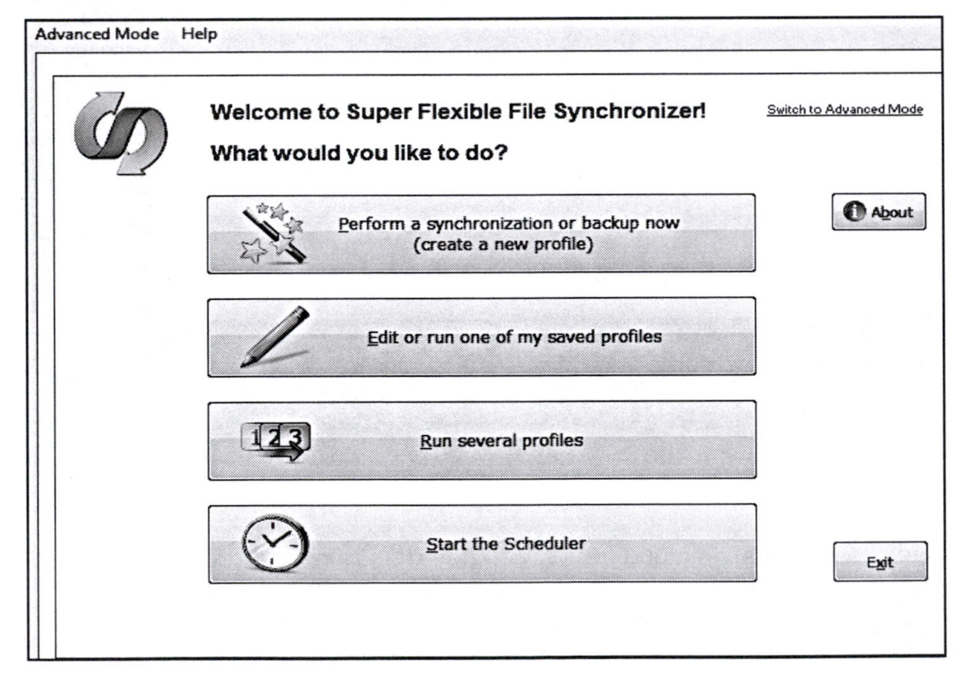

Figure 10–16. *Super Flexible Backup's wizard*

Once you select an option, the appropriate wizard will walk you through the process of completing the selected task. Like **Time Machine**, **Super Flexible Backup** can perform both standard and encrypted backups. And like **Carbon Copy Cloner** (which we'll discuss next), **Super Flexible Backup** can perform drive image-based backups, as well.

In short, **Super Flexible Backup** is a single easy-to-use application that duplicates the features of both **Time Machine** and **Carbon Copy Cloner**. **Super Flexible Backup** can also handle multiple tasks at once, and it offers you a clean view of exactly what is taking place right now in your backup, as well as a view of what has already taken place (see Figure 10–17).

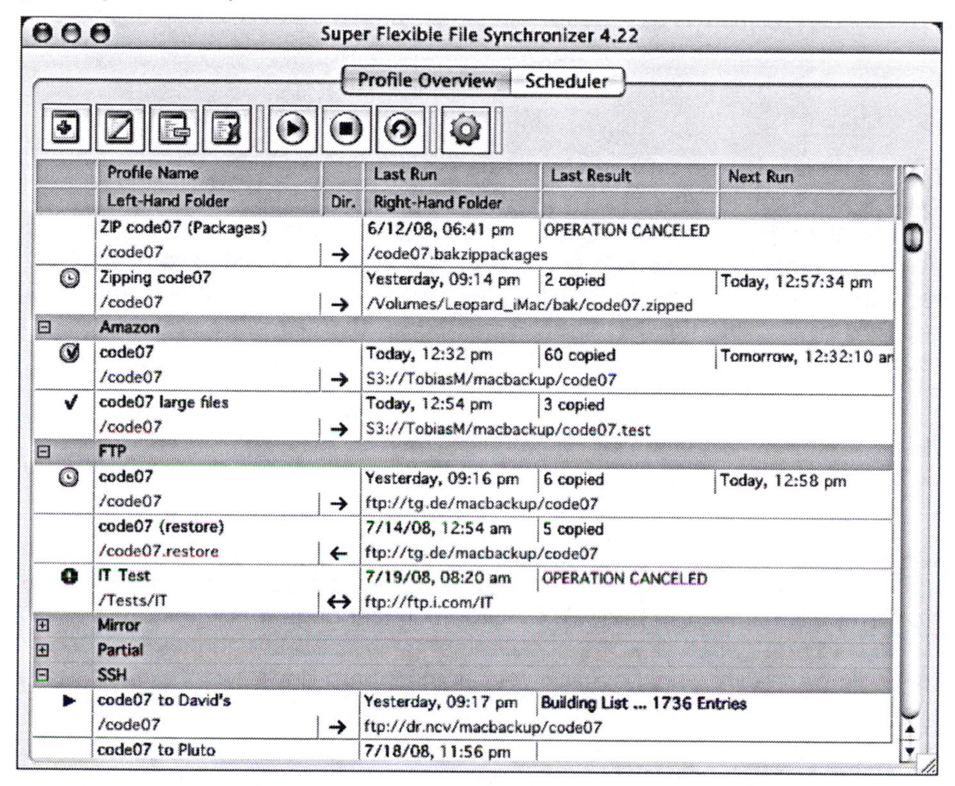

Figure 10–17. *Super Flexible Backup's processing view*

Super Flexible Backup can run in the background or the foreground; it can also be set in motion and left alone once you have programmed it to do what you want it to. There is no backup software quite like it, and I highly recommend it to Lion users looking for a simple, all-in-one solution that completely backs up all their files over both local and remote media, but without compromising performance or security. You can find **Super Flexible Backup** at `www.superflexible.com/`.

Carbon Copy Cleaner

Carbon Copy Cleaner literally allows you to swap drives (if necessary) and/or to boot from another drive without making any other changes. In the next couple sections, we'll delve into why this is a fantastic piece of software for backing up files. We'll also cover how it complements the features of **Time Machine** quite well.

This chapter's earlier discussion on **Time Machine** noted that that program lets you back up your files by putting duplicate copies of them onto another media device for later retrieval; however, this is not the same thing as replicating your Lion hard drive. **Time Machine** does not keep an exact replica of every file on your hard drive. Rather, it keeps the files needed to restore your system completely by copying the files to a designated location after the system has been repaired, or by restoring individual files to a specified location should they be lost or corrupted. **Carbon Copy Cloner** takes this idea one step further.

Carbon Copy Cloner literally makes a mirror image of your hard drive, not just duplicates of your files. Every byte is duplicated, so that you essentially have two working hard drives at the same time.

Carbon Copy Cloner is an excellent utility for disaster recovery because it allows you to simply swap out one hard drive for another or even to boot from either hard drive should the need arise. There is no need to perform a restoration (although this is fully supported). You also don't need to worry about missing files because the backup does a one-to-one backup of every single byte on your primary hard drive.

Using Carbon Copy Cloner

You have heard me say this time and time again; however, it is relevant each time I say it: like most Mac applications, **Carbon Copy Cloner** is extremely easy to use. To use this app, simply download it from `www.bombich.com/` and install it. When you first launch it, you will be prompted to select the backup source and the target for your backup process (see Figure 10–18).

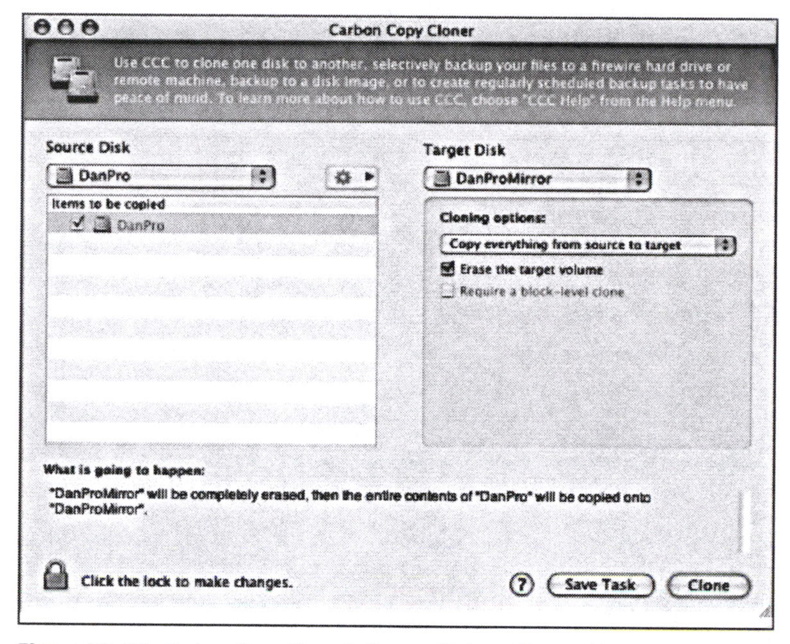

Figure 10–18. *Carbon Copy Cloner's Source Disk and Target Disk selectors*

Be sure to choose the option to copy everything from the source to the target. Also be sure to select the **Erase the target volume** option if this is your first backup (see Figure 10–19).

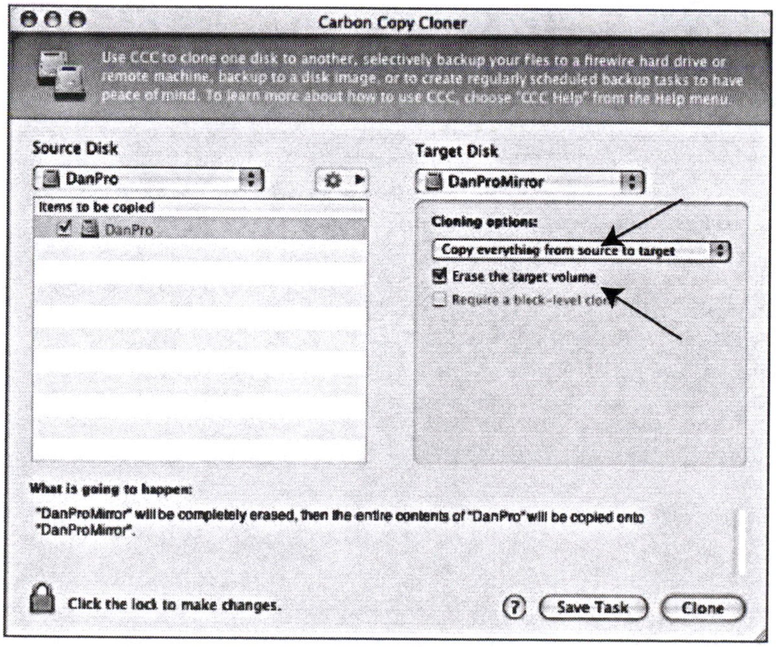

Figure 10–19. *Carbon Copy Cloner's copy options*

Once you have selected the appropriate hard drives for the source and target devices, simply click the **Clone** button. You will then see your files being copied between the two drives (see Figure 10–20).

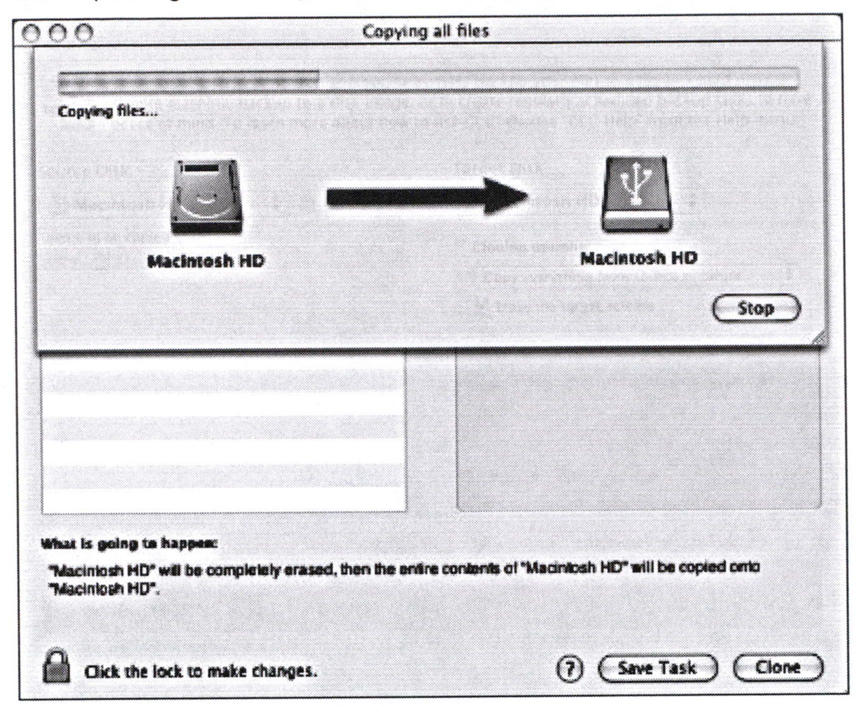

Figure 10–20. *Copying files with Carbon Copy Cloner*

Like any good backup utility, **Carbon Copy Cloner** also allows you to copy your files on a schedule. To enable this feature, simply follow the aforementioned steps, choose your source and target hard drives, and then click the **Save Task** button to fire up the app's scheduler (see Figure 10–21). There is one catch to using the scheduler. **Carbon Copy Cloner** backs up to hard drives, so it will only work when the two hard drives are connected physically to the same Mac.

External USB drives work great with **Carbon Copy Cloner**, and I recommend you use them as your primary media type when backing up your hard drive with this application. USB hard drives are easy to connect and remove; they are also light enough to be carried around with a MacBook, if need be.

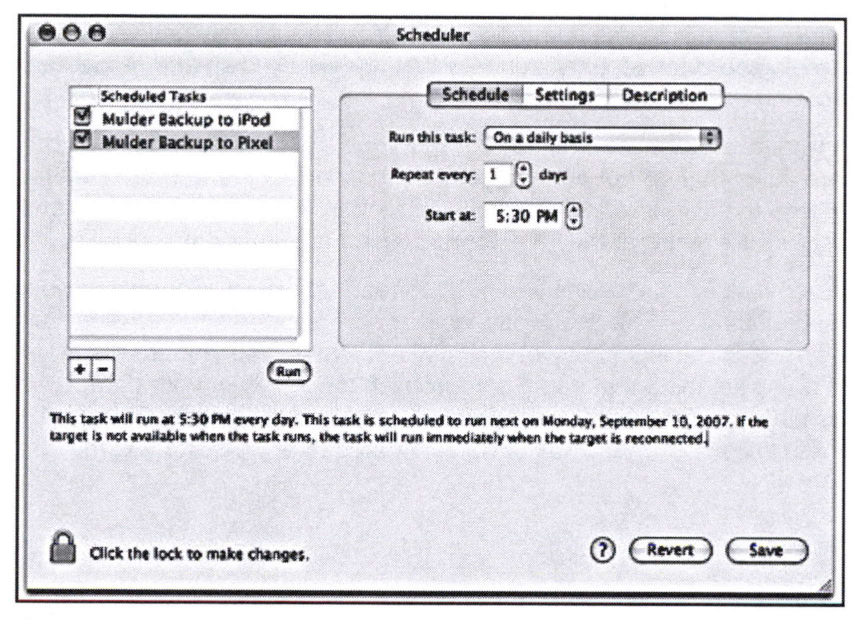

Figure 10–21. *Carbon Copy Cloner's Scheduler*

In any case, **Carbon Copy Cloner** is an extremely powerful backup utility, and it offers Lion users an easy way to make disaster recovery a one-step process. It does not get much easier than that.

Securing Your Lion

We have discussed security in many of this book's chapters, emphasizing the need to make protecting your computer's security an essential part of your computing habits. In the remainder of this chapter, we will look at a few things you can do to make backing up your Mac a secure process, making it even tougher for would-be cyber criminals to acquire your all-important data. Specifically, we'll take a brief look at a few applications and practices that can help you maintain copies of your data, but do so in a safe and secure manner.

Cloud Storage and Physical Security

There is no better defense against theft than knowing where your information is physically being stored; of course, that also includes knowing where your Mac is at all times. Following these principles is your first line of defense in protecting your Mac, whether you are performing backups or just trying to keep your private information private.

You may have heard about a buzz word in IT called *cloud storage*. This is a great technology that allows you to offload the storage responsibility of your hard drives to service providers who store your information online (i.e., *in the cloud*) as a premium service. The rule of thumb here is to use common sense. You should only use vendors that have a proven track record for security, vendors that are well-known and respected throughout the computing community.

If you decide to use remote storage for backup or file storage, be sure that you encrypt your data. Service providers that do not encrypt your data cannot guarantee that others who have privilege rights to their storage facility will not look at your data. Nor can they offer you any security in the event that they are compromised and your data is stolen.

Again, just use common sense. This means you need to read up on any storage provider you're considering subscribing to. The goal when looking up a vendor is to see whether you can uncover any holes in the legitimacy of their claims; that is, you want to make sure that they aren't doing anything that might compromise the safety of *your* data. Cloud storage is a great technology, and I encourage its use wholeheartedly. That said, it's also critical that you know the who, what, and how related to any vendor you might select.

Summary

In this chapter, we explored some of the ways you can keep your data copied and safe. We also took a deep look at some of the applications and practices that best serve the security-aware user, and then looked at how to best implement strategies that can keep your computer information safe, but without that safety being a burdensome task. Your Lion is a caged beast, with the potential to let you create anything you can think of. Like any beast, however, it needs to be watched. Computing with common sense requires heeding the lessons that have been hard-learned by other computer users. Specifically, you must take steps to embrace beneficial technologies, but take equally strong measure to avoid what is harmful. Neglecting backup and security when you use a computer is like putting your Lion on a leash and expecting others not to notice. Be aware that others are aware of you. Compute responsibly and enjoy your Mac.

Chapter 11

Automating Tasks and Customizing Lion

Just about every computer user knows that using a computer means doing a lot of the same things over and over. Whether you need to attach an image to an e-mail, insert pictures into your **iPhoto** library, or download digital content from the Internet, you're going to be performing a lot of repetitive tasks. Regardless of the type of computer system you have, repetition is typically just part of using a computer; however, that does not have to be the case when you use a Mac.

Lion comes with an extensive toolset for automating those repetitive tasks that you have to contend with everyday. The Lion operating system was designed with the user in mind; and as a result, it has powerful tools that allow you to fine-tune and control what, when, where, and how things happen. In this book's final chapter, we will look at a few applications and preferences that use automation to dramatically influence the way you interact with Lion, greatly reducing the repetition inherent in accomplishing tasks on your computer. We will pay particular attention to Lion's built-in automation tool, **Automator**. Learning to use automation effectively will enable you to tap more deeply into the awesome power of the Lion operating system.

Automation can be a tremendous time saver, but what makes Lion especially powerful is that you can automate just about anything you do on Lion. Automation on the Mac is limited only by your enthusiasm and creativity.

NOTE: Lion ships with **Automator** and other great tools for automating tasks; however, I strongly recommend that you use fake data as you learn to take advantage of these tools. This will help you avoid making a mistake that accidently deletes or irrevocably damages an important file. Until you can use these tools flawlessly, you should keep your automation workflows and applications away from your real data. The last thing you want is to lose an important business contact or that photo of your daughter taking her first step.

Understanding Automation

Automation is the core principle behind all computing. Computing in general is meant to save us time by allowing the computer to respond to and address our needs with as little manual input from us as possible. As I prepare this final chapter, several of Lion's built-in automation features are helping me do so. Most of this help occurs in the background, out of sight; however, a handful of these automation features are visible to me as I type.

For example, I am currently connected to the Internet. This enables me to look up information instantly and to be notified when I have new e-mail. For as long as I'm connected to the Internet, my Mac's internal firewall is protecting me from various Internet threats. At the same time, various applications are using that Internet connection to determine whether updates are available. And, right in front of me, I can see my word processor's spelling and grammar checker working away—correcting my misspellings, repositioning my punctuation, and alerting me to grammatical anomalies such as incomplete sentences. As all this goes on, my clock is dutifully tracking the time. And, without any input from me, my word processor is talking to that clock, saving my document every five minutes. At the same time, my music player is randomly selecting tracks from my iTunes library and playing them. That is a lot of automation taking place, and this list is far from comprehensive. Managing all this automation is exactly what operating systems are intended to do.

We'll begin our survey of Lion's built-in applications and tools for automating tasks with one of its most important: **Automator**.

The Basics of Automator

Most operating systems require you to purchase expensive software before you can start doing any real programming. Others offer free tools that are cumbersome and difficult to learn, which creates a steep barrier to entry for those interested in learning how to make program their computer. Fortunately, this isn't true of Lion, which comes with one of the most powerful automation tools ever created—a tool that can be used by even the most novice Mac user.

Automator empowers Mac users by decreasing their reliance on expensive programming solutions that require either an expert or college courses to use. Apple created **Automator** using many of the founding principles of the Mac operating system; that is, it made **Automator** easy to use, accessible, powerful, and secure. **Automator** can be picked up and used by anyone who can read and use a mouse and keyboard. When using **Automator**, implementing basic automation is very easy and requires almost no training whatsoever.

To use this app, locate the **Automator** icon in your Applications folder and open it (see Figure 11–1).

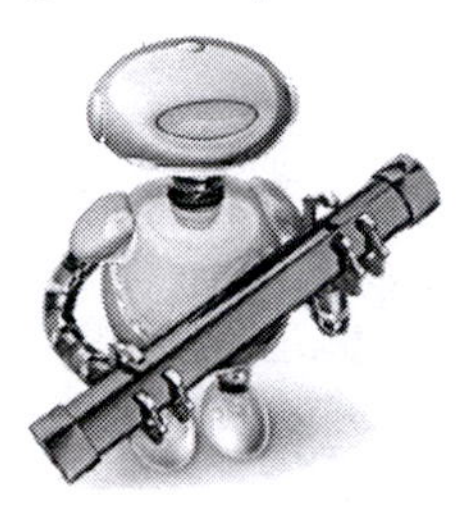

Figure 11–1. *The Automator icon*

Once **Automator** opens, it will present you with several workflow templates for automating your computer (see Figure 11–2).

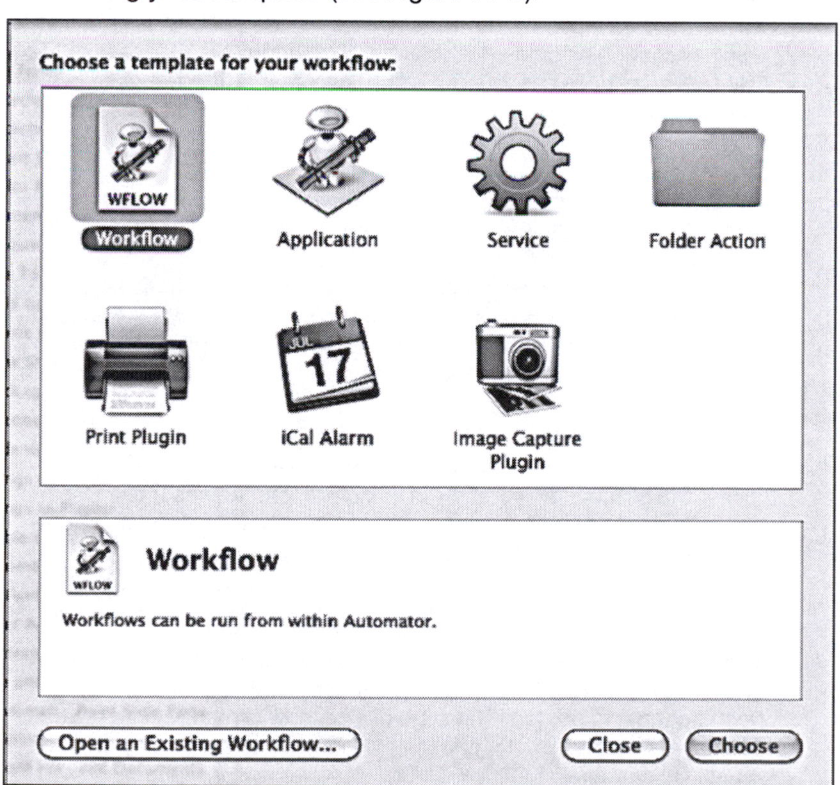

Figure 11–2. *Automator's workflow template selector*

Each of these programming workflow templates is intended to help you accomplish a specific type of automation. Table 11–1 lists the automation templates available and explains how you can put them to use.

NOTE: Clicking each template item will give you a description of each template's intended purpose.

Table 11–1. *Drilling Down on Automator's Workflow Templates*

Workflow Template	Description
 Workflow	You can run the **Workflow** template from within **Automator**. When workflow applications are executed, **Automator** is automatically opened. In most cases, you will be able to see the flow of events and actions in a workflow in real-time. This is the simplest type of automation template available in Lion.
 Application	The **Application** template enables you to create self-running workflows. Any files or folders dropped onto an application workflow will be used as input for that workflow. In this context, an *application* is a self-executing workflow that has been compressed into a single file that other file types can interact with. The **Application** template is a step up in complexity from what the **Workflow** template. As such, it is moderately difficult to use and understand.
 Service	The **Service** template enables you to create service workflows that are available throughout Mac OS X. Service workflows accept text or files from the current application or the **Finder**, and then call on the operating system to execute particular commands on those files. Service workflows appear in the **Services** menu. Ultimately, this type of workflow allows you to bind automation to any application that can support the particular commands included in a given service workflow.
 Folder Action	The **Folder Action** template lets you create workflows that are attached to a folder in the **Finder**. When you add items to such a folder, the associated workflow is launched, and it uses those files as input. This type of workflow can usually be accessed through a right-click, and it is always folder-specific.
 Print Plugin	The **Print Plugin** template lets you create workflows that are available in the **Print** dialog. These workflows accept PDF versions of the document being printed. This type of workflow proves valuable when you have extensive printing needs that vary from day-to-day, but are repetitive in nature.

Workflow Template	Description
 iCal Alarm	The **iCal Alarm** template lets you create workflows that run when triggered by an event in **iCal**. Such workflows receive no input, but they are extremely useful because they let you execute any number of commands at a specified time. For example, you might have your computer automatically print out a report of relevant traffic conditions before you leave for work.
 Image Capture Plugin	The **Image Capture Plugin** template lets you create workflows that are available in the **Image Capture** app. These workflows receive image files as input. This high-end programming workflow allows you to take images, video, or stills, and then process them immediately or at a scheduled time in the future. These workflows are great for on-the-fly batch rendering of videos and images that rely on filters and special effects that must be applied to each recording or shoot.

All of these workflows have their place and can save you a great deal of time when used appropriately. In this chapter, we will focus on workflow basics, walking you through how to use the **Workflow** template for a pair of examples. The first example combines some simple and advanced tasks for automating dictionary terms, while the second leverages intermediate-level tasks to download an image from the Internet.

Example 1: Automating Text Audio

In our first workflow example, we'll create a process that asks the user to type in a dictionary term, so that Lion's **Dictionary** application can read that term back to the user. Begin by opening **Automator** and choosing the **Workflow** template (see Figure 11–3).

This will cause **Automator** to bring up a **Library** dialog that displays a submenu consisting of pre-built **Automator** actions organized by category. Our sample application is considered advanced because it uses all five of **Automator**'s available automation layers. These five layers consist of the following actions:

- prompting the user
- receiving user input
- processing the user input
- providing a response to a request
- using and/or processing multimedia files

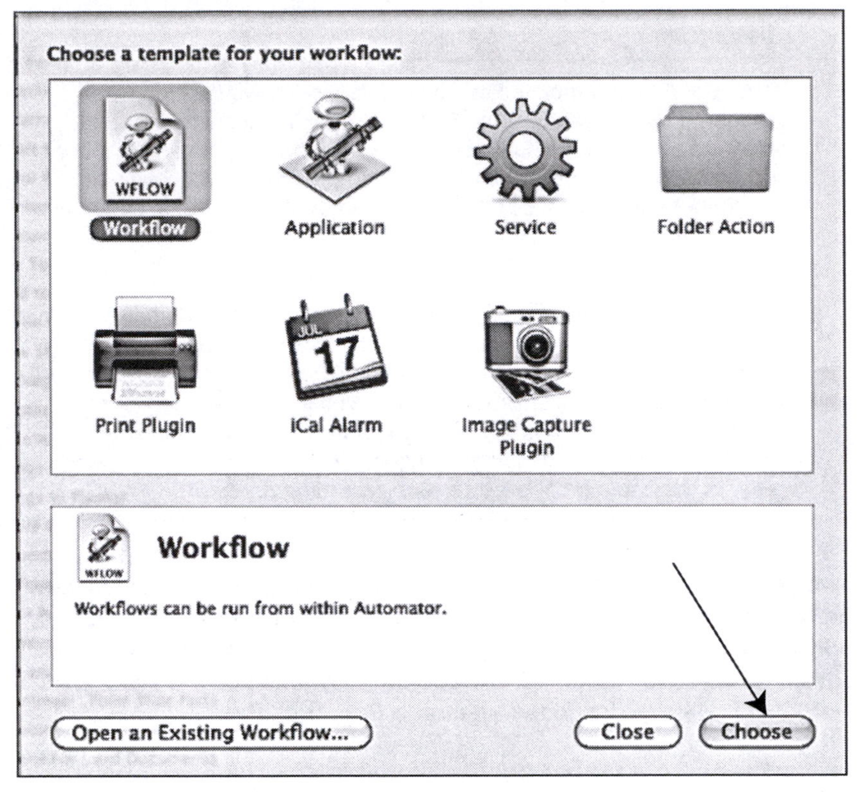

Figure 11–3. *Selecting the Workflow template in Automator*

Implementing the workflow is as simple as following these steps:

1. Select the **Utilities** option from the **Library** menu.
2. Type "wait" in the **Search** bar to bring up the **Wait for User Action** window.
3. Drag the action to **Automator**'s **Builder** window. The result should look exactly like Figure 11–4.

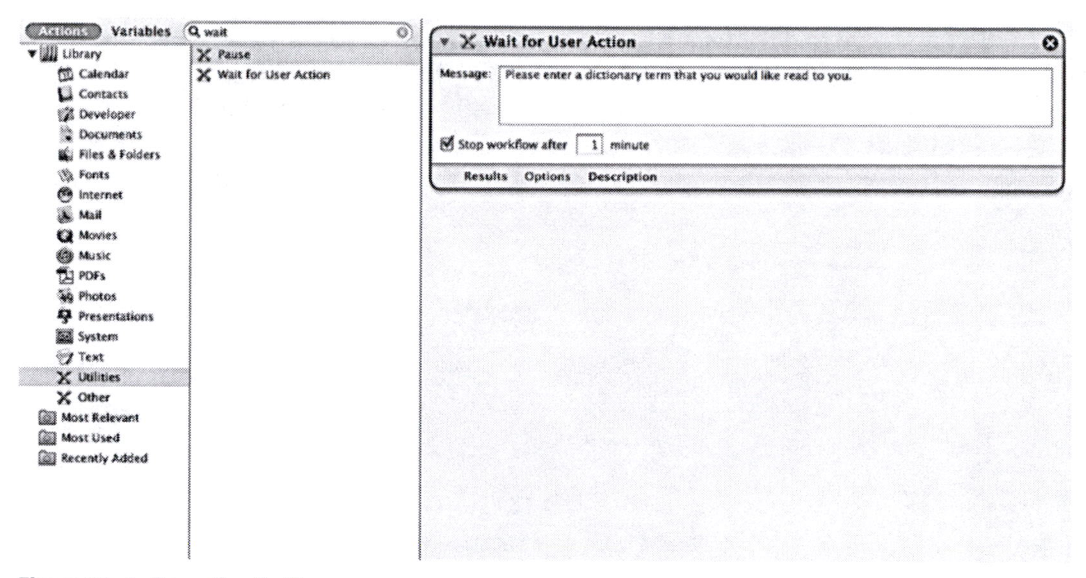

Figure 11–4. *Prompting the User*

4. Replace the message text shown with "Please enter a dictionary term that you would like read to you." Leave everything else the same.
5. Clear out the search context by pressing the **x** icon in the **Search** dialog (or simply delete the word "wait").
6. Go to the **Library** submenu, select the **Text** option, and drag the **Ask for Text** action until it's under the **Wait for User Action** dialog (see Figure 11–5).

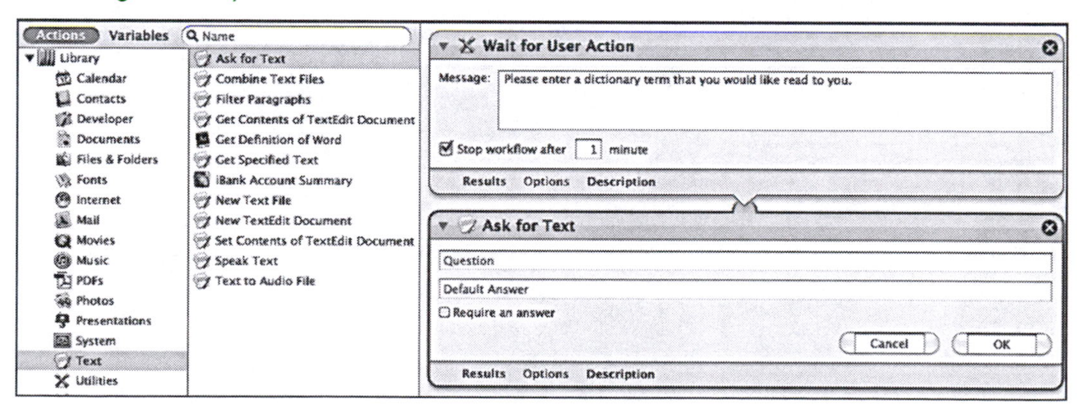

Figure 11–5. *Accepting user input*

7. So far you've told the user what you need and accepted his input. Now it's time to process that input. Select the **Get Definition of Word** action from the same submenu, and place it beneath the **Ask for Text** dialog (see Figure 11–6).

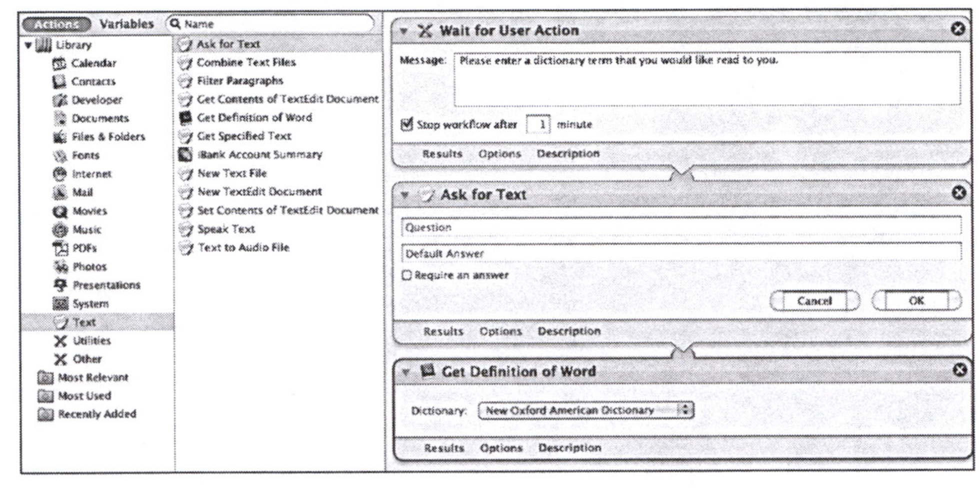

Figure 11–6. *Sending input to the Dictionary*

8. The user's input is now being processed by Lion's built-in **Dictionary** app; however, you have yet to implement the steps necessary to make this app talk. From the same submenu, select the **Speak Text** action and drag it under the **Get Definition of Word** dialog (see Figure 11–7).

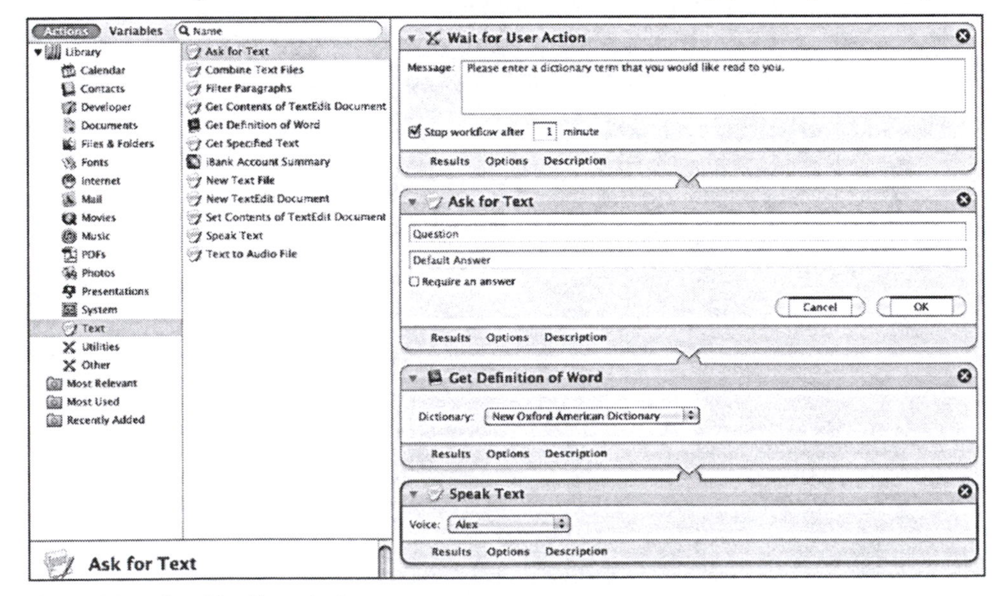

Figure 11–7. *Speaking the output*

9. You now have all of the required components in place, so it's time to run the program. Do so by pressing **Automator**'s **Run** button (see Figure 11–8).

10. Once the program is running, enter the word "summer" when asked to input a dictionary term. You will hear the **Dictionary** speak this word back to you.

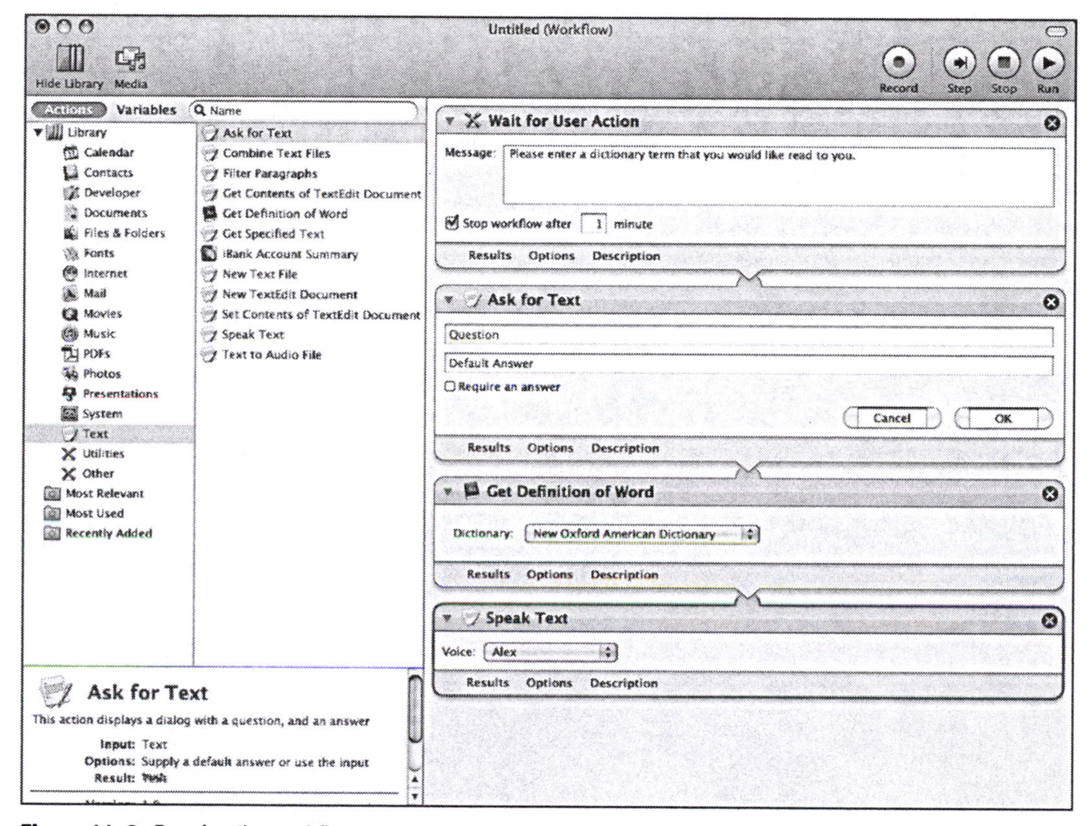

Figure 11–8. *Running the workflow*

Voila! In less than ten minutes, you have created a workflow program that can be used to teach users how certain words are pronounced. It would be easy to extend this functionality to provide even more real-world value. For example, you might combine this functionality with other workflow actions to create a program that teaches visually challenged children definitions from the **Dictionary** app. Or, you might use **Automator** to alter many different aspects of the **Dictionary**'s basic features, including the voice type, prompt, or dictionary type. The sky is the limit, even with a program as small as this one. Let's try one more example.

Example 2: Automating Internet Downloads

In this example, you'll learn how to automate downloading image files over the Internet. This workflow will prompt the user for input, ask her to give provide an image URL address for an image she would like to download, and then proceed to download the image file to the folder she specifies. This type of automation is extremely useful, and it can save you a lot of time once you learn how to use it. It is also applicable to other files you might want to download because you can use this same technique to download any other type of Internet media or even multiple files. For now, let's keep things simple, so can you get a basic understanding of what is going on. Follow these steps to automate downloading that image file:

1. Select **Utilities** from the **Library** menu and type "wait" into the **Search** bar to bring up the **Wait for User Action** window.
2. Drag the action into **Automator**'s **Builder** window (see Figure 11–9).

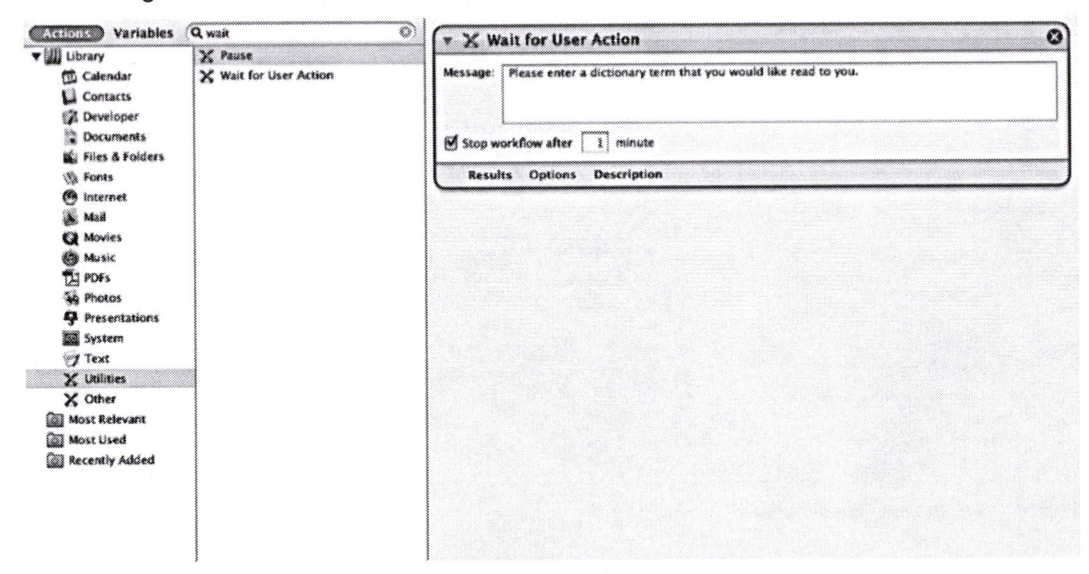

Figure 11–9. *Prompting the User*

3. Replace the message text with "Please enter image URL you would like to download." Do not make any other changes and remember to clear out the **Search** box of all text.
4. Select **Text** from the **Library** submenu, drag it over the **Ask for Text** action, and then place it under the **Wait for User Action** dialog you dropped into **Automator**'s **Builder** window (see Figure 11–10).

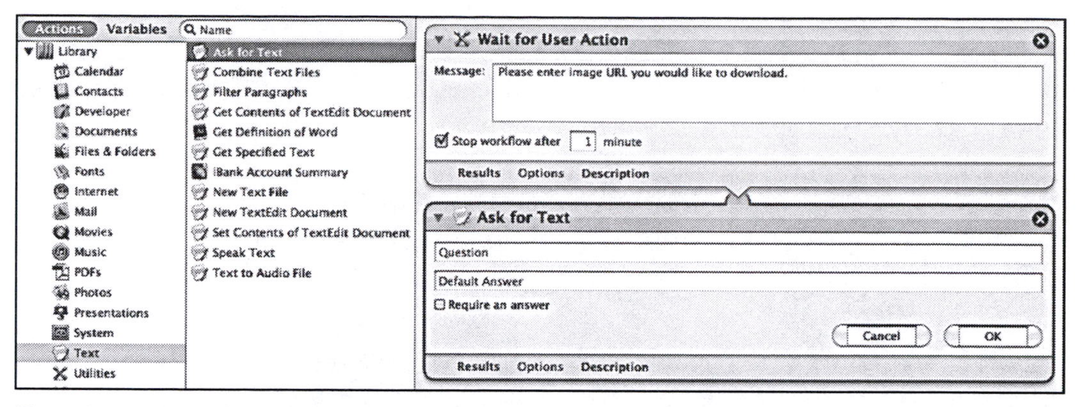

Figure 11–10. *Accepting User Input*

5. Go to the **Internet** submenu and select the **Download URLs** action (see Figure 11–11).

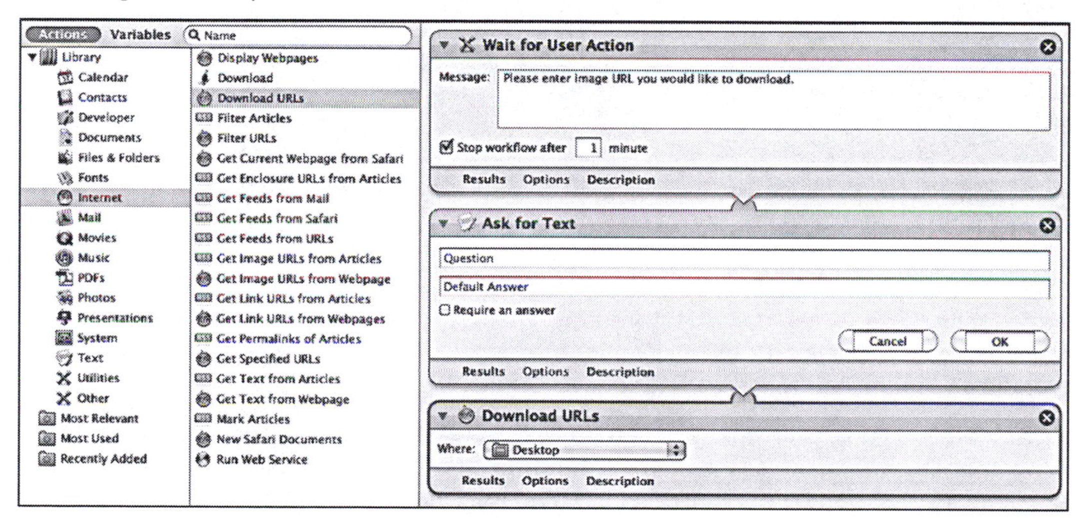

Figure 11–11. *Automator's Download URLs action*

6. Now it's time to download the image by running the workflow (see Figure 11–12). When prompted, change the download destination to your desktop and use the following URL as your input:

   `http://www.linuxwallpapers.org/apple/free-wallpaper-apple.png`

7. Depending on the quality of your Internet connection, this could take a few minutes or a few seconds. Either way, once the process completes you should see the image shown in Figure 11–13.

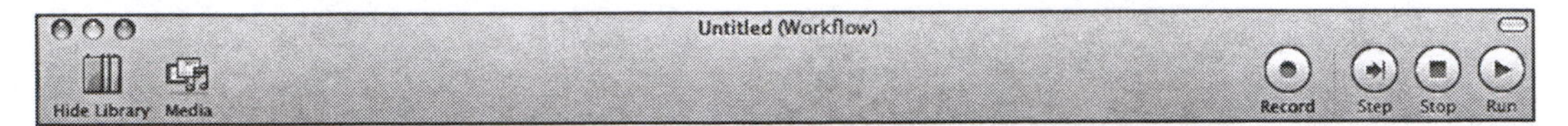

Figure 11–12. *Running the Internet download workflow*

Figure 11–13. *Downloading the image from Exercise 2*

These two examples should give you a good idea of the power and flexibility inherent in automating tasks. What makes **Automator** especially powerful is that you can use it to launch other applications such as **iCal** for alarms. Moreover, you can execute the workflows that launch these applications as frequently as you need to.

Again, there is no limit to what you can do with **Automator**. In fact, there are many Mac programmers who make a living turning **Automator** routines into fully functional applications that can be purchased at the Mac App Store. Cultivating and building your **Automator** skills could pay off in more ways than one.

Customizing Lion

There are literally more than a million ways to customize your Lion operating system, and this book would be as thick as 100 encyclopedias if I decided to describe each one of them. Of course, you don't personally need quite so many customizations; you just need the right customizations for you. In the remainder of this book, I will cover some essential customization secrets that can make a world of difference in getting the most out of how Lion presents resources to you. Specifically, I'll help you understand how to maximize your use of folder organization, indexing, and the screen saver.

Folder Organization

One thing you might notice as you begin to use Lion is that its folders are initially somewhat disorganized. They seem to just sit there, without structure or order. You can change this by right-clicking in the empty space of any of the **Finder's** windows and selecting **Show view Options** from the context menu that appears (see Figure 11–14).

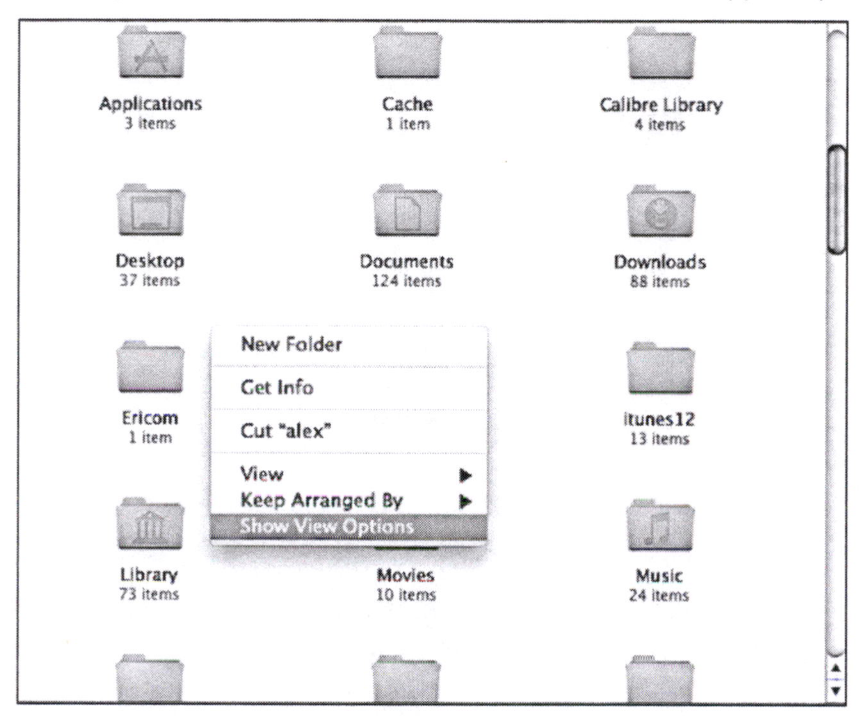

Figure 11–14. *Lion's folder view options*

After selecting this option, make your view options mimic those shown in Figure 11–15.

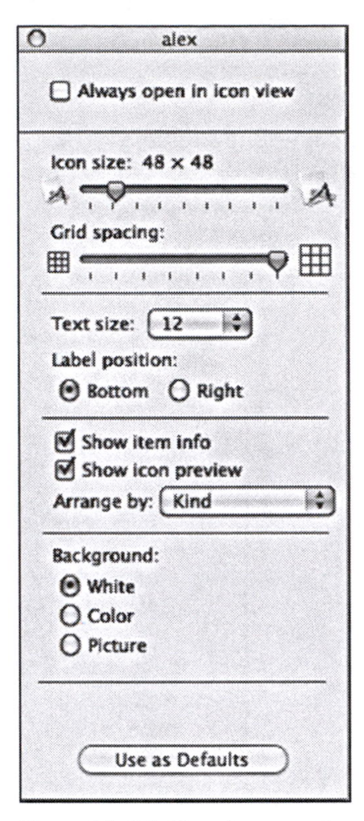

Figure 11–15. *Choosing your view options*

After you make these changes, you will notice that your folders and files now line up nicely and evenly in alphabetical order. This is a much better way to organize them.

Indexing with Spotlight

Another crucial customization you might want to do involves **Spotlight**, an OSX desktop search feature that indexes everything on your computer. One set of information you do not want **Spotlight** to index is your fonts, as this will slow down your Mac considerably.

To ensure that **Spotlight** is not indexing your fonts, go to your Mac preferences, open the **Spotlight** options, and remove the check from the box next to **Fonts** (see Figure 11–16).

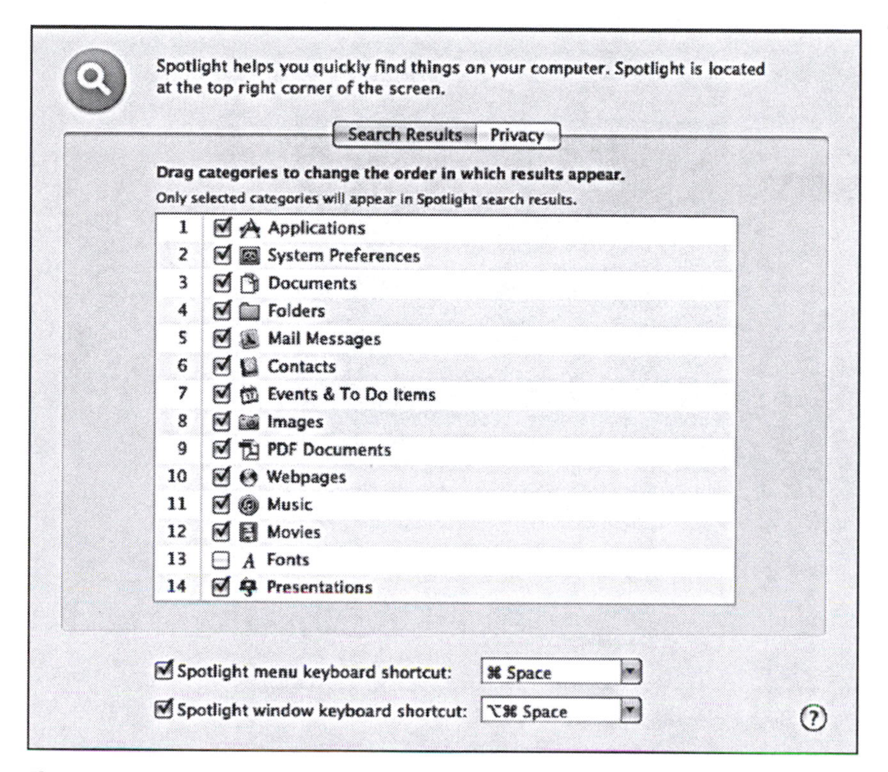

Figure 11–16. *Deselecting Fonts in Spotlight*

Making this change can speed up your Mac considerably because it decreases how much work the **Finder** must do when you conduct broad inquiries with **Spotlight**.

Customizing the Screen Saver

Finally, I recommend you make an important change to how your screen saver works. Screen savers can be beautiful and fun to watch, but they also eat up your Mac's precious memory when they run. Using either the blank or **Computer Name** screen saver will consume less battery life on your portable Mac. Just as importantly, choosing one of these options will consume less RAM (random access memory) on any desktop or portable Mac you might use (see Figure 11–17).

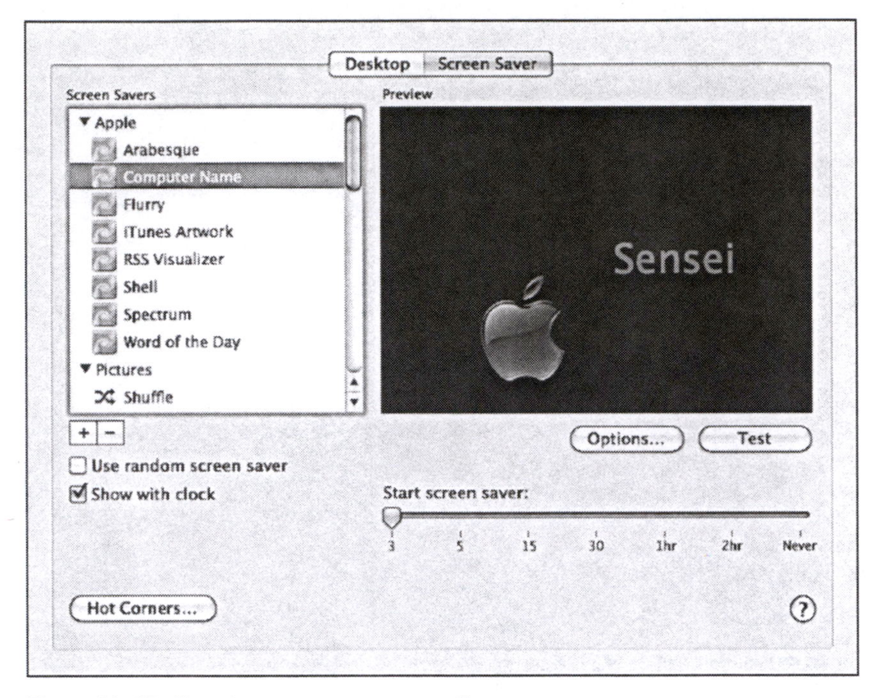

Figure 11–17. *Changing your screen saver options*

Summary

In this chapter, you learned just how versatile your Lion operating system is. For example, you learned you can fine-tune just about anything in it; but more importantly, you learned that you can make it do just about anything you want it to with a little time and practice.

You also learned that automating things can be fun and educational, as well as save you time and—in some cases—money. The Mac OSX Lion operating system is a true beast, one that is limited only by the imagination, talent, and curiosity of its user.

This book just touches the tip of the iceberg when it comes to what Lion can do, and it should be considered an in-depth teaser to get you started. My hope is that it motivates you to explore your OS in much greater depth, so that you can exploit the true potential of your Lion operating system.

Lion was created to roam the digital Safari (pun intended). Feed it with good intentions, the will to learn, and the power of curiosity—and you never know what you might discover.

Index

A

About Finder option, 56–57
About iMovie option, 110
About iMovie window, 111
About option, 110
Accept cookies option, 171
accounts, sharing, 102
Activity Monitor utility, 136, 138
Activity section, in Mail, 179
Actual files feature, 32
Add to Library option, 73
Address book icon, 27
Address entry bar, in Safari, 158–159
Advanced Encryption Standard (AES) encryption, 142
Advanced menu, in iTunes, 74–76
Advanced tab
- of Finder utility, 40
- in Safari, 169–170

AES (Advanced Encryption Standard) encryption, 142
Appearance tab, in Safari, 167
Apple icon, 23
Apple Mac OS X Lion, 21–28
Apple MacBook Pro
- keyboard, 6–7
- ports, 4–6

Apple menu, 10
application menus, 55
application templates, 144
applications
- finding similar, 106
- icons and, 25
- Image Preview section, 105
- Information section, 104
- origins of, 104
- purchasing, 103
- reviewing, 107
- updating, 100–101

applications menu, 9
Ask for Text dialog, 216
Ask for Text option, 215, 218
attachments, for messages in Mail, 182
attributes, 141
Authorize This Computer option, 74
Autofill tab, in Safari, 168–169
Automator tool, 209–224
- downloading example, 218–220
- overview, 210
- text audio example, 213–217
- workflow templates for, 210–220

B

Bento application, 151–155
Blues option, 128–129
Bookmarks menu, 65–67
Bookmarks tab, in Safari, 167
Browse Help option, 112
Builder window, 214, 218
Burn to Disc option, 42

C

Carbon Copy Cloner utility, 198, 204–207
Categories icon, 99
cautions, 18
Charts submenu, 84
Civilization V application, 103
Clean My Mac application, 140
Clip menu, 118

cloud storage, and security, 207
CMS (customer management system), 151
Cocktail application, 141
Colors feature, 86
Column view, 34
Comments option, 84
Commonly used folders feature, 32
Content window, in Mail, 180
contextual menus, in Mail, 181
Controls menu, in iTunes, 73–74
Copy option, 42, 58–59
Cover Flow view, 35
Create option, 75
customer management system (CMS), 151
customization, 220–224
  folder organization ", 221
  folder organization, 222
  indexing with Spotlight, 222–223
  screen saver, 223
Cut option, 58

D

DaisyDisk application, 141
data security
  augmenting built-in, 143–146
  overview, 142
Deauthorize Audible Content... option, 75
deleting files, 28
desktop, navigating, 21–25
Disk Utility application, 138
Documents feature, 87
documents, Versions feature for
  duplicating, 200
  locking, 200
  reverting to version of, 200–201
Download URLs option, 219
Drive Genius application, 141
Duplicate and Revert option, 200
Duplicate option, 42
duplicating documents, with Versions feature, 200

E

Edit menu, 58–59, 73
editing, in iPhoto, 124–125
Empty Trash option, 40, 57
Enter Time Machine option, 195
Erase the target volume option, 205
Espionage application, 143, 145
Event Library menu, 118
Event Manager window, 118
extensions, for Safari, 172–174

F

Faces feature, in iPhoto, 122–123
FaceTime, and Mail, 186–187
FaceTime icon, 27
Featured icon, 99
feedback, address for sending to author, 18
File menu, 58, 72–73, 113, 199
FileVault application, 142–143
Finder application, 10, 26, 30–31, 55–64
  Edit menu in, 58–59
  File menu in, 58
  Go menu in, 60–64
  Preferences menu, 35–40
    Advanced tab, 40
    General tab, 36
    Labels tab, 38
    Sidebar tab, 39
  right-click options, 41
  View menu in, 59
Finder icon, 26, 30
Finder menu, 36
Finder Options, 37
Finder views, 35
Finder window, 31, 196
Flagged option, 123
folders, organization of, 221–222
Font feature, 86
fonts, for messages in Mail, 183
Footer menu, 118, 125, 130
Formula List feature, 93
Full Screen option, 82
Functions menu, 93

G

GarageBand, 126–134
  Media Browser utility in, 131–133
  Playback submenu in, 131
  Share menu in, 133
  Track menu in, 133
  Tracks submenu in, 130
  Welcome window pane in, 126–129
General tab
  of Finder utility, 36
  in Safari, 166
Get Definition of Word dialog, 216
Get Definition of Word option, 216
Get Info option, 42
Getting Started option, 112
Go menu, in Finder, 60–64
Google, using in Safari, 159–160
Graphics feature, 89
Guides menu, 95

H

hard drives, maintaining health of
  overview, 138–139
  third-party utilities for, 140–141
Hide option, 57
Hide Others option, 57
History menu, 65–66
History window, 163

I, J

iCal application, augmenting with utilities, 150–155
iCal icon, 27
iCal interface, 150
iCalViewer application, 155
IceClean application, 141
iChat, and Mail, 185
Icon view, 33, 35
icons, and applications, 25
identity, securing, 101
iDeskCal application, 155
iLife, 109–134
  GarageBand, 126–134
    Media Browser utility in, 131–133
    Playback submenu in, 131
    Share menu in, 133
    Track menu in, 133
    Tracks submenu in, 130
    Welcome window pane in, 126–129
  iMovie, 110–119
    creating new project, 113–114
    interface of, 114–116
    menu for, 111–112
    preparing videos for editing, 117–119
  iPhoto, 120–125
    editing in, 124–125
    Faces feature, 122–123
    overview, 120–121
    photo information in, 124
    Places feature, 123
Image Preview section, 105
iMovie, 110–119
  creating new project, 113–114
  interface of, 114–116
  menu for, 111–112
  preparing videos for editing, 117–119
Import option, 117
indexing with Spotlight, customizing, 222–223
Info icon, 139
Information section, 104
Information utility, 124
Information window, 114, 140
input, adjustments to
  overview, 146–147
  third-party utilities for, 148–149
Inspector feature, in Pages, 86–90
Inspector option, 85
interfaces
  of iMovie, 114–116
  of Mail, 176–180
    Activity section, 179
    Listing and Content windows, 180
    menu functions in, 177–178

of Safari, 158–164
Address entry bar in, 158–159
Search bar in, 159–162
tabbed browsing in, 164
Top Sites section, 162–163
Internet submenu, 219
iPhone Ringtone option, 129
iPhoto, 120–125
editing in, 124–125
Faces feature in, 122–123
overview, 120–121
photo information in, 124
Places feature in, 123
iStat Menus application, 138
iStat resource-monitor utility, 138
iTunes, 72–76
Advanced menu in, 74–76
Controls menu in, 73–74
File menu in, 73
Store menu in, 74
iTunes icon, 27
iWork '09, 79–96
Keynote, 94
Numbers, 91–93
Pages, 80–90
Inspector feature in, 86–90
navigating, 81
using, 80–81

K

keyboards, Apple MacBook Pro, 6–7
Keynote, 94

L

Label option, 42, 53
Labels tab, of Finder utility, 38
Launchpad application, 52
Launchpad icon, 26
Layout feature, 87
Learn to Play menu, 127
Lesson Store menu, 127
Library dialog, 213
Library menu, 214–215, 218
Library submenu, 121
Link feature, 89
Lion clock, 23
Lion Dock, 24
List view, 33
Listing window, in Mail, 180
locking documents, with Versions feature, 200
Loop Sampler utility, 131–132

M

Mac App Store, 97–107
apps
finding similar, 106
Image Preview section, 105
Information section, 104
origins of, 104
purchasing, 103
reviewing, 107
updating, 100–101
description of, 98–100
securing identity, 101
Mac App Store icon, 26, 103
Mac App Store menu, 98
Mac OS X Lion, 15–18
address for sending feedback to author, 18
locating tips and notes, 18
navigating, 8–12
Finder application, 10
trackpad, 11–12
preview of Quick Start Guide, 17
MacBook Pro, Apple. *See* Apple MacBook Pro
Magic GarageBand feature, 128
MagicPrefs app, 148
Mail application, 175–189
composing messages, 182–184
attachments for, 182
fonts, 183
photo browser, 183
stationery, 184
contextual menus in, 181
and FaceTime, 186–187
and iChat, 185
interface of, 176–180

Activity section, 179
Listing and Content windows, 180
menu functions in, 177–178
and Skype, 187–188
Smart Mailbox folders in, 181
Mail icon, 26
Mailbox menu, 181
main contextual menu, 9
Make Alias option, 42
Masters option, 96
Media Browser utility, in GarageBand, 131–133
Media Browser window, 114, 117
Media feature, 85
menu functions, in Mail, 177–178
Metrics feature, 90
Microsoft Word format, 40
Mission Control icon, 26
monitoring
accounts, 102
system, 136–138
Mouse application, 146–147
mouse gestures, right-click options, 41
Mouseposé application, 149
MouseWizard application, 149
Move to Trash option, 42

N

NAS (Network Attached Storage), 194
Native Lion utility, 142
navigating, Mac OS X Lion, 8–12
Finder application, 10
trackpad, 11–12
Network Attached Storage (NAS), 194
New Email Attachment option, 42
New Message window, 182
New option, 94
New Playlist option, 73
New Project menu, 126
New Project... option, 113
notes, 18
Notes and Folders menu bar, 178
Numbers application, 91–93

O

Open Audio Stream... option, 75
Open New Tab option, 164
Open option, 41
Open "safe" files after downloading option, 166
Open With option, 41, 52
operating system (OS). *See* OS
organizing utilities
augmenting iCal application with, 151–155
overview, 150
OS (operating system), 21, 29–54
Finder utility, 30–31
Preferences menu, 35–40
right-click options, 41
Launchpad application, 52
searching with Spotlight box, 53
View Options window, 33–35
Column view, 34
Cover Flow view, 35
Icon view, 33
List view, 33
Other networked computers and devices feature, 32
Outline option, 82

P

Pages, 80–90
Inspector feature in, 86–90
navigating, 81
using, 80–81
passwords, 102
Paste option, 58–59
Photo Booth icon, 28
photo browser, for messages in Mail, 183
photo information, in iPhoto, 124
physical security, 207
Places feature, in iPhoto, 123
Play option, 94
Playback submenu, in GarageBand, 131
ports, on Apple MacBook Pro, 4–6

preferences
for Safari, 165–170
Advanced tab, 169–170
Appearance tab, 167
Autofill tab, 168–169
Bookmarks tab, 167
General tab, 166
RSS tab, 168–169
Tabs tab, 168
Preferences menu, of Finder utility, 35–40
Advanced tab, 40
General tab, 36
Labels tab, 38
Sidebar tab, 39
Preferences... option, 57
Preferences window, 194
Preview icon, 27
Preview window, 114
Prey application, 146
Print dialog, 212
privacy, in Safari, 171–172
Private Browsing... option, 171
Purchased icon, 99
purchasing applications, 103

Q

Quick Look option, 42
Quick Start Guide, 3–12
Apple MacBook Pro
keyboard, 6–7
ports, 4–6
navigating Mac OS X Lion, 8–12
Finder application, 10
trackpad, 11–12
QuickTime feature, 90

R

RAID (redundant array of inexpensive disks), 6
Really Simple Syndication (RSS), 26
Recent submenu, 123
redundant array of inexpensive disks (RAID), 6
Reorganize feature, 93
resources, of system, 138
retrieving data, from Time Machine, 195–198
reviewing applications, 107
reviews, using, 102
right-click options, of Finder utility, 41
RSS (Really Simple Syndication), 26
RSS tab, in Safari, 168–169

S

Safari, 157–174
extensions for, 172–174
interface of, 158–164
Address entry bar in, 158–159
Search bar in, 159–162
tabbed browsing in, 164
Top Sites section, 162–163
menus in, 64–72
preferences, 165–170
Advanced tab, 169–170
Appearance tab, 167
Autofill tab, 168–169
Bookmarks tab, 167
General tab, 166
RSS tab, 168–169
Tabs tab, 168
privacy in, 171–172
security in, 171
Safari icon, 26
Safari menu, 165, 170–171, 173
screen saver, customizing, 223
Search bar, in Safari, 159–162
Search box, 32
Search dialog, 215
Search feature, 32
searching, with Spotlight box, 53
Sections options, 82
securing, identity, 101
security
and cloud storage, 207
of data
augmenting built-in security, 143–146
overview, 142

physical, 207
in Safari, 171
Security icon, 142
Self-Monitoring, Analysis, and Reporting Technology (SMART) system, 141
Services menu, 212
Services option, 57
Sesamouse application, 149
Set Desktop Picture option, 42
Set Up Time Capsule option, 194
Shapes submenu, 83
Share menu, 118, 133
Share option, 84
sharing accounts, 102
Sheet menu, 92
Show All option, 57
Show Original option, 41, 52
Show View Options option, 42, 221
Show warning before emptying the Trash option, 40
Sidebar menu, 39
Sidebar tab, of Finder utility, 39
Skype, and Mail, 187–188
Smart Mailbox folders, in Mail, 181
SMART (Self-Monitoring, Analysis, and Reporting Technology) system, 141
Smart Utility application, 141
solid state drives (SSD), 191
Speak Text option, 216
Spotlight
indexing with, customizing, 222–223
searching with, 53
SSD (solid state drives), 191
Start-up menu, 21
stationery, for messages in Mail, 184
Store menu
in iTunes, 74
Mac, 98
Subscribe to Podcasts... option, 75
Super Flexible Backup utility, 198, 202–203
System Preferences icon, 28
systems, monitoring, 136–138

T

tabbed browsing, in Safari, 164
Tables menu, 83, 92
Tabs tab, in Safari, 168
target phones, and this book, 17
Template Chooser window, 80–81
Text Box option, 82
Text option, 88, 215, 218
Themes feature, 95
third-party application, 136
third-party utilities
for input adjustment, 148–149
for maintaining health of hard drive, 140–141
Time Capsule, for network storage, 194–195
Time Machine, 191–208
alternatives to, 202–207
Carbon Copy Cloner, 204–207
Super Flexible Backup, 202–203
retrieving data from, 195–198
setting up, 192–194
and Time Capsule for network storage, 194–195
using, 194
and Versions feature, 198–201
duplicating documents, 200
locking documents, 200
reverting to version of document, 200–201
tips, 18
Tiptoe application, 146
Top Charts icon, 99
Top Free menu, 100
Top Grossing menu, 100
Top Paid menu, 100
Top Sites section, in Safari, 162–163
Track menu, in GarageBand, 133
Trackpad application, 11–12, 146–147
Tracks submenu, in GarageBand, 130
Trash Bin application, 24, 28, 141
Trash Bin icon, 25, 28
Turn on Home Sharing option, 75

 U

Updates icon, 99, 101
Updates menu, 101
updating applications, 100–101
utilities, 135–155
  data security
    augmenting built-in, 143–146
    overview, 142
  enhancing experience with, 136
  input adjustments
    overview, 146–147
    third-party utilities for, 148–149
  maintaining hard drive health
    overview, 138–139
    third-party utilities for, 140–141
  monitoring system, 136–138
  organizing
    augmenting iCal application with utilities, 151–155
    overview, 150
Utilities option, 214, 218

 V

Versions feature, 198–201
  duplicating documents, 200
  locking documents, 200
  reverting to version of document, 200–201
View menu, 59, 73, 82, 92, 95
View Options window, 33–35
  Column view, 34
  Cover Flow view, 35
  Icon view, 33
  List view, 33
VigiMac application, 146

W, X, Y, Z

Wait for User Action dialog, 215, 218
Wait for User Action window, 214, 218
Watchmac application, 146
Welcome menu, 112
Welcome to iPhoto screen, 121
Welcome window pane, in GarageBand, 126–129
Window Title feature, 31
Window view options feature, 31
Windows Phone 7 User reference, 17
workflow templates, for Automator, 210–220
Wrap feature, 88

CPSIA information can be obtained at www.ICGtesting.com
Printed in the USA
LVOW111910181011

251041LV00001B/4/P